DRAMATIC STRUCTURE
THE SHAPING OF EXPERIENCE

University of California Press   Berkeley, Los Angeles, London   1970

DRAMATIC
STRUCTURE

THE SHAPING OF EXPERIENCE

Jackson G. Barry

University of California Press   *Berkeley and Los Angeles, California*
University of California Press, Ltd.   *London, England*

Copyright © 1970, by The Regents of the University of California
Standard Book Number 520–01624–6
Library of Congress Catalog Card Number: 78–100607

Printed in the United States of America
Designed by Ikuko Workman

To Edith J. Barry and John F. Barry in fond Memory

ACKNOWLEDGMENTS

One of the most enjoyable aspects of a writer's work is the help he receives from others. Advice, encouragement, and frank criticism make what could be a very lonely task into an exciting project. For their help with this book, I am grateful to William G. McCollom, Edward Evans, Thomas Munro, and Albert Cook, all of whom generously contributed to the first shaping of concepts. Monroe Beardsley was most helpful with encouragement and suggestions as I worked out the final formulation. Chapter V benefited from several suggestions from Richard Schechner. David Lewin was kind enough to discuss with me my treatment of *The Marriage of Figaro*.

I am pleased to acknowledge the American Society for Aesthetics, which through its journal and its members has developed an interchange which has benefited all who work in the field.

To all whose words and thoughts I have borrowed I am deeply grateful, particularly to the following, who have granted permission for the use of longer than usual quotations: Duell Sloane and Pearce, Inc., affiliate of Meredith Press, for permission to quote from "An Army Nurse at Bataan and Corregidor," From *History in the Writing* edited by Gordon Carroll (New York, 1945); Theodore Presser Company for permission to quote from Percy Goetschius' *The Structure of Music*, (Philadelphia, 1934); F. W. Bateson, publisher of *Essays in Criticism*, for permission to quote from Robert Heilman's article "More Fair than Black: Light and Dark in 'Othello' " in Volume I of that journal (1951); and to G. Schirmer, Inc., N.Y., for permission to reproduce the Trio #13 from *The Marriage of Figaro* from their vocal score. The American Educational Theatre Association has kindly granted permission for me to use as Chapter XI a slightly revised version of my article, "Form or Formula: Comic Theory in Northrop Frye and Susanne Langer" which originally appeared in the *Educational Theatre Journal*, *XVI* (1964).

Finally, for a task I could not do myself, I am grateful to Miss Barbara Zimmerman for her patient editorial work.

The Notes appear at the back of this volume at my request.

CONTENTS

INTRODUCTION

This book approaches a general theory of drama by examining its structure. The problem will be to supply an analysis of why the playwright organizes the elements of drama in the particular way he does, where these organizational schemes (structures) come from, how they relate to our real life experience, and how the structures typical of drama differ from those of narrative, poetry, and music.

It is possible to practice drama, to read drama, and even to criticize drama without ever attempting to answer these questions. Yet an inquiring mind is bound to encounter problems which can be fruitfully explored only on the basis of a lucid and consistent notion of what drama is.

Playwrights, directors, designers, even audiences must make constant decisions about interpretation and evaluation. Each is faced, either as an immediate practical problem or in an after-the-theatre-debate, with such questions as: Is verse a valid medium for a play about a middle class American suburb? How many liberties with realism can a designer justly take in setting a play whose text is realistic? What meaning or enjoyment can a spectator derive from a play that is deliberately meaningless? Can an improvised confrontation, taking place in separate arguments spaced around a whole auditorium, be understood as drama in the usual sense of that art form?

Persons of a theoretical bent may ask about the possibilities and nature of a "nonobjective" drama analogous to nonobjective painting or to music. Those interested in the dramas of the past may want to compare the excellences of different periods where, for example, the tight unity of Greek drama, if taken as an absolute good, must rule against the sweep and clutter of Elizabethan drama, and dismiss the unfocused activity of "event" theatre altogether.

Not all of these questions receive specific answers here, but a careful analysis of the process of organizing the materials of drama may suggest better ways of framing and investigating the problems, which may lead to a fresh understanding of the dynamics involved.

Dramatic structure has not been extensively covered in a systematic way, but where I overlap ground which has already been explored, I must plead as excuse my attempt to bring together in one analysis two qualities which have generally remained apart: philosophical sophistication and practical theatre experience. I have tried to avoid disappointing the scholarly reader with logical inconsistencies or vague and old fashioned concepts, and at the same time, I have tried to avoid angering the practicing theatre artist with a book which, however fine its theory, seems to have nothing to do with what really happens on a stage.

It is inevitable that particular phases of the study will suffer from the tight leash which must be kept on any general theoretical investigation. This restriction has prevented a number of intriguing explorations, such as a study of the bearing of recent linguistic studies on the structure of drama.[1] Yet it is necessary to first define a general theory in which subsequent special studies may eventually find a place.

For practicing artists of the theatre, critics, and writers of texts on drama, the term and the concept "structure" are central in their handling of dramatic materials, but existing definitions, either explicit, in drama textbooks, or implicit, in the assumptions which guide a playwright's, a director's, or a critic's choices, are vague or contradictory or both. In a survey of the field, René Wellek commented, "It would be easy to collect hundreds of definitions of 'form' and 'structure' from contemporary critics and aestheticians and show that they contradict each other so radically and basically that it may be best to abandon the terms."[2] No one, however, including Mr. Wellek, seems willing to abandon them.

We inherit a field in which Aristotle's suggestive idea that drama is the imitation of an action continues to stimulate critics as different as R. S. Crane and Francis Fergusson. Unfortunately, Aristotle's fragmentary treatise, despite the accumulated scholarship up to and including the recent elucidations by G. F. Else,[3] cannot be made to yield a definition of either "action" or "imitation" clear enough to satisfy contemporary aestheticians, although no one can deny that Aristotle said something that everyone who deals with drama must acknowledge, at least in its outlines.

Those who speak on dramatic structure today seem to fall roughly into four camps: philosophers, literary critics, anthropologists, and practicing theatre men. The first three camps are often hard to distinguish and may indeed be simultaneously occupied by one man with the sweeping interests of a Northrop Frye.[4]

In general, philosophers and anthropologists tend to talk about drama in terms of symbolic forms, myths, and aspects of reality. The literary critics, on the other hand, often look at the drama—particularly that of Shakespeare—so closely that they look right through the text to elaborate poetic structures which, following their trade instead of the dramatist's, they have fabricated underneath. At their best, professional theatre people who write about dramatic structure possess the great resources of practical experience and a contagious enthusiasm for theatre; but not unnaturally their work usually divides between sound dramatic technology (the standard playwriting text, for example) and hortatory pronouncements like "Drama is Magic!" or "Ritual" or "Music."[5]

The philosopher has sometimes relied on notions from other fields such as anthropology. Thus, the work of a philosopher who was profoundly influenced by the influx of data on primitive culture, Ernst Cassirer,[6] stands behind the investigations of Susanne Langer, whose very interesting theories on drama are to be found in *Feeling and Form*, and who is probably the one recognized contemporary philosopher to have achieved popular notice for her works on drama.[7] The general weakness of Mrs. Langer's theories is their tendency to see structure as a musical pattern of emotion in which specific meanings become a matter of indifference. Except for Mrs. Langer and Paul Weiss, who devoted an interesting chapter of his *Nine Basic Arts* to drama,[8] most philosophers writing general works on aesthetics stop cautiously short of an extended treatment of the complex mixture of arts found in a play.

Professional anthropologists can be separated into two more or less antipathetic groups: those whose work has been largely in the study, and those whose work has been largely in the field. Of the first group, those who have had the greatest influence on theories of drama are the so-called Cambridge Anthropologists, for whom Jane Ellen Harrison may serve as a representative.[9] The influence of this group, particularly through their writings on religious rites in Greece, spread to specialists in classical drama, like Murray and Cornford,[10] and their theories of drama as ritual have an enormous, if highly speculative, appeal.[11] Francis Fergusson certainly has incorporated ritual, among other influences, into his highly sophisticated criticisms.[12] Psychology, particularly that branch influenced by the mystic leanings of C. G. Jung, has lent this approach a kind of support which, though questionable in itself, takes some of the pressure off the meager and debatable evidences of an historical proof for the ritual origins of drama.[13] In any case, while myth, ritual, and archetype are valuable in their suggestion of the primitive patterns which undoubtedly underlie much of our drama, they inevitably lead away from just those sophisticated nuances which we are most anxious to explain.

The field anthropologists have not had as widespread an influence on dramatic theory as has the other group. This is hardly surprising, because on the whole they have not much dealt with drama. However, their observations of the dynamics of story telling, dancing, and drama among primitive peoples yield some valuable hints on such structural techniques as repetition, and on the demand for realism.[14] Although essentially a classical scholar rather than an anthropologist, A. B. Lord, carrying on the work of Milman Parry, has brought from the field many helpful suggestions on the technique of the oral composition of folk epic.[15] If Lord's painstakingly transcribed epics are inferior to the *Iliad* and the *Odyssey*—supposedly composed in the same improvised way—they still cast valuable light on creative composition, much of which applies *mutatis mutandis* to drama.

The cases of Gilbert Murray, Northrop Frye, and Francis Fergusson indicate the influence of anthropology on many literary critics. Critics so influenced are apt to see dramatic structure in terms of archetypal or mythical patterns. This view is indeed productive when one wants to consider the larger patterns of drama, but when one wants to consider a specific play it raises problems in two areas: (1) the mystic nature often imputed to archetype or myth may obscure the straightforward logic of a simple structure; and (2) the significance accorded to these gross and abstract patterns may overwhelm the details of the play itself.

Many literary critics loosely allied with the "new criticism" have offered analyses of dramatic structure in terms of the development of image clusters or themes. These works at their best, as in Cleanth Brooks' "The Naked Babe and the Cloak of Manliness,"[16] have made those already aware of the plot structure of a play also aware of the elaborations of poetic image and theme within a drama. This admirable approach, however, when carried too far, leaves one with the logically inconsistent notion that plays are really poems or essays.[17]

Aristotelian criticism has generally had the healthy effect of reminding the reader of the structural basis of drama in plot and action, which "old fashioned" but sturdy notions have been championed by R. S. Crane.[18] Most critics with strict allegiance to Aristotle, however, inherit the problem, if not of the "imitation" theory, at least of the narrow notion of plot which The Philosopher drew from the comparatively limited quantity and variety of dramatic literature of his time.

Critics of all kinds have had valuable ideas about dramatic structure, sometimes dropped as a passing hint, sometimes developed in a chapter or two. I can only offer a blanket acknowledgment of these insights and hope that the best of them have not been forgotten in my own systematic description of dramatic structure.

Practicing theatre men have a rule-of-thumb theory of drama that *works*. John Gassner, who has pleaded exemption from the necessity of erecting a formal aesthetic of theatre, has given this theory what is perhaps its most succinct statement in his introduction to *Producing the Play*.[19] Essentially an amalgam of Aristotle and Brunetière, action generated by conflict, it is a sound theory which only fails to stretch wide enough to cover the immense range of drama confronting us, or to supply convincing principles for determining why and how a *variety* of dramatic patterns might be generated. Jean-Louis Barrault, on the other hand, might be called a "theatre magician" because he advocates a mystique of production, not entirely inconsistent with the "art of illusion." Both approaches are fruitful in their own ways, but neither camp wants to take the time for the sober logical analysis which might find a middle ground, the one because the time may be better spent building a flat, the other because it may be better spent in incantation.

John Gassner's career was spent in the midst of the experiments which swept the Victorian stage clear for "modernism." Theatre people of his day could usually agree on what terms like "audience," "play," and "actor" meant. Within this relatively secure working state, they could easily agree with Gassner that extended aesthetic argument was a waste of time. Now, when each production tests the conventional limits of drama, to question our major concepts is no longer a luxury. Now, artist and theorist are frequently one, and their productions become laboratories.

This theorizing and experiment have received considerable impetus from the work of Antonin Artaud and Bertolt Brecht.[20] Both men revolted from the *entre deux guerres* theatre of realism and psychology: Artaud toward an orgiastic and essentially non-verbal "theatre of cruelty," Brecht toward a narrative, didactic, "epic theatre." Current experimenters are combining portions of Artaud's direct primitive involvement of the audience's senses with portions of Brecht's illusion-shattering techniques of alienation.

Peter Brook and Joan Littlewood in England, Jerzy Grotowski in Poland, Judith and Julian Beck, Joseph Chaikin, and Richard Schechner in the United States have contributed both statements on dramatic theory and productions where we can judge—not always favorably—how these theories work.[21] Their active questioning of the basic tenets of drama has led them to substitute, in theory and practice, the structure of a game, a protest march, or a trip for the more conventional dramatic patterns. The issues are still unresolved, and while it is stimulating—and sometimes even a bit tiring—to have so much thought stirred up, it is still too early to evaluate the results.[22]

On the other hand, critical evaluation of the works of one practical man of the theatre, Constantin Stanislavsky, is long overdue.[23] His insights are both highly pragmatic—Stanislavsky doggedly pursued himself and other prominent actors with questions about how they achieved their successful performances—and eminently suited to theoretical development; they seem so rooted in the natural process of creation that they reflect modern theories of creativity in other arts, notably in the teaching at the Bauhaus.[24] Stanislavsky's thoughts on the drama have not passed extensively into the serious theoretical literature on the subject, the notable exception being found in Francis Fergusson, who put the Russian director's insights to good use.[25] The neglect is not surprising, because acting texts are not given serious consideration by most literary critics and philosophers and, in any case, little can be gained just from *reading* Stanislavsky. It is precisely the critical habit of mind of the literary critic which would alienate him from Stanislavsky's "uncritical" acts of faith and, given the desire to learn, be the prideful deterrent to his novitiate. Yet it is precisely the creation by the actor of a moment to moment life on stage through involvement in immediate tasks or "actions," the experience of the actual theatrical event, that has most eluded the theoretical description of structure.

This, then indicates something of the area covered by the many theories of drama already proposed. The major positions will receive more extended treatment in the chapters to come. Large or small elements have been drawn out of past theories to contribute to the theory of drama I have constructed here. My desire has been to approach the drama from an area where little investigation has been done and, in moving from this perspective toward a more encompassing theory, to cast a fresh light on some of the notorious cruxes of the subject.

Specifically, I hope to contribute to the study of drama an analysis that will show how the peculiarly dramatic structure is derived from reality. Most of the existing remarks on structure, however illuminating, have been descriptive of an existing entity. I shall attempt to show both how and why the dramatic structure is derived, which will provide, as one result, some breadth for viewing and comparing those studies which describe dramatic structure in terms of one period or tradition, for example, Greek or the "well-made" play.

I attempt, from the perspective of the long and philosophical look, to say what drama *is*. I shall investigate the nature of drama by posing the following questions: What compels and guides us to select certain experiences from life and to arrange them in a certain pattern? What, if anything, is a permanent dramatic "form"? What becomes altered in dramatic form as the nature of our experiences and our thoughts about them change, and under what circumstances does this occur?

I shall attempt to show how a satisfying aesthetic experience can be made from the pleasure taken in actions that are presumably spontaneous and improvised and, conversely, from the pleasure in a set and prescribed pattern of events. I hope this will cast a new light on both the complete action and the immediate action, illuminating some of the problems associated with melodrama and other "contrived" pieces.

To achieve these goals the materials have been arranged to present in the first five chapters a description of the structure of drama as we have come to view it. In the next three chapters, structure is compared with the notions of "pure form" in the visual arts and with the structures of narrative, poetry, and music, in the hope that these comparisons and contrasts may more clearly illuminate dramatic structure. Other notable descriptions of the forces shaping a play are then examined as typified in the work of Aristotle, the thematic school (Robert Heilman), and the myth-rhythm theories of Northrop Frye and Susanne Langer.[26]

In all this, two concerns have been kept paramount: to do justice to the nature of drama as it exists in the rehearsal halls, scene shops, and production offices; and to examine all concepts with the analytic discipline of aesthetics, hence to keep a tighter rein on the use of such appealing but slippery terms as "poetry," "form," and "ritual" than the hustle of play production usually encourages.

In the chapters to come I shall develop the notions of drama and structure through specific examples, but it will be useful to state here the general definitions of the two terms which are central to the whole study.

"Drama" is meant to signify a play performed by actors on a stage, fairly represented by the plays of Aeschylus, Shakespeare, Ibsen, and the current Broadway fare. It does not seem important to establish hard-and-fast definitions of drama that would rule in a popular comedy performed on the conventional stage and rule out a Happening "performed" all over New York City and its vicinity. It does seem important to indicate the *kind* of event I conceive to be typical of drama, even though certain characteristics may be shared with other kinds of entertainment. As man changes his views on life and his interests in the materials of life, the form of his drama will change, but basically the drama always yields, to the group which sees it as drama, an image of man's interaction in time. Thus, drama must be made up of actions or events with some physical manifestations observable by the audience. These events do not have to be of a particular kind —dialogue, for example, is not the *sine qua non* of drama even though without the communicative power of the spoken word drama would be very limited; the mere employment of dialogue, however, does not guarantee a "dramatic" work. Finally, the events must form a meaningful pattern for that group that takes the work as drama, for whom, as we said, it presents an image of man's interaction in time.

The field of drama is a multidimensional spectrum stretching not only from the sublime to the trite, but from the highly verbal to the highly visual, from the elaborately formal to the freely improvised. In an investigation into the nature of drama, certain events low on the spectrum of artistic value can sometimes indicate more than the masterworks of literature. Just as biologists searching out the nature of life often work with simple organisms on the border of "life," so I shall investigate, where it seems appropriate, such protodramas as spectacles, and acting class exercises, but I expect this knowledge to be used to illuminate the great works of the medium, not to stand as mere commentary upon the insignificant.

It might be valuable to include in this volume a section contrasting the structures of film and drama. This would, of course, complement the sections contrasting drama with poetry, narrative, and music. Arguments either that the film is dramatic or that modern "mixed media" stage events are filmic could be cited in support of an extension of the present subject matter. However, the film is only just beginning to receive the kind of analytic attention which the other arts have had, and it would thus be impractical to discuss it without first devoting an inappropriately lengthy study to establishing its structural features.[27]

That, then, is the nature and scope of what will be referred to here as "drama." Structure is understood to mean the set of relationships between the parts of a given whole.[28] Although this understanding of the term denies a physical nature to structure, one popular image, the bare framework of girders outlining the shape of a new skyscraper, may indicate the idea in question because it strikingly articulates the organization of space and of construction elements in a building, thus the relationship of its parts: its structure. Of course the completed building will be a whole made up of many systems, each with its own relationship of parts (for instance, the structure of the electrical system), and will also participate as a part of other, larger wholes such as the total urban complex.

Mathematics and symbolic logic have gone a great distance toward expressing basic relationships in the realm of pure structure.[29] On the other hand, the arts have continually eluded such structural analysis from Pythagoras to Scott Buchanan[30] while still tantalizing searchers with their obvious regularities.

The verb form "to structure" is usually meant in the sense of "to arrange" and this certainly describes an important part of the artist's activity whether it be arranging the sequence of sounds in a line of verse or arranging the incidents which build to a climax in a tragedy. The noun would then designate the nature of the final arrangement, or relationship.

It must be apparent that, just as in the building, so in the work of art we are almost certain to find not one, but a host of structures describing the web of relationships. The abbreviated form, "*the* dramatic structure," must be understood to designate the totality of relationships in a given drama, which may include the gross, obvious, and basic structure of incidents as well as the structure of an individual sentence, the structure of a costume, or of a stage platform. These latter structures are not unique to drama; indeed, on other occasions they organize quite different entities.

Just as the skyscraper is ordered as a vertical arrangement of floor on floor, so the typical dramatic structure orders its incidents in a causal chain—as opposed to a poetic structure, which might arrange its parts according to the contrast or likeness of the themes or images, for example.

Structures vary widely in their complexity. Some are conventional and may organize such a relatively superficial feature as the rhyme scheme; however, a structure is not necessarily superficial merely because it is conventional. It is important to realize that there are structures of meaning suggested by a work of art as well as structures of its physical parts. In some sense, this differentiates the use of "structure" from the use of "form," which is commonly accepted to mean the arrangement of physical parts.[31]

In some ways the description of a work's structure must seem a fruitless reduction—a description of the obvious and inconsequential—but a description of structure can be undertaken at almost any level and with greater or less perspicacity. It can range, for example, from the offhand statement that *Hamlet* has a beginning, middle, and end to a book-length study of the multiple relationships in that complex play. Yet the pattern which relates them surely contributes to the significance of the parts.[32] The reasonable statement that *Antigone* is built on a temporal pattern of incidents which has been formularized in the warning "pride goeth before a fall," may seem to ignore most of what is usually enjoyed in that drama. In art it *matters* what specific parts are related in the pattern—(the vital characters of Antigone and Creon as created by Sophocles' lines, for example), while it does not matter in mathematics whether it is two apples or two tons of bricks which added to a like quantity make up the four units total. In art there is a power and meaning in the pattern itself. The sequential relationship of ignorance to knowledge is a basic experience of life and becomes more vivid with each repetition of the pattern, whether we find it in the mistaken identity of comedy or in the irony of tragedy.

Ours is a Pythagorean age, whether our contemporary Pythagoras studies computer programming by correspondence course or explores the most sophisticated realms of the philosophy of mathematics. Even toys and games cater to a taste for mathematical amusements. Painters like Josef Albers and Victor Vasarely, sculptors like Tony Smith and Donald Judd give us art works which present simple geometric shapes or masses in relation to each other and the space they occupy. Representational elements —and even the emotional content of the abstract expressionists— are omitted so we may enjoy a picture of pure relationship, which is to say, a picture of structure.[33] In France, contemporary interest in structure has manifested itself in a movement called "structuralism." Using structuralism as a tool, the loosely associated writers who fall under this rubric have investigated such subjects as Brechtian drama, poetry, the novel, women's fashions, and contemporary myths. Generally, however, the French structuralist is less affected by mathematics or philosophy than he is by studies in the structure of language—especially those in the school of Saussure—and by the ideas of anthropological structure put forth by Claude Lévi-Strauss.[34]

The ontology of dramatic structure—the question of whether we actually discern a set of relations in things and events, or whether we impose structure on them—lies at the periphery of this study. The exigencies of keeping an analysis of dramatic structure within manageable bounds dictate that we stop at the border of this and such other philosophical problems as the "meaning" or "truth" of a work of art. However, in all these delicate matters I have attempted to proceed with an awareness of the theoretical depths involved, so that at least the major positions I have taken may be defensible. Full treatments of the philosophical questions, to complement the presentation here, may be found in most contemporary books on aesthetics, of which Monroe Beardsley's *Aesthetics: Problems in the Philosophy of Criticism* is a good example.[35]

Before I turn to the analysis of drama in the next chapter, I must briefly discuss the general structure of time and space within which a play takes place. A play as a theatrical experience begins with the specific time of its performance. The ancient Greek "curtain time" was dawn. For an audience of Shakespeare's day, the play occupied part of an afternoon, and the middle and lower classes attended instead of, rather than after, work. In the early nineteenth century, the appetite of the lower-class audiences was for six hours of assorted melodrama. Our own experience of a given drama is partly influenced by the knowledge that it will occur after supper and in the conventional dramatic period of between two and three hours, and an experienced playgoer will sense roughly what can be done within the given time. He will have a feeling for the beginning, when the play lies before him, the

14

middle, and the end, when the playwright must start wrapping things up.

The ordinary time span of a drama and the time of day at which it is presented become part of the structure of the drama itself, and our conceptions of these contrast not only with the historical variants, but with such exceptions to the contemporary habit as the famous "dinner break" schedule of O'Neill's *Strange Interlude* (1928). But O'Neill's experiments represent only a puffing out of the conventional dramatic pattern. Today restless dramatists are searching further afield for configurations of time which may be more meaningful to our modern experience. The prize fight (which may last fifteen rounds or a few seconds), festivals lasting one or more days, rallies, and vigils have all been mentioned as offering fresh time schemes to a new drama.

This rough structuring of our temporal dramatic experience is paired to the rough structuring of our spacial experience by the nature of the auditorium in which the play is presented. The modern spectator is likely to be seated with from 500 to 1000 others in a large, comparatively dark, ramped space facing a smaller rectangular space that will probably be well lighted. This is only one possible arrangement, supporting through historical accident (or despite it) a concept of our image of action. This image can be radically altered, as it has been in certain contemporary experiments where the performance may, for example, surround the audience.[36]

Within the space of a stage and the time of a performance, however they are arranged, the production team will articulate an image of the possibilities for man's use of that space and time, and these may range, for instance, from the elaborately contrived use of entrances, exits, and hiding places of a farce, to the processions and soliloquies of Elizabethan staging, to the static arrangements of a conversation piece.[37]

Chapter I

ASSUMPTIONS

The most direct way to realize the principles of dramatic structure is to set yourself the task of composing a play from your own experience. As ground rules, accept that whatever you put in your play must be something that you have witnessed, and it must be put down exactly as it took place in real life. You will soon be tempted to "improve" on real life here and there: to change into one unswerving contest the argument which, as you witnessed it, was spread out over several meetings (one of which you only heard about) and which ended inconclusively. You would, of course, only be doing what all playwrights do. Eugene O'Neill compressed a number of incidents of his ragged relationship with his father and mother, which actually took place over a period of months, into the one eventful day of *Long Day's Journey into Night.*[1]

But if a playwright changes that which he is representing, on what does he base the decision that the new arrangement of the incidents is better than the one which at least had the recommendation of being real? Further, an attempt at playwriting will reveal another, more basic, challenge: why arrange a reproduction of experience as a *drama* in the first place? Why not take from the same ground of experience a series of sounds—say, an arrangement of the different automobile noises that drift through the window during an afternoon?

Presumably the playwright has a notion of drama which has accrued from all the plays he has experienced, and, given this pattern, it is possible to construct art works to fit it from the material of experience, almost as Sardou did with his dramatic formulas. But what if he did not have a notion (or tradition) of drama? What could possibly lead him to select and arrange experience in such a structure? Or, to take a more probable, related question: given one form of drama, what principles allow for the modifications which changing civilizations have made and will make in the manner in which experience is imagined?

To answer these questions, and hence to lay a basis for the meaningful discussion of dramatic structure, it is necessary to sketch in what I believe to be the basis of the organization of experience into art. The multitude of sense impressions, feelings, and thoughts that constitute experience may be organized in a number of different ways. As Eugene T. Gendlin says:

> Experience is "multischematic." It is capable of many specifications, many units, and therefore many different kinds of relationships between units. By "capable of," we will mean that experiencing as such is not patterned in any *one* of these schematics, but that when experiences are specified, then schematic relationships between experiences are likewise specified.[2]

If we did not impose order we could not cope with our experience. Before we can choose an ordering, we must make certain assumptions about experience which, from a philosophical point of view, cannot be strictly proved: for example, that sense impressions we entertain correspond to objects "out there" in space. Many assumptions are less basic and some, such as the assumption that the Earth is the center of the universe, have been disproved and replaced with assumptions which better represent the available data and opinions. It should be understood that the degree of sophistication of the assumption is not at issue here. Primitive rain dances based on naive assumptions about the causes of precipitation do not suffer a loss of validity as art.

There are many representations or descriptions of reality—those made by the physicist, the geometer, or the newspaper reporter, for instance. Each may be said to see reality in his own way—with his own assumptions about its basic nature—and each may be said to be looking at different *aspects* of a many faceted reality. It is not my task here to say how these representations are derived or how accurately they describe what they describe.[3] I am interested only in the representations of reality presented in drama, and to a lesser extent the representations of reality in such other arts as poetry, music, and narrative, since their different structures may, by contrast, throw light on the arrangement of experience in the dramatic form.

Assumptions are important to the idea of structure because the kind of structure we impose upon reality to make a drama of it will depend on how we see life. By the same token, the kind of drama we prefer and, indeed, the degree of our appetite for drama (instead of, say, painting, poetry, history, or sociology) will be dictated by these conscious or unconscious views. People of the same age and society often see life with more or less the same assumptions, which is why we do not need a different drama for each of us. Different cultural periods usually entertain different assumptions about the reality of life in time, as I shall later illustrate by considering the effects on their drama of assumptions held by the Greeks, the Elizabethans, nineteenth century mechanists, and modern absurdists; but for now let us examine an assumption generally shared by all playwrights and audiences that may clarify how this notion works in the shaping of a drama.

Most societies have assumed that a person retains the same identity, or "self," throughout his experience. Although common sense suggests that this must be so—that I am essentially the same man I was yesterday—a skeptical philosophy can cast serious doubts on the issue.[4] Yet it is fundamental to most dramas that the protagonist be the same Mr. X in the third act that he was in the first—a sadder and wiser Mr. X perhaps, but sadder and wiser because he is still Mr. X, not Mr. Y or Mr. Z. Only a few of our more inventive playwrights have questioned this basic assumption, as Pirandello did by suggesting in *It Is So, If You Think So* and *As You Desire Me* that a man's identity can change in different situations and with different people. Ionesco in a more radical and more literal way has altered the identity of some of his characters from moment to moment in some of his "anti-plays."

As we structure reality to understand—or, perhaps, just to perceive—it we select a view that admits some things and ignores others. We are capable of seeing, for example, in the *same* neutral series of events, the hand of fate or a strictly calculable causal chain depending on the assumptions we hold. Thus, assumptions are the basis for what might be called the first structural principle, *selection*: a way of looking at reality that sets crude limits. Selection might be compared to the simple aiming of the box camera, which frames part of a view, cutting out the rest. This kind of selectivity is particularly well illustrated in a discussion of James Stephens' poem "The Main-Deep" by Brooks and Warren:

> First, we know that the poet has assumed a particular view of the sea to the exclusion of other possible views. For

instance, the sea in "The Main-Deep" is not a stormy one. The poet, then, has selected the particular view that will suit his purpose.

Second, his selectivity has been exercised further in regard to the details from the particular view. We know that it is obviously impossible for the poet to put into a poem the enormous body of detail in his view of the sea. He must select details to build up the poem.[5]

It is difficult to investigate the effects of assumptions in selection without bringing in another principle that often acts toward the same end—interests. Assumptions are the basic philosophical choices which may influence us to see a unity of experience in the one person of the protagonist or, with less agreement, to assume that "justice triumphs" is a meaningful pattern. Interests, on the other hand, influence an author and audience to choose from among many phenomena those they would most like to see represented. The Greeks evinced an interest in legal debate, while the Elizabethans had an uncommonly great and uncommonly widespread interest in rhetoric. As Moody Prior says of the latter age:

> There was a good deal of interest in allegorical schemes, emblems, witty devices, and the like. Poetry, moreover—both its composition and appreciation—played a large part in the general notion of the accomplishments appropriate to a cultivated person. More specifically, two factors may be isolated for the deep and permanent mark which they left on this drama—the general acceptance of the principle of the didactic function of poetry, and the great interest in the technicalities of rhetoric.[6]

Assumptions and interests dictate the kind of drama a society will produce, and they also account for the differences between dramas. For example, the Elizabethans found their highly verbal drama satisfying to their interests and hence natural, while, lacking the interest, moderns often find this drama unnatural at first glance.[7]

How do assumptions about the nature of human life in time

determine a selection of events from the life around us and thus determine the structure of drama? Four examples may make the process clearer. It is reasonable to suppose that those groups that formed a receptive audience for the following respective periods of drama tended to see the human experience in time as: (1) in the Greek period, threatened by fate; (2) in the Elizabethan period, "chronicle life and death"; (3) in the late nineteenth century, mechanistic cause and effect; and (4) in the contemporary period, absurd and repetitive.

Moving from the general assumption to its consequences in specific details of dramatic structure, let us examine the following observations. The Greek drama supplies several instances of a man of great power and wealth, a king, unexpectedly brought low. Think, for example, of Agamemnon, Oedipus, and Creon (in *Antigone*). Each may be said to have been struck down by fate. For our purposes it does not matter in what exact manner fate is interpreted as acting (whether as punishment for some form of guilt, as blind chance, or whatever),[8] the fact remains that Greek assumptions about life, which find a voice in such sayings as "Lightning strikes the tallest tree," and "Count no man happy until he dies," find their image in these dramas. The fact that Aeschylus, Sophocles, and Euripides all saw fate in different ways gives richness and individuality to the images of life they created. These playwrights may also be said to have modified and explained the primitive notion of "blind" fate.[9] Nonetheless, the assumption that the image of a successful man suddenly struck down, for *whatever* reason, forms a meaningful pattern of experience is a prominent feature of Greek drama.

Some of the structural devices which are derived from the Greek assumption of the insecurity of life are: (1) the contrast of a scene of the king in his power (the triumphal procession of Agamemnon, the appearance of Creon to make his proclamation in person, the appearance of Oedipus to preside over the rites for the purification of the city) with a scene of the king brought low;

(2) the occurrence of the events of the tragedies within a single day, since fate's blow was conceived of as sudden and extreme; and (3) the accumulation of the ironies which modern critics are so fond of describing and for which the suddenness and unexpectedness of the fall provides rich ground. If life were imagined to be a gradual process of events which depended entirely on one's own willing, there would be little point in building a structure which relates the bitter curse Oedipus lays upon the murderer of Laius (245–254) to the moment, later in the very same day, when he enters to the townspeople, having wreaked the punishment upon himself (1309). The poignant irony found in Greek tragedy would not be represented in a situation in which the career of the high school boy voted "most likely to succeed" dragged on for thirty or forty years of undistinguished effort (as opposed, say, to his being struck down as he left the graduation exercises).

The sprawling structure of Elizabethan drama presents a striking contrast to the compact tragedy of Greece. The events in *Oedipus the King* take place within less than twelve hours. Years elapse in *Tamburlaine* and *Pericles*. Yet neither the nature of man nor of time has changed; the change is in the assumptions people make about the nature of human experience in time. Shakespeare's Christian audience no longer believed strongly in fate—though certainly the idea had not disappeared.[10] The Elizabethan was fond of viewing life as a progressive historical process.

For a drama which is an image of the career of a ruler or prominent man, this means, an expansion in structure, because it becomes meaningful to see how the hero arrived at his power, to see his machinations. It also means that he may lose his power more slowly. Oedipus is struck down in a day; Macbeth's decay stretches back many "yesterdays" from the moment of his actual physical defeat by Macduff. The tendency to order events as a chronicle of history also leads to the double plot, because in history many things happen at once, and the story of a hero is likely to be entwined with the stories of those who followed or opposed him.

The late nineteenth-century drama reflects the assumptions of Laplace and his mechanistic theory that given enough knowledge of the mechanisms which control life—a state which he assumed we were rapidly approaching—all events could be predicted from natural laws.[11] Thus the structure of the plays of the period exhibit a carefully ordered progression of events building to climax and denouement according to the "laws" of playwriting (which only reflected the *assumed* laws of natural phenomena). Indeed, all the facts necessary for accurate prediction are thoughtfully supplied by the nineteenth-century dramatist. Each event, even to each entrance and exit, was painstakingly motivated, which is tantamount to saying that a cause was provided *within* the play.

The structure of the well-made play has dominated drama for over one hundred years and it is not yet dead; however, a different form of drama, the "theatre of the absurd,"[12] has attained notice in the 1960s. The assumption about the nature of life in time which one of the outstanding representatives of this school, Eugene Ionesco, shares with his audience is that life is absurd and repetitive. Thus, in *The Bald Soprano*, when the actors reach the end of the play they start all over again. Opposing the carefully motivated structure of the well-made play (which is the target for a number of the satiric devices in *The Bald Soprano*), Ionesco introduces remarks and incidents which the regular gathering of evidence or the laws of cause and effect cannot connect with later remarks and incidents. For example, at the opening of the play the Smiths are talking about the large meal their maid has just served them; a few pages later they complain that the maid has stayed out late and left them hungry.[13]

The simple philosophical notion that what you see depends upon what you are looking for has been adapted to our use in the concepts of "assumptions" and "interests." These concepts will be a starting point for discovering how a drama is constructed because they provide some basis for selecting and ordering the events of experience.

In order to pursue the question further, though, it is necessary to split the investigation and follow, one at a time, the two aspects of dramatic structure which unite in the play: the individual units relating one to the other in their concrete immediacy, and the overall pattern of the whole. They depend upon each other, and whichever we pursue we must soon come back to the other. This fundamental dualism in dramatic structure corresponds, as I shall argue, to the dual nature of our experience of time—of which I have asserted drama is an image—because in time there is both the ever-present now of immediate experience and the sense of pattern in time remembered or foreseen. It is with this latter sense of structure as whole pattern that we shall continue in the next chapter.

Chapter II

THE BASIC PATTERN OF EVENTS

It will be easiest to break into our topic by considering first the general structural principle which orders the play as a whole. Not only will this furnish a broad view of the subject, which will be helpful for orientation, but this is also a reasonably familiar area which a number of theorists have illuminated. Perhaps it will be best to start by stating some of the things dramatic structure is *not*.

Dramatic structure is not a visual shape or line, but graphic representation of nonvisual phenomena, such as the graph of rising and falling action in a play emphasized by Freytag and his followers, has long been a popular and useful visual aid.[1] We have statements such as Marvin Rosenberg's: "I suggest that the form of conventional drama is linear."[2] Concepts of a circular structure, as the death and rebirth cycles, are popular among the anthropological critics. More elaborate shapes are found in "The Shape of Shakespeare's Plays" by Richard David: "*Othello* . . . has no stops; it is one great springing curve. . . . *King Lear* is a double curve."[3]

The visual analogy is a convenient one, but it is an *analogy* to dramatic structure; it does not describe that structure. No play can have the form of a circle. The problem is similar to the one which prompted Bergson to insist, in words which might well apply to dramatic theory, that the nature of time does not accurately fit the spatial analogies by which it is commonly described. "Intensity, duration, voluntary determination, these are the three ideas which had to be clarified by ridding them of all they owe to the intrusion of the sensible world and, in a word, to the obsession of the idea of space."[4]

The surrender of spatial analogies—circular plots, rising and falling action, and so forth—relinquishes the use of an apparently indispensable formal apparatus which has supported innumerable descriptive schemes, including Plato's elaborate cosmology in the *Phaedo*. Without it we must describe a play structure in terms of groups of events. Certainly this seems much less formal than saying it has a circular shape.

The fact that the structure of a play is sometimes identified with an emotional pattern of response, and that usually this identification is made in connection with a graph of rising and falling action leads to another misconception. Because, for instance, the peak of emotional excitement (the highest point of the graph) is usually defined as the climax of the play, there follows an easy but false equivalence between the line of the graph and the structure of the play. Actually the emotional graph is only the *result* of tracing the intensity of emotion stirred in the characters of the drama, especially the protagonist, or of graphing the intensity of emotion which the play induces in the audience.

Certainly the psychological constitution of audiences has some effect on the nature of a play. Man's sense receptors behave in much the same way inside the theatre as they do outside, and audiences are not able to endure a high peak of emotional intensity for very long without a break. Thus it has become a commonplace of playwriting that intense scenes should be built up to in waves rather than assaulted directly and steadily. A continuous and unbroken battering of the emotions produces numbness; therefore, the playwright, who ordinarily wants to represent our sharpest and clearest experiences, avoids those conditions which would dull our senses. To conceive of a play as primarily shaped by the author's desire to produce a certain series of responses in the playgoer is to hold, as Iredell Jenkins puts it, "with the psychologistic schools, that art has no antecedent *object*, but only the *purpose* of exciting certain feelings and attitudes in its audience, that is to say that the aesthetic object is a fiction, fabricated only with an eye to the effect it will have."[5]

Dramatic structure may also be conceived of as a series of purely formal relationships, such as repetition and variation. This concept of aesthetic form is usually derived from the visual or musical arts and extended to literature or drama. The analyst armed with this concept views the structural connection between two scenes in terms of the fact that there is a contrast between a noisy crowd scene and a succeeding intense duet, for example, instead of in terms of the fact that the two scenes may manifest a customary succession of events, such as a battle and a rest to lick one's wounds.

This approach, in which structure is identified with pure form (arrangements of physical materials regardless of meaning) recalls the theories of such men as Clive Bell, who wrote primarily on visual art.[6] Many of the observations of this school are persuasive, and certainly formal considerations of this kind do have an effect on the construction of plays (which will be considered in detail in Chapter VI), but no overall structural principle that disregards meaning can account for the nature of drama.

Yet intelligent critics like E. E. Stoll have been led by easy and inconclusive analogies to pure form in music and painting (Stoll uses both) to speak of contrast as the inner structure of a play.[7] Certainly there are such relationships discernible in many plays, T. B. L. Webster has, for example, painstakingly charted the character contrasts in Sophocles,[8] but to go from this to the statement, in the same passage, that "Sophocles constructs his whole play of character contrasts" is to make a static relationship determine a moving course of events. Character may be revealed by action, but character and action are not the same thing. The contrast provided by pairing a headstrong daredevil and a cautious meticulous planner merely provides a ground for action; it does not give that action its structure.

With these misconceptions removed, it should now be possible to make a case for what I hold to be the gross structure of drama, the gross shaping principle which orders the play in its broadest outline. This pattern, this overall structure, can only be accurately described in terms of a series of events, what we shall call the Basic Pattern of Events.

Certain groups of events seem to recur in more or less the same *order*; for example, the events of a journey: leaving home, series of adventures enroute, arrival or homecoming. Other familiar patterns are: rise to great power and prominence, decision to risk this for greater power, fall, new arrangement of the forces and persons; one person mistakes the identity of another, a series of comic incidents ensues, the mistake is realized. We recognize in these last two typical patterns of tragedy and comedy.[9] Descriptions of structure in these terms are not neat and precise; they lack the obvious formality of geometric description, but are they not more accurate descriptions of general dramatic structures than "circular," and "straight-line"?

The idea that a summary of the plot of a play—which would be traditionally considered "content"—represents the structure or form of the play, may seem galling, even when the problem is

28

approached with modern mistrust of the form-content dichotomy. Plot summary lacks the visual suggestion of "form" and the architectural suggestion of "structure," yet it seems likely that the locus of the relating and ordering principle of drama would be found in a pattern of the major developments of a series of events—a pattern which recurs in that order often enough to impress itself on our memory.

How do events come to be ordered in these patterns? In life, experience may be intense at times, but it does not always have discernible form. One drinks a cup of coffee, phones for a repairman, reads through a circular of new books: the events of early morning. They have a vague form and a certain tenuous connection one with another, but they clearly do not suggest the kind of marked pattern of events which may structure a drama.

Patterns of many kinds can be abstracted from the flow of our lives. A reporter puts events into a terse form that rapidly discloses the famous "who, what, where, when, and why"; biologists find certain patterns in our bodily processes, of which we are often unconscious; and historians, at least those with the leanings of a Toynbee, discover patterns of human behavior so abstract as to be involved with cycles of the rise and fall of cultures over periods of hundreds of years. Among these "stories of life," each of which has its own appeal, popular interest is often drawn to the story which answers the query, "How did he make out?" In other words, from the mass of events we are involved with, we abstract the history of a striving: man sets his mind on a goal, strives for it, and attains or loses it. Certain assumptions affect the decision to view experience in this way, among them the unity of the person who strives, the assumption of free and conscious decision to strive, assumptions as to the efficacy of effort, etc. Pure pattern is rarely found in any one personal experience though, for the strivings we know are intermittent and frequently inconclusive.

There is, however, considerable interest in the kind of shaped experience we have called "the history of a striving."[10] In primitive times, the success or failure of striving to capture an animal in a hunt or striving to defeat an enemy presumably meant a great deal to the person involved, as well as to his tribe. In our own society the success of our effort can win us a nicer house, a desired bride, even life or death. These rewards give our strivings an emotional importance which most casual series of events do not have. The satisfactory Basic Pattern of Events, then, no matter what its nature, must be emotionally meaningful to its audience. They must care about the results, not in the sense of being in suspense, because the pattern may be enjoyed in retrospect when the conclusion is known, but in the sense that the pattern as a whole must stir our feelings about living. Such is the nature of a Basic Pattern of Events, the gross structure of a drama. Not every Basic Pattern of Events need be the history of a striving (although this is a common type), but the origin of other patterns is generally similar.

The Basic Pattern of Events is a pattern of "the way things may go" in human life. It need not necessarily be realistically feasible, probable, or "average." Nor must a specific historical pattern (as in a biography) contain a meaningful Basic Pattern of Events, although it may, because as Aristotle saw, history does not always have the compulsion of what he called the probable and the necessary (*Poetics* 9. 1451a 37–1451b 32). The Basic Pattern of Events is a pattern which seems to the people who accept it to illustrate a significant aspect of human life in time. What people take as being a significant aspect of our life in time is going to change, of course, as our basic philosophical assumptions of life change; the assumptions of an inexorable fate at work on the lives of man or of a universe of random and meaningless flux would bring about different kinds of drama (Greek tragedy or absurdist farce), as we saw in the previous chapter.

One source of the confusion may be cleared up by noting the difference we assume to exist between the Basic Pattern of Events and the plot, because if no conceptual difference separates them, surely the more familiar term would be preferable. The kind of pattern referred to by "Basic Pattern of Events" is of a general nature, a pattern usually recognized because of frequent repetitions and/or the importance attached to it as a root pattern of experience. In this way it acquires the strong sense of pattern necessary to give it authority as artistic structure. Plot, on the other hand, refers to the actual mechanisms by which the Basic Pattern of Events is made to take place in a particular play.

What Sam and Bella Spewack satirized in *Boy Meets Girl* (a favorite Hollywood Basic Pattern of Events—boy meets girl, boy loses girl, boy gets girl), could in one sense be said to be a plot; however, we would take "plot" to involve the mechanisms by which the boy met the girl: that he followed her to the top of the Empire State Building, as in *The Moon Is Blue*, that he lost her temporarily when she mistook some token to indicate that he was already married, and so on.

Clearly we are dealing with stages of abstraction, where the Basic Pattern of Events quoted above could equally well be stated as "possession, loss, repossession," but the point is to distinguish a particular *pattern* of events, at whatever level of generality it seems most meaningful, from the specific mechanisms for working it out. A Basic Pattern of Events may serve for several different dramas, a plot for only one.

A few illustrations—statements of the Basic Patterns of Events of two well-known plays—may help to clarify the notion of this root pattern. First it must be taken into account, though, that there are many ways of seeing the gross structure of a play. As noted, there are several levels of abstraction on which one could operate. Also, especially in those great dramas we have always conceded to be packed with meanings, several different yet intertwined patterns of experience—each with a high emotional charge—may shape the play.

These multiple patterns can be seen in operation in *Oedipus the*

King. The Chorus, elders of Thebes, see life, as the old often do, with the benefit of hindsight and hence often in patterns. They offer us:

> What man, what man on earth wins more
> of happiness than a seeming
> and after that turning away?
> Oedipus, you are my pattern of this,
> Oedipus, you and your fate!
> (1190–1194)[11]

The elders stood by while Oedipus taunted Tiresias, accused Creon, and probed Jocasta and in the third choral ode warned of the fall of those who are haughty or insolent. Thus, by using the Chorus as sensitive observers, we come up with the following statement of the Basic Pattern of Events for *Oedipus the King*: The haughty man who seeks too much knowledge may destroy himself with that which he seeks.

This pattern seems to organize the events of the play correctly if somewhat abstrusely. It reflects the Greek ideal of "nothing in excess" and the terror of knowing too much about oneself, and it suggests a concrete temporal pattern of probing for knowledge with relentless curiosity: the interviews, the threats of torture, and the ultimate destruction as the knowledge forms its own awful pattern. This is assuredly a pattern of time and hence of drama because the knowledge must be built up bit by bit and cannot be dismissed once gained. The Basic Pattern of Events for *Oedipus* the play, as opposed to the myth, does not, of course, contain the events of the murder of his father and the wedding with his mother because these take place before the drama begins. This fact makes it clear that in whatever sense *Oedipus* is "punished" in the play for his haughtiness he is punished by knowledge, not by the incestuous acts themselves.

A different approach might state that whatever else it may be, this play is certainly a murder mystery. It contains the statement of the crime, the summoning of the witnesses, the demonstration of guilt, and the carrying out of the sentence. In contrast to the usual detective story, however, this investigation is not carried out in an indifferent city of "innocent bystanders" nor is the detective himself an innocent instrument of the law.

And on a third level, it would be easy to see *Oedipus the King* as structured by a pattern of striving, which, as we have suggested, is a common way to view events. It could be interpreted in the play at hand as: decision (to investigate), effort (the calling and examination of witnesses), and outcome (the success of the investigation, which is the defeat of the investigator). This is to read in *Oedipus the King* roughly the same basic pattern that Francis Fergusson found and abstracted to the tragic rhythm of "purpose, passion, perception."[12]

Thus by slightly shifting the frame of reference, the pattern of events in which Sophocles involves King Oedipus assumes a slightly different logic of construction: the intemperate search for knowledge, the detection of a crime, or the working out of a purpose. Each pattern organizes the same events, each pattern is contained in the other, and each pattern involves the protagonist in a deeply affecting way. It is part of the endless fascination of this drama that these several patterns *do* cohere in the specific events which transpire within its bounds, and they immeasurably deepen and broaden its meaning, as Aristotle realized long ago when he pointed out the effect of having the discovery (the climax of the quest for knowledge) coincide with the reversal of fortune (the climax of the striving) (*Poetics* 11).

For another brief example of Basic Patterns of Events, consider how *Macbeth* may have been selected and arranged by assuming a meaningful pattern for an image of experience as follows: the unleashing of ambition in an unnatural deed may return evil upon the perpetrator a hundredfold until the evil is stamped out by a return of natural order. Thus in Macbeth's career his murder of the "divinely ordained" monarch leads to his involvement in progressive evil—indeed a sickness in the land—which is finally ended when the rightful heir, aided by other victims of Macbeth's treachery, reclaims the throne.

If we have perhaps been able to give some notion of what the Basic Patterns of Events is, we must now add a few notes about its importance in the art of drama, because a good deal of confusion has been induced in this area. First, the obvious but necessary reminder that although the Basic Pattern of Events is usually intimately wedded to the specific power of a great drama, it is also frequently used in hack works simply as a framework on which to hang miscellaneous materials. "Boy meets girl, boy loses girl, boy gets girl" serves as story device for all kinds of displays of sex, fast cars, sunny beaches, and other pleasant sights, but for a different audience the same basic formula may tie together displays of verbal wit, as in *The Importance of Being Earnest*.

The Basic Pattern of Events shows the kind of fundamental ordering of experience which has probably aided the author in making his play and the audience in understanding it (although these two functions may be performed without either author or audience having explicitly stated the formula). It shows, then, how the play is structured. The Basic Pattern of Events does not represent a "deeper" or "real" meaning which is the valuable nugget extractable from the dross of the play.

This should suggest that the Basic Pattern of Events is of limited significance to the worth of the play as a whole, because it is after all only one—and that the most abstract—of the principles of structure which will be described here. A work *without* a strong Basic Pattern of Events would probably be of very little artistic worth (as I attempt to demonstrate in one of the examples of narrative in Chapter VII), but a good Basic Pattern of Events alone guarantees nothing. It is in those cases where the material of immediate appeal—even the sunny beaches—enforces the emotionally compelling pattern of experience in a specific way that we find worthwhile drama.

The description of a Basic Pattern of Events as a kind of root pattern of experience is sufficiently similar to the two related concepts of myth and archetype that the distinctions which forced the coining of this new term should be set forth. The Basic Pattern of Events is not a story or a myth; it precedes these possible manifestations of itself. Aristotle considered that story or myth was a structural cause of drama (*Poetics* 6. 1450a. 37–38). This, of course, was true in the sense that the Greek myths existed before the dramas did, and the Greek playwrights used the myths as a basis for making their dramas. On the other hand, the myth itself was an art form with its own structure, and, as we see in Aristotle's example (*Poetics* 17. 1455a 31–1455b 15), many of the events in the myth of Iphigenia as he quotes it do not find a place in the drama of Euripides. This leaves us still in need of a principle of dramatic structure which dictates which events in the myth are used and which are left out. The nub of the problem lies in the fact that instead of identifying a source for the formalization of experience in drama, Aristotle merely refers back to a cruder and more general art work. In modern drama, where there is usually no story source, this principle will not work, yet the sense of a pattern of events, which underlies myths, proverbs, stories, and the most sophisticated dramas, *can* serve to organize the traditional or the modern play.

In some respects the Basic Pattern of Events resembles what are called archetypal patterns. The meaning of "archetype" varies with the user; we shall be concerned here only with its use by the three writers who have contributed most to its popularity: Northrop Frye, Maud Bodkin, and C. G. Jung. Frye, who inherits the term from the other two, uses it in a very wide sense:

> I mean by an archetype a symbol which connects one poem with another and thereby helps to unify and integrate our literary experience. . . . A symbol like the sea or the heath

cannot remain within Conrad or Hardy: it is bound to expand over many works into an archetypal symbol of literature as a whole.[13]

In Frye, then, the sea can be an archetype, a character can be an archetype, and a plot (in the loose sense) may be an archetype. It is in the latter sense, where Frye's archetype covers a root arrangement of actions or events, that it coincides with the sense we intend for the Basic Pattern of Events. As Frye explains this aspect of his concept:

> The archetypal analysis of the plot of a novel or play would deal with it in terms of the generic, recurring, or conventional actions which show analogies to rituals: the weddings, funerals, intellectual and social initiations, executions or mock executions, the chasing away of the scapegoat villain, and so on.[14]

Frye is not interested in how the archetypes are derived—he notes that they exist. In this he differs particularly from Jung and Bodkin, who are primarily interested in the psychological aspects of the archetype in literature.

C. G. Jung may be considered the "inventor" of the archetype, and at the very beginning of her book—significantly subtitled "Psychological Studies of Imagination"—Miss Bodkin summarizes Jung's theory of the archetype as it would pertain to her investigations into its appearance in works of poetry and drama —and, hence, its pertinence to our study:

> In an article, "On the relation of analytical psychology to poetic art," Dr. C. G. Jung has set forth an hypothesis in regard to the psychological significance of poetry. The special emotional significance possessed by certain poems—a significance going beyond any definite meaning conveyed— he attributes to the stirring in the reader's mind, within or beneath his conscious response, of unconscious forces which he terms "primordial images," or archetypes. These archetypes he describes as "psychic residua of numberless experiences of the same types," experiences which have hap-

pened not to the individual but to his ancestors, and of which the results are inherited in the structure of the brain, *a priori* determinants of individual experience.[15]

The most controversial aspect of the Jungian archetype—which Miss Bodkin neither wholly accepts or rejects[16]—is the idea that these archetypes are "inherited in the structure of the brain." Jung claims:

> Typical mythologems were observed among individuals to whom all knowledge of this kind was absolutely out of the question, and where indirect derivation from religious ideas that might have been known to them, or from popular figures of speech, was impossible. Such conclusions forced us to assume that we must be dealing with "autochthonous" revivals independent of all tradition, and, consequently, that "myth-forming" structural elements must be present in the unconscious psyche.[17]

It is very hard to say what these archetypal structures are, for being "essentially unconscious, . . . it is impossible to say what they refer to." An archetype, however, seems best described as a "nucleus, an unconscious core of meaning."[18] Some further description in Jung's "Conclusion" may throw a little more light on the problem—if not on the archetype itself:

> No archetype can be reduced to a simple formula. It is a vessel which we can never empty, and never fill. It has a potential existence only, and when it takes shape in matter it is no longer what it was. It persists throughout the ages and requires interpreting ever anew. The archetypes are the imperishable elements of the unconscious, but they change their shape continually.[19]

Criticisms of Jung's archetypal theory by psychologists and physiologists are clearly outside the bounds of this essay; however, two more relevant criticisms should be noted briefly because they have been influential in our abandonment of the term. In discussing Jung's theory of the archetype and quoting passages from the *Essays on a Science of Mythology*, Melville J. and Frances S. Herskovits state: "To those who have had first-hand experience with nonliterate peoples . . . the passages we quote from Jung take on an air of fantasy."[20] In a more generous mood, they conclude, however, that "the *mystique* of the archetype falls into that large body of theoretical formulations that explains universals in human behavior without the benefit of empirical proof."[21] Rudolf Arnheim has also undertaken to displace the archetypal theory of structures by endeavoring to show that dynamic properties in simple geometric shapes lead to the "spontaneous perception of symbolic meaning."[22]

This is perhaps enough to show that our Basic Pattern of Events is not coincidental with the Jungian archetype because: (1) no claim is made (or denied) that any Basic Patterns of Events are inherent in the structure of the brain, or even that they are primordial or traditional—some patterns certainly are ancient, like the birth-death-resurrection pattern, but other patterns, like the wait for narcotics in Jack Gelber's *The Connection* and Samuel Beckett's *Endgame*, are very recent and "special"; and (2) the Basic Pattern of Events is precisely a *pattern of events*, a series of happenings which seem to have some importance as collected and ordered. The Basic Pattern of Events is not a symbol or core of meanings like Frye's sea or heath.

The Basic Pattern of Events does share with the archetypal pattern of events the sense of existing prior to any specific instance of itself. That is, we sense a pattern of events in our experience before it is set down in any drama and as distinct from those dramas which manifest it. These sensed patterns could be verbalized in such general statements as "That which goes up must come down" (surely general enough to qualify as an archetype), yet the fact that we do make these generalizations hardly involves a mystery deep enough to entail the usual archetypal theories.

In this chapter I have outlined a gross structural principle—the Basic Pattern of Events—which describes what is sometimes (inappropriately) called the "shape" of a play. There is, however, a large step between the Basic Pattern of Events and the individual actions which body it forth. It will be suggested that this area is organized both by set patterns (such as the ordinary progression of a day) and what will be called the improvisational structure, essentially undetermined, moving always into the future one step (one action) at a time. Thus we shall turn in Chapter III to some of the intermediate patterns which organize the materials within the Basic Pattern of Events.

Chapter III

INTERMEDIATE PATTERNS

In *The Birthday Party*, Harold Pinter has skillfully utilized a familiar temporal pattern: the preparations for the party, the drinking and games, the giving of gifts, and even the recovery, next morning, from the effects of the party. Of course, a birthday party is not what Pinter's play is about, but the familiar organization of behavior allows him to move his characters through the sinister cat and mouse game which culminates in the frightening climax to the party—and the play—when the blindfolded Stanley stumbles into his musical present: the pathetic toy drum. The pattern of the birthday party has been employed by Pinter as an intermediate pattern; that is, a retrospective temporal pattern organizing some large or small part of the play *within the Basic Pattern of Events.* Thus such patterns as the meal-time chatter of Meg and Petey, Goldberg's jokes, and the party itself, including the pattern of their game of blind man's bluff, all organize larger or smaller bits of the play within the Basic Pattern of Events, the progressive destruction of a man's mind.

Such patterns are impossible to catalogue; they spread through the whole realm of living. They appeal most obviously to the representational sense when, for example, a familiar pattern makes us recognize the life around us in the life on stage. But the significance can go much deeper when the patterns used transcend the reproduction of life to present an image of the patterned nature of our passage through time. The experienced playwright and director will be aware, also, that these patterns can shape and color the actors' behavior in a scene, giving it purpose and direction as, in Odets' *Awake and Sing*, the characters, while pursuing their more abstruse goals, gather for Sunday dinner, or play a game of cards. Poor plays often ignore the help that well chosen intermediate patterns offer and seem pallid and abstract as a result. Great plays, from the Greeks on, are redolent with processions, prophecies, trials, and all the ritual elements which mark our lives with specificity and excitement.

Here we must see the place of these intermediate patterns in the analytic picture being developed. The play as a whole is shaped by the Basic Pattern of Events. This is the most general and most inclusive structural force at work. At the other extreme stand the individual single units of which the play is composed, the immediate actions. In rough analogy this would correspond to the simple drawn outline of a house—an abstract indication of over-all shape—and the individual concrete bricks which in combination will fill up this outline. The actions (bricks) do not constitute a structure because structure is the relationship among units, and the decision to designate the action as smallest "indivisible" unit is an arbitrary one because the action could as readily be broken into constituent parts as the brick could be analysed into grains of clay.

Given this gross outline and the concrete units which will fill it out, the task becomes one of describing the structural forces between: the structures which shape parts of plays within the outline of the Basic Patterns of Events—in terms of the analogy given, a door, a fireplace, a room. It has been suggested that there are two different kinds of structural forces: one which organizes events into patterns seen, as if in retrospect, as complete—such patterns as birth, death, and resurrection or morning, noon, and evening fall into this category; and the other we shall call improvisational, moving forward in a perpetual now which can never be complete. The latter is the kind of relationship which is continually linking one moment to the next toward an unknown future, the perpetual process as opposed to set pattern.

It will be convenient now to round out the discussion of retrospective patterns in drama. Within the Basic Pattern of Events there are many temporal patterns organizing larger or smaller parts of the play. Since these patterns fall within the gross shaping of the Basic Pattern of Events and above the improvisational linking of one action to the next, we shall call them "intermediate patterns."

Intermediate patterns differ from the Basic Pattern of Events, which always shapes the play as a whole and is completely exemplified in the play. The intermediate patterns are utilized as they become convenient to the playwright and order as much or as little of the play as he may desire. For example, in *Long Day's Journey into Night*, within a Basic Pattern of Events involved in a child's acceptance of his parents as human beings with human failings (in the specific plot, the father's stinginess and the mother's addiction),[1] O'Neill has skillfully employed a number of intermediate patterns, such as the pattern of mealtime activities. In fact, the pattern of a day from just after breakfast to time for bed can be found in the play as a whole—while other patterns, such as those of the meals, govern only parts of the play. The pattern of the day is, in this case, coextensive with the Basic Pattern of Events. It is not a Basic Pattern of Events for *Long Day's Journey into Night*, however, because (1) it does not really govern the events of the play but merely supplies a temporal scheme for them; and (2) it is not, as the Basic Pattern of Events always is, completely exemplified in the play. It does not matter, thus, that parts of the day have been left out. In *Death of a Salesman* the pattern of a family reunion is coextensive with the Basic Pattern of Events for that play but does not really shape the events of the play and is not wholly exemplified.

The intermediate patterns, as conveniences to give a logical order to events, are not necessarily significant to the play, although they may be utilized with significance. O'Neill has made the progress of his long day suggest the movement from the hope of clear morning sunshine, through the haze of noon, to an afternoon of fading light and drifting fog, which gives way to midnight—dark, fogged in, and hopelessly focused on the past. The progress of such a day also suggests, by analogy, the turn of the seasons or the movement of a life toward its "evening."

There are a number of temporal patterns which have been utilized effectively in dramatic structure. Chekhov made use of external temporal patterns to provide structures of activity within which he could bring his characters together. Act I of *The Cherry Orchard* is a homecoming; Act IV a leavetaking (as is Act III of *The Sea Gull*); the activity in Act III is a party; and Act I of *The Three Sisters* represents Masha's name-day party. C. L. Barber presents a well-documented case for the use of holiday as a structural device in a number of Shakespeare's comedies.[2] The device has been of use also to O'Neill, who patterned the first two acts of *Ah, Wilderness!* around the Fourth of July, and Inge, who used Labor Day to structure his *Picnic*. The list could be greatly extended.

The patterns just discussed have been external to man, impressed upon him by the rising and setting of the sun, the turning leaves of a calendar, or by conventional formulas that govern the etiquette of a meal or a party. It appears that the specific possibilities for finding patterns that will allow the creation of images of our experience in time are limited only by the vision available to grasp them. This is a real yet incalculable limit, for who can predict a Shakespeare, Molière, or Ibsen—even a Gelber or Beckett? After all the countless images of temporal experience: as seasonal, as fate controlled, as plotting, as endlessly pleasure bent, and so forth, each with its own structure, we have from two contemporary playwrights two images of our temporal experience as *waiting*. Thus, in Jack Gelber's *The Connection*, the pattern of killing time (in this case while waiting for narcotics) becomes a powerful image of desperation. Samuel Beckett's Estragon and Vladimir wait on two successive *almost* identical days for the mysterious Godot. Much of the reduced life of Hamm, the invalid character in Beckett's *Endgame*, is patterned around the wait for a narcotic, in this case, the periodic injections of his pain-killer.[3]

The Italian aesthetician Gillo Dorfles has pointed out the change in temporal patterns forced upon man by a technology which has given him motion at speeds formerly impossible:

> But, while man has been conditioned ever since his appearance in the world, and is constituted in all his physiological structure to obey and respond to a "cosmic rhythm" (bound obviously to breathing, to cardiac pulsation, to the mysterious rhythms of the universe, alternating like day and night, the tides, the months, etc.) it is probable that only in our era has he found himself in contact with mechanical rhythms which interfere profoundly with his interior rhythms.[4]

One could add to Dorfles' examples the incredible speed-up in information processing. This has already had its effect on the temporal patterns of popular crime detection and adventure dramas, where the computer room with its blinking lights and spinning tapes becomes operational headquarters. It becomes apparent that any aspect of our temporal experience can be treated. The few examples already given, of images of our experience in time which have determined the inner structures in different plays illustrate the way this principle works for patterns external to man.

One of the most pervasive psychological patterns for relating temporal experience in drama is expectation and fulfillment. This pattern is only really possible in the temporal arts, because while it is not meaningless to say that a color or shape on one side of a painting fulfills an expectation set up by some device on the opposite side, the figure is stretched and metaphorical. Even expectation and fulfillment, which might seem to underly all drama, actually varies widely in both the amount and kind of use it receives according to the assumptions about life held by playwright and audience. The realistic drama, inheritor of nineteenth-century mechanistic assumptions, finds great significance in the pattern. When we see a play or motion picture which, by its general tone, indicates it is of conventional stamp and in which there is a man exhibiting the usual signs of a drinking problem, we firmly expect he will succumb to temptation at a crucial moment of his career. Each glance sets up an expectation which must be satisfied before the final curtain descends.

This is literally true of *Picnic* by William Inge, who covers his poverty of language with gesture. In *Picnic* the mere glance between Hal and Madge sets the audience on edge until the pair brush aside the conventional restraints to run off together. Many other details of the play function in this same way, as signs pointing ahead: Madge disobeys her mother and wears her new dress, supposed to be saved for later dates with the conventional boy her mother favors; Madge and Hal dance better than any of the other couples, setting up the expectation fulfilled by their coming together. The structure of expectation and fulfillment supplies the basis for the theory of the *scène à faire*, which in *Picnic* means that Hal and Madge must have their scene together. As John Gassner explains it:

> The so-called *obligatory scene* or, as the French critic Francisque Sarcey called it, the *scène à faire*, is nothing more than a scene made obligatory by the expectations created by the logical trend of the individual events. There is a place, at least once in a play, when we expect that characters will come to grips with one another or will grapple with their problem.[5]

Not all audiences have entertained similar expectations, however, and while the pattern of expectation and fulfillment is widespread in drama, if not universal, signs are read in different ways by different cultures. The Elizabethan drama, for example, does not usually load expectations upon relatively minor events. In *King Lear*, Kent's tripping of Goneril's steward, Oswald (I.iv. 93), brought no direct consequences and would thus have frustrated any expectations entertained by Shakespeare's audience. Avant-garde plays of today often make a point of breaking rather than fulfilling our expectations, as Ionesco does in *The Bald Soprano*.

It is easy to see how this pattern of expectation and fulfillment is suggested to the dramatist by our temporal experience. In daily life one foresees dangers—a sudden coolness on the part of the boss, an ominous knock in the car engine, a girl friend making flustered excuses for missed dates—these are read as signals of consequent events. Often we fill in imaginary endings to bits of information picked up. It said that Mr. X has begun to gamble heavily, and we expect financial ruin to make his family homeless; we may never hear that within the month Mr. X moved to another town and never picked up a pack of cards again. This may seem a trivial example until it is compared with the fact that Eugene O'Neill's mother was cured of the use of narcotics despite what the behavior of her fictional counterpart in *Long Day's Journey into Night* would lead one to expect.[6]

Since each event in a drama is included because it is in some way meaningful, the usefulness of the pattern of expectation and fulfillment lies at least partly in the meaning it lends to events. One kind of meaning that an event may have is as a sign of another event. This is not necessarily the same as cause and effect: although arthritic pains may be a sign of damp weather, they certainly do not cause it.

The popular assumption is that signs are meaningful, that most events are interconnected; therefore, in the drama—which is an image of our beliefs about our life in time—the man who buys a gun uses it before the play is over. The pattern, as suggested, is not universal. Although the "laws" of dramatic technique at the beginning of the century dictated that each event should have its "preparation" or "foreshadowing,"[7] this can clearly be a "law" only for the playwright who believes that events in life are meaningfully connected in this way. For a playwright who believes that events are random, following the laws of preparation and foreshadowing could only result in a mechanical and hollow play. The connectedness of the events is not the criterion of excellence in all drama, and as beliefs or assumptions change the overprominence of expectation and fulfillment in dramatic structure will fade, as it seems to be doing today.

These larger patterns, like expectation and fulfillment, are seen *as* patterns primarily by the audience or author and not always by the characters of the play. The characters of the play in generating their own future *do*, though, see and give the illusion of creating the improvisational structure discussed in Chapter V. It might be argued, too, that at least in the best plays the important characters have some sense of the larger patterns.

A less precisely temporal scheme lies in the structure of the trick, two superb and fairly extended examples of which may be found in the similar tricks played on Falstaff and Parolles in *Henry IV-1* and *All's Well that Ends Well*. It is easy to see how this pattern derives from life, but the image of trickery is perfected in the drama. Falstaff does not "catch on" and spoil the joke, as he very well might have; and what is perhaps more miraculous, Malvolio in *Twelfth Night* does not see or hear all those chattering cursing tricksters who watch him pick up and read Maria's note.

Even a short joke, a conventional formula of greeting, or repartee gives structure to its small section of the play. One thinks for example, of certain formalities of conversation, common to the Restoration, which provide the patterns which could turn any gallant's conversation into "wit."

As a final example of the kind of temporal pattern a playwright may borrow from life to use as a dramatic structure, there is the interesting case of the *contest*. In this pattern the succession of events is well provided for: decision to enter the contest, taking cognizance of the chances of winning and the payment for defeat, the contest itself (horse races and automobile races have been the center of a number of motion pictures), and acceptance of the results. In real life the outcome depends on some mixture of skill and chance, but in the drama the outcome depends on what might be called "poetic justice." In other words, chance does not operate in the play, but the outcome (an image of what we assume to be a meaningful result of chance operation in real life) is pre-set in the Basic Pattern of Events. "Poetic justice" in this case is an excellent example of an assumption at work: we assume that in the meaningful instance, when the chips are down, chance will favor the pure in heart.

This has been only a sampling of temporal patterns that have been utilized in dramatic structure. Some patterns are not of immediate concern here because they come from poetry or the other arts. These are, for example, the rhetorical devices which organize much of classical Spanish and Elizabethan drama, including the charming speech in *As You Like It*, "For your brother and my sister no sooner met but they looked, no sooner looked but they loved, no sooner loved but they sighed, no sooner sighed but they asked one another the reason, no sooner knew the reason but they sought the remedy." (V.ii.35–40)[8] Some patterns, such as prologue and epilogue devices and the play-within-a-play, are metapatterns, derived from the literal nature of the process of presenting a drama.

I have not attempted a rigorous and exhaustive classification and description of all the set patterns that, within the Basic Pattern of Events, organize parts of plays.[9] I have, however, tried to suggest the sources and uses such patterns have. Since the examples of intermediate patterns could be expanded enormously—without any appreciably greater clarification of the principles involved—it seems appropriate to turn now to the basic building blocks in our structures, the immediate unit actions.

Chapter IV

ACTIONS

THE NATURE OF ACTIONS

The enjoyment we experience when Lady Macbeth breaks in on her wavering thane (I.vii.28) to draw him back to Duncan's side and to their purposed murder is only partly attributable to our sense of the development of the gross patterns of the play, because both the development of these patterns and our moment to moment stimulation are dependent on the texture of the immediate moment of the drama. To describe the structural place of this component of the dramatic experience we have designated a basic indivisible unit or building block termed an "action."

Clearly the establishment of such a unit is an arbitrary though useful fiction. As Eugene T. Gendlin points out in his analysis of experiencing to which we made reference in our discussion of assumptions, "Experiencing is not constituted of unit experiences (but only symbolizing makes it so)."[1] Actions viewed as units are constructs, symbolizations, or abstractions (all of which amount to much the same thing in this context) which the playwright makes in representing experience and which the analyst makes in looking at the drama of life. The idea that life can be meaningfully represented or analysed in terms of actions is an assumption which we make about reality—the basic assumption involved in the decision to write drama.[2]

Susanne Langer's thought reinforces this point when she develops her central notion that "The arts, like language, abstract from experience certain aspects for our contemplation,"[3] to yield a basic abstraction for each of the arts which, in the case of drama, leads her to say, "Its basic abstraction is the act."[4] The suggestion of a basic abstraction, thus, is a fruitful one, though the notion of art as *abstract* needs careful qualification and Mrs. Langer's elaboration of the nature of the act in dramatic structure has weaknesses which will be dealt with below.[5]

An action is here being taken to mean the basic unit of striving, an act or deed, which may be pursued with words and/or physical movements. An action *may* be purely mental, but the number of mental actions in a drama must be limited if the audience is to follow what is happening on stage. Two well-known uses of "action" in dramatic theory color the term and require that its usage in this book be carefully distinguished, especially since its usage here, although concurrent with the main critical tradition, has a more limited special sense.

For Aristotle an action was the thing which drama imitated and he so presented it in the famous definition offered in *Poetics* 6, "Tragedy, then, is an imitation of an action that is serious, complete, and of a certain magnitude." The word Aristotle used is *praxis* which commonly means a doing and in this respect accords with the usage here. The difference is that Aristotle is clearly thinking of one large action which constitutes the whole play. In this sense the action of *Oedipus Rex* might be "to cleanse the city."[6] An action in the sense understood in our analysis, while similar in kind (a doing), is much smaller in scope and constitutes one of the individual acts which are the concrete steps in the accomplishment of Aristotle's one over-all action. An example of this smaller unit action from the same play might be "to demand evidence," when Oedipus in lines 300–315 bids the blind prophet Teiresias to tell all he knows of the crime which is polluting Thebes.

Actions are like the popular trick boxes each of which is found to contain a smaller one. In a simple example, the action "to go to New York" might be broken down into units like "to phone for a reservation," "to get to the airport," and "to board the plane," but each of these could similarly be analysed into such smaller actions as "to pick up the phone," and "to dial." The object is not to find a basic element which it is impossible to subdivide, but to *assume* convenient analytic units which will serve in both the study and the rehearsal hall.

The second use of the term "action" has actually found its way to us from the rehearsal hall where it is popularly used by actors and directors influenced by Stanislavsky (but not limited to them). Here the word has a wider scope and—usually qualified by an adjective—can take in either the whole play or one small unit. When the actor speaks of an action for the whole play he usually speaks of an "over-all action" or sometimes "spine." In this sense *each character* has an over-all action which, at least in modern drama, is a little neater than thinking of the play itself as being an action. The unit actions undertaken to achieve the over-all action are called "immediate actions."[7]

Immediate actions have the same scope as what we term "actions," but the meaning has a shade of difference because what American actors have come to call "actions" are more accurately described by Stanislavsky's term "objectives." The Stanislavsky action is not so much something done as something *intended*. From the point of view of the actor, which was, of course, Stanislavsky's point of view, it was necessary to know one's action (purpose) *before* it was performed. From the point of view of our analysis, though, an action is understood as something being done, not something intended.

Ideas of intent, will, or goal are definite components of any process of doing, and mixed with the present there is always a part of the past and the future; thus it will be seen below how important Stanislavsky's emphasis on the given circumstances and the purpose, intent, or objective are to the concept of the action, but an "objective" written in an actor's script only becomes an "action" for us when it forms part of the actual performance of the deeds undertaken to accomplish that objective.

Having clarified our use of the term "action," we can now turn to the important matter of how this basic abstraction introduces a number of elements which sometimes confuse the descriptions of drama's structure. A simple illustration may be drawn from the works of Tennessee Williams.

By scene seven of *A Streetcar Named Desire*, the past has begun to catch up with Blanche, the frail heroine of the piece, who has taken refuge (a "last stop on the streetcar named 'Desire' ") in the New Orleans Latin Quarter apartment belonging to her younger sister and the sister's lower-middle-class husband, Stanley Kowalski. At the opening of the scene, Stanley, whom Blanche has inevitably rubbed the wrong way with suggestions that he is common and unrefined, returns to his apartment with the story of Blanche's career as a nymphomaniac in Laurel which he hopes will fulfill his objective: to discredit Blanche and reestablish himself as the rightful ruler of his home and his wife's affections. To do this he must tell his story to his wife, Stella, and must tell it in such a way that she will believe of her own sister the lurid details of Blanche's disgrace.

As usual, Stanley's communication with Stella is curtailed by

Blanche's presence in the small apartment and by Stella's attendance upon Blanche—at this moment Stella is fixing a birthday party for her sister. As Stanley takes up his objective, which in shortened workable form is "to reestablish his right," he first determines what Stella is puttering around for, then locates the object of his story as out of earshot (meanwhile depreciating her for soaking all afternoon in a hot tub when the temperature is "100 on the nose"), and finally fixes Stella's attention in the fifteenth speech of the scene with "Set down! I've got th' dope on your big sister, Stella."

The place of the immediate action, "to fix Stella's attention," as contributing to Stanley's over-all objective for the scene, "to reestablish his right," should be clear, and the combination and progression of actions will be discussed in the next chapter. Here the concern is with the immediate unit action as basic building block. Given, then, Stanley's immediate action, consider how it forms the basis on which the dramatic image grows. This action may be accomplished by either words or gestures or, more likely, a combination of the two. Stanley could simply grab Stella to stop her puttering with the birthday cake or he could speak to her. Here we see that neither words nor gestures are primary for drama but that both serve as tools for the accomplishment of an action. Certainly the richness of verbal communication adds weight to an art which without that depth would be a minor one, but the words, or what is sometimes taken as the literary aspect of drama, is not structurally primary.[8]

In any case, Stanley does not merely grab but speaks—probably moving to face Stella at the same time—and the words he uses *enrich* the action because they strive not only to fix Stella's attention but her attitude, particularly as he speaks of getting the "dope" on Blanche and pointedly refers to her not by name but at a distance, as Stella's "big" (i.e. *older*) sister. An inseparable part of this dramatic image which is spun around the action is the element of character: Stanley, the lower-middle-class Pole says "set" instead of "sit."

The nature of presenting an action introduces physical materials which must be organized to some degree. That is, the action must take place in some space, however well- or ill-defined, people are present as visual elements, movement or its lack will be noticed, and usually some sound will result. In staging our brief action from *A Streetcar Named Desire* the basic visual materials will be two figures grouped before a background. This will be articulated to suggest the restricted shabby space which seems to trap Blanche, and which at the moment under consideration enforces Stanley's action by limiting his privacy with his wife and creating his sense of urgency about giving Blanche the bus ticket back to Laurel that he has purchased. At the same time, the necessity to create a physical environment for the actors provides the opportunity for formal elaboration of color, line, texture, shape, and mass. If the restricted space in which Stanley's action must be performed is well designed it will provide a dramatic image which succinctly presents relationships beyond those conveyed by the words alone.

There is also an aural component to action which would come from, say, the sound of footfalls, the scrape of a chair, and the sound (as separated from the sense) of the words spoken. This aural component may be elaborated in various ways according to the structural systems of music and poetry. The movement in space, although extremely simple in our example, is also the basic material of dance and could be elaborated as such.[9]

No other art contains so many different materials, which explains why people are apt to see it as structured by the rules of other arts, particularly of the other principal temporal arts: music and poetry. But although in elaborating the image which is an action, the structures of the other arts may organize their materials in their own typical ways, they ordinarily do so *under* the basic structure of drama. The competing arts are restive, however, and raise their own typical structures to challenge dramatic structure, sometimes even to dominate it. Verbal structures overwhelmed much of the early nineteenth-century poets' attempts at a "literary" drama. Opera has sometimes eluded the ideal of musical drama to be a composition in which the musical interests lead the characters through the most illogical actions. Even designers have usurped a dominating place for their art as, in the baroque era, Vigarani arranged a number of court spectacles just to display the elaborate workings of his scenic machines.[10] In succeeding chapters the structures of poetry and music (as well as narrative) will be examined to show what similarities and influences may exist between the typical structures of these arts and those of drama.

The foregoing has indicated the nature and workings of the action within dramatic structure. My other purpose in this book has been to advance an hypothesis about how the dramatic image is shaped from the materials of experience. It is to this matter that attention must now be turned. In this pursuit the shadowy areas where drama and life are sometimes indistinguishable may offer the best clues to the transformation of the action. The drama, it must be remembered, offers less of a reduction of life than any other art (music, for example, reduces experience to only the aural aspect), so while it is more easily confused with life, perhaps its greatest strength is that it offers the most direct image of life.

THE SIGNIFICANCE OF ACTIONS

There are many examples of people mistaking drama for life. If, in our sophisticated society, it is hard to find a yokel who would rush up on the stage to save the heroine, still millions of Americans were shocked to find that the quiz shows, which they had taken as televised broadcasts of real events, were actually "scripted" and rehearsed dramas. An Italian walking in on Pirandello's rehearsals for *Six Characters in Search of an Author* (or an Elizabethan walking in on a rehearsal of the speech to the players in *Hamlet*) might well have assumed that he was seeing raw life at that moment instead of a play. Improvisations in acting studios provide further illustration and have indeed fooled the author occasionally. That one would be unlikely to be deceived for long in no wise mitigates the point that deception *is* possible; our concern here is with the momentary action, not with a whole play or scene.

If we cannot tell whether a bit of action is art or life, could not a bit of life, which we know to be life, be considered art since it is indistinguishable from art? Certainly there are many cases of this identification. The theory and practice of the so-called *cinéma vérité* in which motion pictures are made up of unedited "candid" photography verifies this.[11] But even more to the point, for drama, are the experiments of the creators of Happenings which, although widely various in their nature, have in some instances taken just this approach of making a "work of art" out of experience in no way distinguishable from ordinary life. The stroll through New York past an arguing couple, a man in a parked car eating celery, and other events contrived by Ken Dewey, Anthony Martin, and Ramon Sender and graphed out in *The Tulane Drama Review*, X (Winter 1965), serves as a case in point. These cases recall the practice of certain dadaists earlier in the century who exhibited *objets trouvés*, ordinary articles of everyday life, as works of art when, for instance, they mounted a piece of driftwood or a urinal in gallery shows. The dramatic analogies to the *objet trouvé* pose extremely interesting questions in the avant-garde aesthetic which stresses experience and practically excludes connection and meaning.[12]

So there is a kind of *objet trouvé* action which may constitute a work of dramatic art to those who choose to see it as art. The assumption of a specific attitude, or way of looking, that is peculiarly invited by works of art is problematic but it will be sufficient here if the piece of driftwood or observed incident is regarded carefully and principally—though not necessarily wholly —for itself.[13] It must also be taken into account that the person presenting these *objets trouvés* suggests that we look at them aesthetically by lifting them out of their usual mundane context and setting them in a place where we are accustomed to regard objects aesthetically; that is, the driftwood is mounted on an art gallery pedestal and the chance event is somehow induced upon a stage. Indeed, we commonly forget how important are the separations made by architecture and light in letting us know what parts of our experience within a playhouse are to be taken as drama. Pirandello nearly lost his life at the hands of an angry audience when he confused the usual arrangement.

The determination to call an observed event "art" is only part of the distinction we are trying to build up in the shadowy area which separates proto-drama from "mere" life. The other distinction is between dramatic art and other kinds of art. The interesting phenomena of the Happenings of the mid-sixties are more often related to kinetic sculpture and to dance than to drama, as may be seen from the fact that they have been primarily created by painters and sculptors. This fact may make them all the more valuable in vitalizing little-explored aspects of the dramatic image, but nevertheless, many are not in themselves what has been understood as dramatic.

The isolation of an object or event for contemplation, which we have just discussed in terms of the *objet trouvé* and the Happening, is, however; only one aspect of its nature as art (if such it becomes for us). Another important function of a piece of art is to suggest, in widely varying degrees, qualities outside itself. Sir Russell Brain offers an excellent example of this mental process in which his experience of the flying fish, isolated and viewed aesthetically, became not only a beautiful object but a suggestion of more profound meanings:

This brings me back to the dolphins and flying fish, which I described in my first lecture, flashing in and out of my thoughts as I sailed home from South Africa, the dolphins leaping in lovely curves from the waves, and the flying-fish rising in company from the sea into the sunlight, shaking the shining drops from their wings. To me they were images as well as objects, and it is the mystery of beauty that it should be an image, as many have felt, of the nature of things, triumphant over all the accidents and agonies of life.[14]

This is precisely what can and does happen to parts of life: we recall certain incidents, separate them from the rest of our experience, and look at them as images. The experience of going through (or failing to go through) a door into a garden became an image for T. S. Eliot.[15] A poet's memory is ordinarily filled with particular sights, smells, sounds, etc. which function for him as images even before he has set them in a poem. The dramatist too has his stock of images, although the precisely dramatic image is usually of human interaction: the sorry spectacle of a man boasting to a group that knows the truth of his inadequacies, or a witty and charming girl fending off a too-chummy admirer, for example. These real-life incidents may be justly described as little dramas when they are selected to function as an image for the beholder; that is, when they are viewed (usually in retrospect) aesthetically.

The concept of art as an image of reality is of great importance to this study. We have defined drama as an image of man's interaction in time (p. 10). An image presents to the mind a perception of sensuous material which may be present or suggested, that is, the man in an image may be real or described. Use of the word "image" instead of "iconic sign," which denotes Charles Morris' model of art, is intended to emphasize the idea that the work of art draws our attention into itself rather than beyond itself to some external meaning, as signs and symbols tend to do. The image may be taken as a sensuous epitomization of an aspect of our experience. And while the work of art as a whole is an image, the parts may also be images, as I suggest the individual actions are.

Perhaps because it is so suggestive of qualities found in works of art, the word "image" is widely—and sometimes ambiguously —used in literary and art criticism. Critics who refer to "Shakespeare's images," for example, have in mind a restricted usage, such as that which refers to the "naked newborn babe" to which Macbeth compared the pity for Duncan (I.vii.21). My position is that the work of art *qua* art functions in the manner of an image.[16]

Our appellation "image" must not be understood to limit "true" art to one vision or, the corollary of this technique, interpret the variety of art with one set intention. Although perhaps "image" implies a kind of art which is high in reflected content, it is meant here to include art which may fall anywhere on the spectrum from highly referential art, modest or naive in its own formal qualities —such as naturalistic drama or the lesser medieval morality plays—to the purest formalism where reference to systems outside the art itself, be they the literal physical aspects of life or conceptual systems, are minimal—as can be most strikingly demonstrated in music or abstract painting but which Wilde approximated in his dramas. We would hold—without affording the space to argue the view—that neither end of the spectrum allows a pure case, that is a work of art purely referential (a transparent counter pointing beyond itself), or a work of art, even music, which gains its power by referring to nothing else in our experience. The image which is art, and thus interesting in itself to some degree, is an object or event, ordinarily refined, which reflects *some* aspect of our literal or formal experience as suggested by the interests and assumptions the artist and his audience take as important and/or interesting.

We have suggested so far that a "found" event may, by selection, be taken as a work of dramatic art, implying an interest in it for itself alone and some degree of reference beyond itself, even

60

to the class of events for which it stands as example. It may become, then, a work of art or image. While it is possible to use these moments as images, and hence as at least borderline art, they have two limiting aspects. First, we stumble on them usually by chance and unpredictably. Even at the local bar it is uncertain that you will chance upon a drama every night, and certainly one of the conveniences of art is that we can "order up" the experience. Second, even when these images do occur they are most often imperfectly realized; for example, a tragic moment may be glimpsed in distracting surroundings which disturb and obliterate parts of it. Hence it has become the standard practice of artists to compose our images for us. Despite the fact that the phrase "composed image" may suggest a contrived and traditional art having none of the vitality, complexity, and randomness sometimes attributed to raw life, the phrase need not have that connotation; it is here taken to allow all the compositional strategies of the avant-garde, including chance composition.

Turning our attention to the method by which these dramatic images are composed, we find that some very interesting insights may be gleaned from the work involved in training actors to perform these actions. It is especially here that the work of Stanislavsky, who was a superb investigator and critic of the mysterious acting process, throws valuable light. Stanislavsky, revolting from the stereotyped acting of the nineteenth century, eschewed copies or clichés of life in favor of a freshly created image.[17] In the process of creating this fresh image for which the actor is to live his part, not imitate it, the conception of actions bulks large, because basically the actor was supposed to *do* not *show* in his work. Stanislavsky saw drama as based on action. *"On the stage it is necessary to act, either outwardly or inwardly."*[18] But not just any action was suitable for the stage. "All action in the theatre must have an inner justification, be logical, coherent, and real."[19] Thus, Stanislavsky stressed the purpose or motive in action.

While one concept in Stanislavsky's system looks toward the

future in terms of a clear and precise motive or objective, another key concept looks toward the past in terms of a clear and precise understanding of the situation in which the character finds himself. This is the concept covered in the "given circumstances."[20] Those effects of clear purpose and given circumstances with which we are concerned are brought out by Stanislavsky as follows:

> "If you speak any lines, or do anything, mechanically, without fully realizing who you are, where you came from, why, what you want, where you are going, and what you will do when you get there, you will be acting without imagination. That time, whether it be short or long, will be unreal, and you will be nothing more than a wound-up machine, an automaton."[21]

In classes stressing this approach toward the freshly created image instructors often use as an exercise the performance of simple actions such as "to comb your hair," "to tie," "to open." The object is to see that the student actor learns to perform these simple actions so that they become charged with dramatic meaning, that is, become suitable images. With practice, the student will be capable of charging a long string of actions in this manner, and will be capable of working as a professional actor in a play.

What gives the simple action a significance is, first, that the actor perform it with a strong sense of purpose—a compelling and personal belief in the urgency of achieving whatever goal the action of the exercise is to lead to (as "to comb your hair" may be done under some urgent reason for looking attractive); second, these everyday actions seem to be dramatically interesting (significant) only when they are supposed to take place on some special day—that is, the everyday act of combing your hair becomes interesting only when the actor supposes the action to take place not any morning but, for example, the morning he or she first reports to a new job. The quality of being special refers not just to the popular idea of being exciting and pleasurable, but to a time which throws enough importance on the action to make it a conscious and unique act, not a kind of reflex action. Strictly speaking, every day is a unique day and could be made the "day" of an exercise or drama; however, in practice, it is only the special day which etches events in our minds strongly enough to lend significance through the clarity of their detail.[22]

Since the average audience member rarely pays much attention to one single action in a play, nor does he usually possess the experience of seeing an actions exercise performed and perfected in training classes, the "artistic" quality of the brief event in which a person combs his hair may be hard to imagine. Nevertheless, the single event can, for those patient enough to watch it, become a striking, if minuscule, drama as the student goes from the generalized and mechanical effort which usually characterizes first attempts to the fully informed and purposive behavior which shows (in the rhythms of the movements, the spontaneous reactions to the finished combing job, etc.) the nature of a person involved with time and process. With addition comes complexity, but however complex the whole drama is built of just such individual units as our single action example.

Stanislavsky's directions to his students have the effect of relating actions specifically to time. The given circumstances place an action in relation to the past; purpose places the action in relation to the future. This is close to Susanne Langer's statement about the drama referred to at the beginning of this chapter: "Its basic abstraction is the act, which springs from the past, but is directed toward the future, and is always great with things to come."[23] Mrs. Langer deplores the Stanislavsky idea of "living the part,"[24] but the material from the Stanislavsky System developed in this chapter may be used to fill in an important point on which Mrs. Langer is vague (*how* the action may be "great with things to come") as well as to clarify the nature of the action as image.

Mrs. Langer offers the following statements:

> As literature creates a virtual past, drama creates a virtual future.[25]

> Dramatic action is a semblance of action so constructed that a whole, indivisible piece of virtual history is implicit in it, as a yet unrealized form, long before the presentation is completed. This constant illusion of an imminent future, this vivid appearance of a growing situation before anything startling has occurred, is "form in suspense."[26]

Despite the confusion resulting from the fact that Mrs. Langer sometimes refers to drama as virtual *history* and sometimes as virtual *future*, I think it is clear, at least in the passage just quoted, that she sees the drama as looking to time ahead which, as Mrs. Langer sees it, is "virtual," or illusionary (on the analogy of virtual images in optics, such as rainbows and mirages).[27] Because Mrs. Langer is committed to a doctrine in which only the organic whole of a work of art has meaning, she runs into a problem in drama, where the work is not given all at once. This forces her to overextend the amount of "virtual future" contained in any one action or group of actions until, as she says, "a whole, indivisible piece of virtual history is implicit in it." This unfortunate and unnecessary pressure distorts a valid insight into a mystical belief.

But, of course, there is the hint of future in each action. It need not be a mystical presence, however, and a further look at the student actions exercises can point to the concrete evidences of the future in each dramatic moment. These evidences must come from the strong sense of purpose that Stanislavsky insisted is necessary to make an action significant. The classroom audience at an actions exercise can tell from the care the student takes with the action "to comb your hair" the importance of the situation for which he or she is preparing. They can tell from the general attitude of the performer whether the situation is expected to be a pleasure or a duty, and from the degree of haste, how close the

64

situation is in time. In well performed actions exericses (those in which the performer has a deep belief in his purpose) the students are often able to guess in detail the kind of situation being prepared for.

Where suspense is important, as in the melodrama, the action strains toward the future, sometimes with a loss of present reality. The most obvious device is for a character to make a prediction: "I'm going to kill you at midnight!" But a director's bag of tricks also includes such stratagems as having a character glance nervously at a door, then at his watch. In these cases there is a danger that the performer's sense of the present situation and of his purpose will be submerged in the sign language pointing toward the future; at that point drama ceases to be an image of human striving in time and becomes a series of theatrical clichés and indications.

It is not difficult to embody an intuition of the future in a dramatic action. In life we constantly make guesses about what a situation may become from our assessments of what it is. The dramatist, recognizing this aspect of our experience with time, contrives his images in such a way that every aspect of the act is significant. In this way an action, our basic building block of the drama, may be selected from life (as Sir Russell Brain selected his perceptions of the dophins and flying fish to serve as images of beauty for him) or, more likely, may be freshly constructed by theatre artists who utilize their trained bodies and imaginations to charge their actions with a sense of the given circumstances and purpose.

Construction of more complex actions follows the same pattern. The playwright, for example, certainly creates his dialogue with the same kind of imaginative grasp of purpose and given circumstances which the actor uses to direct a physical manifestation of the actions. At crystalizing purpose and given circumstances in precise dialogue, Shakespeare can hardly be outdone. For example, the exchange between Macbeth and Lady Macbeth in which she presses him on to the murder ("Was the hope drunk/ Wherein you dress'd yourself?" I.vii.35–82) is a brief verbal action full of Lady Macbeth's purpose (taunting her thane into courage), and of the given circumstances (her discovery that he is wavering in his determination to kill the king).

An action performed is performed in some *place*. This involves visual components which are articulated by theatre artists. The actor reacts to the space (its degree of confinement, heat, etc.) and the scene designer defines it with the pieces of furniture and set he places around the stage. Thus we come, *from life*, to the kind of action explored earlier in this chapter when, in *A Streetcar Named Desire*, Stanley Kowalski tried to fix his wife's attention by his speech and movement in a given spacial and aural environment. The process of refining each aspect of the dramatic image is essentially the same as the one employed by a poet, who makes each word, sound, and rhythm function as meaningfully as possible in the expressive whole.

Some further clarification of the function of the brief dramatic images constituted by individual actions may be found in an analogy to cartoons such as those featured by *The New Yorker*. These represent a single dramatic situation with a visual component (usually static, although occasionally movement is represented in a series of pictures) and dialogue (usually the equivalent of one "line"). A good cartoon or joke is quintessential, it epitomizes recurrent human situations, as a dramatic action does. A cartoon is a particularly clear-cut example of a type of situation. For instance, the *New Yorker* cartoon showing the chorus from *Aida* roaming through the audience demanding, "What are *you* doing to help Aida and Radames? Will you just sit and let them die?" summed up the feeling of a theatrical season which featured the return of the Living Theatre. A cartoon gives the "meaning" of a situation by giving us a tag for it and contributing, as it were, a "proper name" for handling and identifying that class of situation in the light of its clear-cut and attractive epitomization.

The following words of Kenneth Burke's indicate that he has found a similar analogy to the effect of literature (using the proverb as his illustration-in-little where I have used, as more appropriate to the dramatic situation, the cartoon.) "Examine random specimens in *The Oxford Dictionary of English Proverbs. . . .* They name typical, recurrent situations. That is, people find a certain social relationship recurring so frequently that they must 'have a word for it.' "[28] The sociological frame which Burke is anxious to annex goes beyond the pleasure I have posited to the discovery of the sharp image in and for itself and implicates Burke in the problems of literature as (useful) knowledge. It also has the effect of playing down the obvious formal value of such of his quoted proverbs as "He that hath lands hath quarrels."

The use of the dramatic situation, the punch line, to sum up situations in our lives takes place after initial experience of the art work. We experience a work of art with our total selves, including our memories of similar situations, or the work would not be understood at all. At the moment of experience, however, our attention is primarily with the work of art itself. The aesthetic experience would be clouded, if not destroyed, if we tried to bring all these analogies immediately to bear. Iredell Jenkins suggests how this may work:

> The aesthetic life always contains two moments. During one of these, which can be called that of discovery, we accept the aesthetic object as a unique particular which requires no context and has no ulterior relevance. During the other, which can be called that of assimilation, we make the aesthetic object a part of the body of experience, and it assumes a universal reference because of the content and the direction that it gives to our regard of other particulars.[29]

It must not be imagined that each individual action in a play has the striking individual significance displayed by the cartoon, which is a work of art by itself. There are striking individual moments, but most of the actions of a play are no more significant by themselves than is the word "chariot" without the rest of the text of Marvell's "To his Coy Mistress." Even the memorable moments of drama are as striking as they seem only because of the weight given them by the development of the whole play.

Many examples of the way in which individual actions in a play epitomize or form an image of life may be recalled by actors and directors. When a play is in rehearsal or performance, cast members are apt to be struck by lines from their play which aptly sum up common situations. This was particularly true of a production of *Macbeth* which I directed. Many of Shakespeare's lines, even some that on first reading seemed distant or overly poetic, with familiarity became the most natural and apt way of responding to contemporary situations. In their depth and precision they seemed to lend a clarity and meaning to the situations from which they arose.

Before concluding the discussion of actions it might be well to point out that although the examples used in this chapter were drawn from real life and from exercises in acting class, we must recognize that most theatrical moments are clearly artificial and some, to which we could scarcely deny the label "drama," are blatantly unrealistic. The examples have allowed me to speak of the manufacture of actions from the stuff of life without undue complication from the intricacies of the complete drama. The basic points hold for any play: once a dramatist selects an action he gives it significance by the methods described. This certainly does not mean that this action is bound to follow the surface aspect of natural life. Depending upon the particular interests of the artist and his audience, the dramatic image can stress any aspect of an action, including, as the advocates of "poetic" theatre would insist, the formal aspects.

The actions of Antipholus and Dromio in Shakespeare's *The Comedy of Errors* are basically natural. They contain a clear sense of the present situation and a strong sense of purpose; so much so, in fact, that they epitomize the condition of mistaken identity. Far from losing point by being set in a highly improbable situation, they gain from Shakespeare's inventiveness. On the other hand, *The Comedy of Errors* represents an amusing but limited image of human striving, and such naturalistic dramas as Gorky's *The Lower Depths* may have their point to make too.

All the individual actions should have significance, although they are rarely seen as separate. We cannot, however, consider that we have a drama until a number of these immediate actions are bound together in an over-all action "of sufficient magnitude," so the greatest significance of actions in drama must come from their relations to one another and to the parts and whole of the play.

Chapter V

IMPROVISATIONAL STRUCTURE

It is easy to see dramatic structure in terms of a pattern such as "boy meets girl, boy loses girl, boy gets girl," or in the events of a royal wedding (as in *A Midsummer Night's Dream*, which combines both), but it is apparent that these gross patterns have little effect on the immediate level, relating speech to speech, action to action. It is here that improvisational structure operates.

The nature of time suggests that two structural assumptions govern the drama. From Saint Augustine (*Confessions*, Book XI) to Pirandello men have been torn between the concept of a "now" which is ever present—moving continually step by step into an unknown future—and a sense of patterned time—time viewed retrospectively and essentially statically: a life, a career, even a hand at bridge begun, played, and completed. These two views yield the improvisational structure, which is the subject of this chapter, and the "retrospective structures," such as the Basic Pattern of Events and intermediate patterns, which were discussed earlier. Inevitably the sense of time as Heraclitean flux opposes the formal sense of patterns; inevitably man's image of time—his drama—reflects the facets of this conflict.

Literary composition alters radically from the univocal lyric when two independent forces affect it. In this alteration lies the basic identifying quality of the drama; in it also lies the basis of the moment-to-moment structure of the drama, which I call the improvisational structure. The most obvious example of two independent forces in drama is found when two characters confront each other: the standard dialogue situation.

It is tempting to follow Brunetière's analysis of the dramatic situation as having a conflict of wills as its prime mover,[1] yet many dialogue situations contain conflict only if the sense of that word is widely stretched. For example, the idea of conflict does not explain very much in the merry movement of joking between Maria, Toby, and Sir Andrew which occurs early in *Twelfth Night* (I.iii.47–142). It seems more expedient to say that the basic idea can, and often does, expand into conflict, but need not always be so identified.

The idea, the generating force for drama, is posited here merely as *difference*. Take two people and let them converse on any subject within the ken of both, and there will be a dramatic interplay—of however low voltage—because they will always differ in some small degree from each other, because, in short, of each person's unique personality. Dramatic interchange does not always occur when two people talk; in fact, both ordinary "small talk" and bad acting avoid it. In life the use of formulas (Hello, how are you? Fine; and yourself?) maintains a minimal contact without real interplay. In acting, interchange is prevented when the actors use what Stanislavsky called the rubber stamp clichés: a rise in pitch at the end of a sentence to indicate "questioning," a frown to indicate "displeasure," etc.[2]

Consider an exercise intended to stimulate beginning actors to dramatic interplay. In this exercise a student actor utters a word and his partner replies with another word suggested by the first word, and so on, back and forth. ("House, door, open, latch," etc.) This might be called a protodramatic situation because the partner is the necessary factor in the composition of the chain of words. Any one person can make such a chain of related words, but the dramatic progression is only possible where another person provides interplay by altering the progression in a way the single person could not have entirely foreseen. This is the essence of improvisation, and the relationship built up by this force is referred to here as the improvisational structure.

A number of clarifications are necessary, even at this elementary level. (1) Certainly *one* person may write a play in which a number of different people react. This is possible because the playwright composes in terms of the interaction of more than one personality,[3] as opposed to the lyric poet, who uses the progression of only one personality's thought. The nature of the playwright's creation is suggested by the simple but basic phenomenon with which the play is "brought to life" in production: the speeches and gestures are divided among individual actors, who do interact in what is essentially the manner described above. Dialogue which lacks the interplay, the unexpectedness, the *improvisational* quality of the partner situation is often referred to as mechanical; in these cases, the playwright has usually composed either in clichés, in which two people avoid interaction despite their differences, or from a single point of view, where the author proves unable to break outside one train of thought, even though he may assign various passages of this discourse to different "characters." Some of Shaw's arguments in *Heartbreak House* have this latter quality.

(2) Some monologues and scenes of individual business have

proved not only feasible but highly dramatic. Actually, although the interaction between persons provides the normal, and probably the most interesting, dramatic situation, the two independent forces need not be two people. Where only one person is present or active, he may be acted upon, for instance, by time, each unique moment bringing its own unpredictable force which interacts with the single actor in place of his partner.

Consider *Macbeth* V.v.: essentially this scene belongs to Macbeth; Seyton and the Messenger merely bring reports of off-stage action (the queen's death and the "moving wood"). Shakespeare, the consummate dramatist, includes some interplay between Macbeth and these two reporters, but the dramatic quality of the scene comes from interplay between Macbeth and the force of time bringing change. Macbeth moves from a defiant confidence in the security of his besieged stronghold, through bitter thoughts on the meaninglessness of life, to the bravado of his suicidal decision to force a showdown in hand-to-hand combat against Malcolm's vastly superior forces. This change from defiance to suicide is encompassed in 52 lines, 41 of which belong to Macbeth. The scene is intensely dramatic because Macbeth moves not in the timeless world of logic and free association, but in the irreversible progression of the "now."

A student actor performing a simple actions exercise must see to it that his purpose interacts with the ever-changing physical conditions with which he is involved. These will be slightly different every time the exercise is performed and will often admit of the little accidents which keep the actor in touch with a progressing reality. The situation is often made more complex by adding a "deadline," or time by which the given tasks must be completed. Thus, the single actor is involved not only with the progress of his task, which must be unpredictable in its details, but also with a measured time, which, although it will run out at a predictable point, leaves unpredictable how much of his task he will be able to complete.[4]

For example, the greater urgency of limited time drives on Macbeth's monologue of Act II, Scene i ("Is this a dagger. . .") because Lady Macbeth's deadline will end his innocence in a bloody deed. This scene is like a hissing fuse leading up to the summons of the bell (line 61).

To see the improvisational structure at work now in an actual dialogue situation it will be convenient to utilize a passage between Macbeth and Lady Macbeth appearing just after the monologue "If it were done when 'tis done. . ."

> [Enter LADY MACBETH.] How now! What news?
> *Lady M.* He has almost supped. Why have you left the chamber?
> *MacB.* Hath he asked for me?
> *Lady M.* Know you not he has?
> *MacB.* We will proceed no further in this business.
> He hath honored me of late, and I have bought
> Golden opinions from all sorts of people,
> Which would be worn now in their newest gloss,
> Not cast aside so soon.
>   (I.vii.29–34)

At the beginning of the quoted section Macbeth is on stage immersed in a situation which would require a long summary of the play and our independent knowledge of related matters to describe, but which may be summed up as follows: Macbeth realizes he has a perfect opportunity to fulfill the witches' third prophecy and win the crown because his king, Duncan, is within the castle. Macbeth's purpose is to decide whether or not he should commit the murder which would place him on a bloody throne. This debate with himself has been the business of the monologue that precedes the quoted dialogue above. Macbeth (the host) has absented himself from the banquet to consult with himself before he is catapulted into an action which can bring so many consequences. At the end of the monologue he has presumably still not determined to do or forbear, although he admits that the single

74

voice of his vaulting ambition is perhaps not sufficient counsel for committing such a black deed.

The first action following the monologue is the entrance of Lady Macbeth, which is a direct result of the temporal progression of the play. Macbeth has very little time to think since he will be missed at the banquet. His wife's entrance means the end of his soliloquy and the end of wavering; he knows he must take a stand. But the entrance means more than this, of course, for Macbeth is confronted not by a page sent to fetch him, but by Lady Macbeth herself, who is both decided on the murder and watchful for any inconstancy of purpose in him. On the occasion of her entrance cutting short his agonizing debate and forcing the rapidly approaching murder on him again, he stalls her: "How now! What news?"

Lady Macbeth is involved in the same general circumstances as is her husband, added to which is the problem of having a husband who not only shrinks from the necessary foul play to consummate their high ambitions, but has so far departed from looking "like the innocent flower" (I.v.66), as she commanded him to do, as to make himself conspicuous by his absence from his fond king's banquet. Her purpose is both to find Macbeth and return him to the business of beguiling the king and company, and to prevent her thane's having time to think on the evils of their plan. Her reply comprehends the situation she comes upon— Macbeth found alone and brooding: "He has almost supped. Why have you left the chamber?" She will press the urgency of the situation, the pressure of time, upon him and ask an account of his inconstancy.

Macbeth, hearing his lady speak of Duncan, makes an adjustment from his moralizing speculations toward a practical decision. But he has not made the decision yet and he passes almost incidentally through a thought suggested by Lady Macbeth's mention of Duncan at supper. "Hath he ask'd for me?" We know the thoughts from which this question came ("I am his kinsman and his subject"), and from his next speech we know where it is heading ("He hath honor'd me of late"). Yet the wheel of drama does not progress by itself, and Macbeth's mental progression needs the impetus of Lady Macbeth's prodding.

Hearing Macbeth's presumably ingenuous question, Lady Macbeth presses him further to make him drop his play of innocence and face with her the keen reality of the plot. "Know you not he has?" Macbeth's mental progression brings him now to a decision pressed on by Lady Macbeth's appearance and her relentless calling him to account. He takes the control of his life back to himself. "We will proceed no further in this business." He will stop the horrible movement which is carrying him at a pace he cannot control into evil for which he has no appetite. This speech arises directly from the situation, which must always be understood as moving and progressing.

In a proper drama, time's wingéd chariot is always at the back of the characters, whether it seems to be flying too fast or dragging unconscionably, as in *Waiting for Godot*. In our example, the last speech is the precise sum of all that has gone before. It could not have happened earlier, nor could it happen later. Indeed, Macbeth's soliloquy in the next scene ("Is this a dagger which I see before me?") is in a changed frame of mind, although it too carries the sum of all that has gone before, including this reluctance to perpetrate the deed. This dependence on the change and accident of progressing time, including the progression of dialogue with another person—the trial and adjustment of purpose—is precisely the quality of drama and the basis of the improvisational structure.

The specific nature of this quality needs to be examined further, however, for it transcends what can appear in a printed script. It depends upon the full and lively circumstances of presentation on the stage. Macbeth's speech above ("We will proceed no further in this business.") springs not just from previous printed speeches

—set down in a given order to be sure, but carrying neither in fact nor in symbolized form (as music notation does) a measured time—but from a *situation* which, to use a loose if popular figure, has the four dimensions of life. In other words, this speech takes shape not only from the considerations enumerated above in the examination of the text, but from these as a part of a situation which includes the physical presence nearby of Duncan, Banquo, and the other lords at banquet. This factor is so important that the particulars of it—their presence, their occupation (eating), the time of night, and their direction from Macbeth—were indicated at the beginning of the scene by the business, *"Hautboys. Torches.* Enter a *Sewer,* and divers *Servants* with dishes and service over the stage." The pressure of time, the increasing need for Macbeth to follow these "sewers" back to the banquet, is urged in the lines "Hath he ask'd for me?" "Know you not he has?"

Finally, the physical presence of two individuals confronting one another is an inseparable part of the situation. This is the dramatic fact of which the separation of speeches under character names in a text provides only a notation. Aristotle seems to have had some intuition of the importance of the physical presence of the characters when he wrote, "In constructing the plot and working it out with the proper diction, the poet should place the scene, as far as possible, before his eyes." (*Poetics* 17. 1455a 22–26.) A play takes on different aspects, and in just this improvisational quality, not in the larger patterns, when scripts are handed out and the different characters speak to one another. Most directors can testify to the new insights into the dramatic meaning of a play which becomes apparent when, in the course of rehearsal, they listen to the play read by individual actors. This is true no matter how carefully the director may have analyzed the text in his study (unless he is intent on transferring his preconceived notions of the play onto his actors as Reinhardt is reported to have done).

I have described a scene in terms which bring out the progress in time of the characters' actions, both as these actions emerge from the given circumstances and as they represent adjustments of the mode of operation to the status of the characters' intentions in the exigencies of the present moment. This is to *describe* a series of relationships exemplified in the scene; it does not specifically *name* the relationships. It would be possible to say, however, that action *x* is related to action *y* as representing the progress of purpose and to name the relationship generally as "later than." The difficulty is that the description of the relationship (which is to say the description of the structure) between Lady Macbeth's line "Know you not he has?" and Macbeth's "We will proceed no further in this business" fits too loosely in the designation "later than" because it is a special instance of "later than." Also, between the two lines one may find many other specific relationships which help to weave the taut net of our improvisational structure. Only the specific work of art itself has *precisely* the structure it has, and the only reasonably accurate description of that structure is contained in such an explication as that given above, even though it does not name relationships.[5]

Although we would not want to admit that the relationship is "*too* subtle for the intellect," the following remark by W. B. Yeats sums up the feeling of one confronted by the complexities of art:

> There are no lines with more melancholy beauty than these by Burns—
>
> > The Moon is setting behind the white wave,
> > And Time is setting with me, O!
>
> Take from them the whiteness of the moon and of the wave, whose relation to the setting of Time is too subtle for the intellect, and you take from them their beauty. But, when all are together, moon and wave and whiteness and setting Time and the last melancholy cry, they evoke an emotion which cannot be evoked by any other arrangement of colors and sounds and forms.[6]

Even though each relation in a work of art is individual, we may consider that we have isolated in our analysis a class of similar relations which are typical of the drama—a class which may find some use in genre criticism. This relationship, basically determined by the fact that one unit is later than the next, but also involving the adjustments necessary to ongoing action between different people and in a changing progressing time, may be contrasted with the relations typifying the structure of narrative and poetry.

The improvisational structure shapes an image of that aspect of our life in time which is concerned with our movement from moment to moment in terms of change and opposing (or simply *different*) wills. These immediate moments of drama are elevated from life to art (1) by being chosen as meaningful and interesting —a determination made through our assumptions about the nature of experience; (2) by virtue of the fact that the performers, through training and innate gifts, are extraordinarily sensitive to the changing conditions separating one action from the next, and are able to reflect their changing awareness in what they say and do. This awareness of the particular (and particularly *dramatic*) aspect of time mirrored in the improvisational structure is the mark of artistic ability in the theatre artist just as heightened vision characterizes the painter.

Perhaps a glance back to the passage from *Macbeth* can make this clearer. Assume, for the moment, that the scene is improvised by two extraordinary actors who invent Shakespeare's dialogue. The actors choose a situation on which to improvise which has to do with human interaction in time, rather than, say, the distribution of racial groups in the geography of the city. The situation has as its core the conflict between ambition and the legal and moral restraints on that ambition—a conflict which works not only within the mind of one character, but between the characters as holding two different views on the problem. The result is drama, not life, because the two improvising actors in the parts of Macbeth and Lady Macbeth are so sensitive to situation, purpose, and change that their physical being, movements, and speech convey in a marked degree what it is like to be in the clutches of time. They also convey what it is like to be an ambitious pair of Scots with a king's life in their hands, and although this is not the kind of information a modern person ordinarily needs, because the situation itself is assumed to be meaningful and because the improvisation is so fully played out, we get from the particular situation in Scotland of the Middle Ages an image of what it is like to be alive in time at any period.

An observant person can find numerous images of what it is like to be alive in time—in short-term improvisational structures —by watching people talk on the streetcorner. The artistic improvisation seen in a theatre presents a scene in which every detail of this changing progressing life in the speech and movement of the actors is charged with meaning, much as a poem, utilizing the same materials as common conversation, presents an image in which each element of sound and sense bears its refined significance.

At this time it will be well to bring back Shakespeare and return to him the dialogue usurped by our improvising actors. An important point, though, was intended by assuming that the great poetry of Shakespeare's lines could be improvised. In this point lies a definition of the genius of Shakespeare's dramatic poetry. It was assumed that the improvisors focused the situation, purpose, and change of drama through their sensitive awareness and responsiveness trained for delicacy and strength. They did this through all their physical means: movement and speech. Shakespeare's genius, then, is to "improvise the words." (Our concern here is still limited to the immediate aspect of improvisational structure, eliminating consideration of Shakespeare as plot maker, "Imagist," etc.) Where the dramatic scene demands of the improvisor the most sensitive awareness of situation, purpose, and change, Shakespeare, the specialist in words, supplies those lines which epitomize the awareness required. This is what every playwright does (with varying degrees of sensitivity and skill).

It may be objected that too much stress has been put upon the awareness and sensitivity of the characters in creating the improvisational structure. Dramatic literature abounds with characters who are neither sensitive nor aware. Eschewing borderline and debatable cases, the Martins in Ionesco's *The Bald Soprano* may be taken as an example. Not only do they communicate in clichés, but they are presumably so unaware that they do not recognize one another on meeting at the Smith's house. Their conversations, in clichés and with lack of communication, however, manifest an improvisational structure that is an image, and a very sharp image, of our human interaction in time. In this case the playwright assumes that human beings do not communicate very much.[7] Thus, the Martins' byplay does give evidence of a sensitive image of interaction *under Ionesco's assumption* of our failures of communication. It could be added that while many images are possible, not all have the same dramatic potential, and assuming a lack of communication seems—offhand—inauspicious for any lasting and widespread dramatic literature.

This returns us to the hypothesis which guides this study, that drama is an image of man's life in time in which the pattern structures represent our view of time as fixed—as capable of being viewed as *pattern*—whereas the improvisational quality corresponds to our sense of time as the eternally changing, eternally present "becoming." There has been, and probably always will be, some conflict between these views, and plays will seem to have more or less of an improvisational nature as their author sees life in time as spontaneous interchange or a fixed and recurring pattern. Racine's plays, redolent with patterns from the oxymoron balanced across his alexandrines to the parallelism of his scenes, represent an absolutist culture whose very garden walks were symmetrical—even though the breath of baroque movement stirred the classical air. In Chekov's plays, on the other hand, his characters move in an oppressive and absorbing present which precludes any meaningful pattern for their lives and gives the (superficial) impression of plotlessness. No play, however, can dispense altogether with either the structure of retrospectively seen patterns or of progressing improvisation. This is the source of the dilemma of *Six Characters in Search of an Author*, in which the characters both know their fate and must endlessly play it out "as if for the first time." Even the radical improvisations of chance theatre, destroying any sense of teleology by destroying any meaningful connection between events, in retrospect produce a pattern—though it might take a statistician rather than a neo-classic poet to see it.

The playwright intuitively recognizes that no play can dispense altogether with either of the two structural forces. A compromise must be made, and as this compromise tends to favor the improvisational force, hostile critics condemn it as formless and vague; as the compromise favors the set pattern, hostile critics call it still and lifeless. The image of time in drama cannot avoid the conflict of the reality it mirrors, and structures of myth, theme, repetition, death and rebirth, or, simply, boy gets girl must stretch with the accidents of progressing time which they enclose, because if improvisational structure compounds the nitty gritty of our theatrical experience, it also materializes the abstraction of a hero's fall.

BEATS

The improvisational structure leading from action to action does not form one unbroken line from the beginning to the end of the drama, or even from the beginning to the end of an act. The human being is not so precise. Instead, drama—and the life it reflects—seems to move toward its purposes in changing directions and at various speeds. When the purpose is changed, a beat is said to have closed. The analytic unit of drama called a "beat" is thus very like a paragraph in prose, and can be divided as arbitrarily in some cases. An example of a marked change of beat taken from O'Neill's *Long Day's Journey into Night* may make the nature of the unit clearer:

> *Mary:* Why did the boys stay in the dining room, I wonder? Cathleen must be waiting to clear the table.
> *Tyrone:* (Jokingly but with an undercurrent of resentment.) It's a secret confab they don't want me to hear, I suppose. I'll bet they're cooking up some new scheme to touch the Old Man.
> (She is silent on this, keeping her head turned toward their voices. Her hands appear on the table top, moving restlessly. He lights his cigar and sits down in the rocker at right of table, which is his chair, and puffs contentedly.) There's nothing like the first after-breakfast cigar, if its a good one, and this new lot have the right mellow flavor. They're a great bargain, too. I got them dead cheap. It was McGuire who put me on to them.[8]

It should be clear that a change of beat occurs between the discussion of the occupation of the boys in the dining room and Tyrone's mention of his cigar. The conversation continues about McGuire for four more speeches, then the beat changes again.

The passage from O'Neill is early in the play, when the characters are still engaged in more or less idle conversation, which naturally tends to short beats and wide shifts in the as yet ill-defined purpose. It is useful as an example, however, because the break is so clear and because, even in the text, a pause and a change of position for the actors is indicated.

The separation of a drama into beats (in which the director follows what his author's text suggests) is the basis for the rhythm of drama—in addition to and working through such metrical rhythms as may be present in verse drama. This rhythm in the beats is a pulse rhythm which, although irregular, can yet be easily felt, and which is manifest in a building tension and a release at the end of the beat. There is usually a variety to the length of beats in any section of a play, for example, the first six beats in Ether-ege's *The Man of Mode* contain twelve, nine, seven, fifteen, twenty-four, and four lines respectively. There is considerable variation in the tension or pulse speed built up in the beat and in the extent of change and release between beats, and smaller beats without marked change between them can be grouped together in larger beats with more marked change.

This rhythm is not the same thing as Francis Fergusson's "tragic rhythm" of purpose, passion, and perception, which uses "rhythm" only in an abstract and metaphorical sense.[9] The beat as analytic unit is, for the most part, a stranger to literary discussions of the drama. It is found almost exclusively in rehearsal parlance or in the writings of those whose experience with drama has been primarily practical.[10] Perhaps the reason for this is that those things which mark off a beat are more noticeable in rehearsal than on the printed page.

Ordinarily the beat is the unit chosen when a drama is to be broken up into small units for rehearsal. Also apparent in rehearsal would be the fact (suggested in our example from *Long Day's Journey into Night*) that a change of beat is apt to involve move-ment, so that shifting stage positions are coordinated with the shifting purposes of the characters. Of course, a move such as James Tyrone's cross to sit in a chair is only one of the many changes which mark the progress of an acted play. Changes of voice, tempo, intensity of light, together with the obvious change from speech to silence in a pause, help to vary this aspect of the play.

This concept of the rhythm of the play looked at more precisely shows itself to be based primarily on the sounds of the play, with the spoken word the most frequent and evident of sounds. How-ever, every sound and movement contributes to and must be made part of the rhythm. The sound of footsteps, the visual rhythm of a cross or a gesture, a quickly or slowly descending curtain, a sud-den "black-out" at the end or a slow fade, all are a part of the rhythm of performance. A rhythm of this kind must come from a sensitivity to the improvisational quality of the script. When the actor is really caught up in a give-and-take with his partner, the changing purposes and situations of the improvisational structure stimulate in him a speeding-up and a slowing-down, a growing urgency and involvement with the partner, or a slacking of interest searching for new purposes. There even appears to be something about the rhythm of a given performance which is fundamental to a judgment of the acting as believable or not, that is, as a performance in which the actor is truly involved or a mechanical performance.[11]

If the kind of rhythmic structure represented by the beats exists in a play, how is it derived for drama from life itself? The question brings up an embarrassment of riches because there are so many rhythms in our lives (both internal, like breathing, heart beat, and external, like pounding surf, click of train wheels). It may be sufficient for the purpose of indicating the derivation of beat structure, to point out that there appears to be a rhythm to striving. This is manifest in a driving toward the goal to the point where our energy seems to reach a peak, then a slacking off before the next surge forward. One would suppose that it is the same type of rhythmic response called for by "Heave, ho! Heave, ho!"

Of course the rhythms of everyday life are seldom developed or sustained. They tend to be brief, shifting, and irregular like the dialogue quoted above from *Long Day's Journey into Night*. As O'Neill's play develops, though, O'Neill draws in the audience by lengthening the beats and carrying purpose further before it is broken off. (Even so there is a characteristic kind of jagged rhythm to this play, since the characters typically agree only for very short periods before they erupt into quarrels.)

This rhythmic potential is inherent in the improvisational quality of movement from action to action and the dramatist, by control and manipulation of the rhythm, sharpens the image of life. The sensitive writer (whom we compared to an improviser in words) composes rhythmically. The director designs appropriate rhythms of performance derived from those put in by the author. The actor, taking the rhythm of the written text, and the rhythm of the performance as a whole, fits himself and all his speech and movement into this patern.

A rhythmic tightening and slacking of interest also satisfies the psychological-physiological needs of the audience, which requires a pause to sit back and catch its breath between moments of tension. Laurence Cor puts this well:

> In view of these conditions, the dramatist is compelled to cope not only with temporal and spatial but also with psychological limitations. As a result, he proportions his effects according to the faculties of the spectators. . . . He varies the dialogue according to the need for diversity that the audience naturally feels. The dimensions of every scene harmonize the necessity of action and the spectator's powers of attention.[12]

An interesting question of the emotional effect of pure rhythm arises in connection with music-drama, opera, melodrama, dramatic dance, and all attempts to abstract drama in whole or in part from the spoken word. Although such a specialized study of rhythm is outside the bounds of this essay,[13] some of the issues it raises are dealt with in our next chapter on the considerations of pure form in drama. First, however, one more aspect of play structure must be examined.

ACT AND SCENE DIVISION

Act division has an ambivalent nature in dramatic structure because it may be either purely conventional or organic and, in either case, its dictated divisions may or may not be physically marked for an audience at the playhouse. In part, act division is certainly conventional, the product of historical precedent bearing the tenuous authority of Terence, Horace, Donatus, and others,[14] and in part, a matter of practical convenience: to shift the set, sell more orange drink, stretch the legs and refresh the spirit of the audience. Act division conceived as a convention presents a mechanical slicing up of the play which would not interest us here; however, even the mechanical division of a play has its ambiguity because the division into acts may be physically marked in the production or may be made only in the printed text so that only a reader would be aware of the division. On the other hand, there are logical divisions of dramatic material into the two to five segments which have traditionally marked the act division of a play. These are analytic divisions corresponding roughly to Aristotle's triad: beginning, middle, and end.

It is well to observe here that this neat division of the ancients would hardly occur to all dramatists of all times; it did not impress the writers of the medieval cycles. Baldwin gives an interesting example of a perfectly logical dramatic division when he notes about John Bale's *God's Promises* compiled in 1538 with seven acts: "Again these seven acts are only the seven major subheads of Bale's argument. There were seven promises, so Bale devotes an act to each."[15] Even so, most of the great dramatists of the western world, through Ibsen and his inheritors, have found it logical to subdivide their total dramatic action. Explanations of this logic vary.[16] When drama assumes the Aristotelian tragic pattern the hero's progress quite naturally falls into stages which might be summarized thus: the hero is found in his position and discovers a challenge to it, the hero locks in final combat with the challenge carrying him through the reversal of fortune brought on by his struggle, and, finally, a new arrangement of the status quo is made either by the hero or his survivors. Where custom requires, this can be easily subdivided to give four or five acts in all, but even in these situations the clearly perceptible stages of striving are obvious in the play.[17]

Where these logical divisions really exist, something may be gained by marking them off into units—even by sending the audience out to smoke in the lobby—but this three-stage pattern cannot be imposed upon all dramatic material. The episodic plays of Brecht suggest no such act division. Samuel Beckett's tightly organized *Waiting for Godot* must be divided in two parts representing the two days of waiting. Much of Ionesco's material has suggested and been cast in one-act form. Motion pictures have demonstrated that even very conventional stories are quite palatable without any division into acts. (Changes of pace or setting do not constitute a cinematic equivalent to the intermission; they may be found also within the acts of regular drama.)

Often the time of a dramatic progress is not continuous, lending further logic to the act break. Here, particularly in modern plays, the authors have utilized certain qualities inherent in the periods of the day or season to underline the emotional feeling for the progress of events. A typical arrangement might be: Act I— early summer; Act II—the end of August; Act III—the first touch of fall. This is roughly the pattern of *The Cherry Orchard*, which begins in May, has a second-act Chekovian interlude in June or July, places the sale of the cherry orchard on August 22nd (Act III), and concludes with the fourth-act departure in October. We noted earlier O'Neill's placement of the action in *Long Day's Journey into Night* as Act I—morning; Act II—lunchtime; Act III—just before supper; Act IV—midnight.

Whether or not any clear case of influence can ever be made, these patterns recall the supposed connections of tragedy with myths based on the seasonal cycle. Certainly the hope of spring, the involvement of summer, and the reintegration of fall suggest the dramatic movements of purpose, passion, and perception. Other atmospheric progressions have underlined advancing dramas, such as the gathering of the clouds, the storm, and the clearing. Since these are readily discernible stages of life experience, they invite use in the dramatic image of life and become the acts of a play.

The progress of a play may also be broken into smaller units which we know as scenes. The beginning and end of a scene is very simply determined: one scene constitutes, by definition, the continuous action in one place. French practice further refines this unit by adding that the action must also involve the same persons; that is, when one or more persons enter upon or leave the stage we get a new "French scene."

The nature and number of scenes in a play (leaving aside now French scene division) depend on the author's assumptions about the essential nature of our life in time. It was demonstrated in Chapter I how an assumption that man's progress was controlled by a blind fate, or was the strict result of anterior causes, or was a meaningless flux would change the nature of the dramatic structure adopted. One such effect would be upon the nature of the scene structure, because a belief in cause and effect, such as was shared by most writers at the end of the nineteenth century, would lengthen the dramatic scene to let us observe this chain in its inevitable development. This logic led William Archer in 1912 to observe that "There is undoubted convenience in the rule of the modern stage: 'One act, one scene.' " (*Play-Making*, p. 90.) In practice we got, typically, the compressed continuous action of Strindberg's *Miss Julie*.

Where people think of the relation of events in other ways as, for example, that they are chronological and in a typical pattern but not necessarily in a cause and effect relationship, we get the episodic structure of scenes in Elizabethan plays or the Brechtian episodic structure illustrating forces—usually economic—outside the play proper. The fact that these scenes may also be connected by such relationships as contrast or similarity leads to setting a brief scene of life in a rich home before an equivalent scene of life in a poor home, or a scene within Macbeth's "constrained" castle just before a scene with the volunteer forces who will storm it (V.iii and V.iv). Such short juxtaposed scenes contrast with the practice of showing the unbroken chain of causal events leading at one time and place to a given result.

In short, division into scenes is really a method of analytically marking off units fundamentally determined by the nature of the dramatic material itself. No widespread formulas for the *a priori* division of this material into scenes exist as they do for act division. Scene division can, then, be most profitably viewed as a formalization of the results of the structural forces already described.

With this discussion we conclude our coverage of the principal elements of dramatic structure. Certainly other organizing forces of greater or less strength may be observed, but those forces which govern the specific shaping of drama have been at least touched upon above. Further light will be shed on the operation of these dramatic structures when, in Chapters VII and VIII, they are compared with the structures typical of narrative, poetry, and music. First, however, we must explore in Chapter VI the relation of structure as described here with certain notions of "pure form" including the effect upon dramatic structure of such highly abstract "formal" considerations as unity, balance, and contrast.

Chapter VI

STRUCTURE AND "PURE FORM"

Our discussion of dramatic structure to this point has implied that these structures are derived, at however abstract a level, from patterns observable in the real world. However, theorists have advanced reasons to believe that more or less of the structure of a work of art is derived from rules indigenous to the art itself, not from an imitation of life. Arguments of this nature are most commonly associated with the idea of "pure form" which has found a fertile ground in the visual arts and music, but little encouragement in literature. Nevertheless, there are elements of literary structure which suggest that they are what they are less through imitation of external nature than in response to the "purely" formal requirements of the work itself. We must, therefore, investigate the nature of these claims about dramatic structure to identify what effect, if any, pure form may have on it and to further clarify what we understand dramatic structure to be.

The value of such an investigation is not solely theoretical because a number of important rehearsal hall questions depend upon decisions about how far art may shape life. This, indeed, was the problem facing the beleaguered Director in *Six Characters in Search of an Author,* who was intrigued by the freshness of these "live" Characters but who wanted to alter their experience to his ideas of dramatic form. Even when we grant, as we must, some necessity for rules of form, there remains room for doubt about the specific rules employed and whether their authority stems from artistic necessity or from tradition.

The extreme, and possibly the most interesting case, is presented by the question of whether a nonrepresentational drama of pure form, analogous to nonrepresentational paintings, is possible. Experiments and manifestoes from at least two groups in this century (the Bauhaus stage workshop and the makers of Happenings) seem evidence enough that it is possible, yet questions remain about the real definition of what these groups have done and of its value as drama. To grasp what is at issue here it will be necessary to see what the advocate of pure form has in mind when he uses those terms and how these notions apply to the drama.

"Form" itself is a slippery omnibus term for which Lancelot Law Whyte listed the following—sometimes overlapping—meanings in his introduction to the symposium *Aspects of Form*: "shape, configuration, structure, pattern, organization, and system of relations. [also] . . . musical form, linguistic form, abstract mathematical form, and the forms of thought, of human personality, and of society."[1] Morris Weitz, examining common usages of the term, narrowed the principal meanings down to "shape, mode of expression, relations, organization, or medium."[2] In the same place Weitz notes Bell's and Fry's understanding of "form" as consisting of "*certain elements in certain relations.*"

Clearly our term "structure" overlaps "form" in some meanings. It may lessen confusion to remind the reader that "structure" has been used here to refer to the pattern of relations between the parts of a work of art. "Structure" generally seems a preferable term to the often ambiguous "form," and it has the advantage of avoiding both the imputation of shape and the seductive overtones of pure form. The concepts of form which Whyte and Weitz bring out present no real problems here but the notion of a "pure" form—the idea that these relationships originate and exist in art alone and apart from the real world—does require investigation.

In 1911 Clive Bell stated what must certainly be the purest position on pure form: "They [persons who can experience true aesthetic emotion, i.e., pure form] are concerned only with lines and colours, their relations and quantities and qualities; but from these they win an emotion more profound and far more sublime than any that can be given by the description of facts and ideas." The obvious ground for theorists of pure form is music, and Bell used the musical parallel, telling us that when he appreciates music *correctly*, "I do appreciate music as pure musical form, as sounds combined according to the laws of mysterious necessity, as pure art with a tremendous significance of its own and no relation whatever to the significance of life; and in those moments I lose myself in that infinitely sublime state of mind to which pure visual form transports me."[3] Bell's youthful position, as he admitted, was a little exaggerated.[4] Obviously it is extremely difficult to maintain the absolute purity of pure form. Even in music the "referentialists" still have not been driven from the field,[5] and the hermetically sealed pure form of Bell and Frye has been punctured by further inquiry. Two objections are the circularity of the argument (Pure form is that which yields the aesthetic emotion.

The aesthetic emotion is that which is yielded by pure form.) and the ambiguity about the rules for pure form (the "laws of a mysterious necessity"). Yet Bell's balloon is perhaps too easily punctured by such criticisms and by the historical observation that he was reacting in favor of modern and primitive art in the heyday of anecdotal art.

There seems to be cogency to the idea that a kind of form exists in art which responds to rules which, if not implicit only in art itself, at least depend on such highly abstract orders of experience as "unity," and "diversity," rather than upon the imitation of the surface aspects of reality. It is notable that at least a modified idea of pure form has persisted through the century, particularly among artists themselves. This suggests that we should explore the notion to see what bearing it may have on dramatic structure.

First we must determine exactly what is meant by *pure*. As Weitz has pointed out in the material referred to above, Clive Bell thinks of form as comprising *both* elements and relations. This allows for four cases of pure or impure art which are rarely discriminated. The possible combinations of elements and relations are as follows:

1. Pure elements in representational relational patterns.

2. Elements seen as representational in representational relational patterns.

3. Pure elements in pure relational patterns.

4. Elements seen as representational in pure relational patterns.

Before examining examples of each case, the concepts of pure and representational elements must be clarified. The elements or raw materials of a work of art are the sounds, colors, lines, masses, movements, etc. (all in themselves meaningless). In a portrait these lines, colors, shapes, etc. might represent a man, but the same elements also can be considered pure by ignoring the representational factor (with or without such tricks as squinting or turning the painting upside down). However, the present discussion depends upon making a distinction between pure elements and elements considered as representational, i.e., a man, a house, or a dog in a painting. It is most important to realize the distinction between what is *there* in the work of art and what is merely suggested.[6] In the painting the lines, colors, shapes, etc. are really there, the man is merely suggested; that is, no real man exists in the painting. On the stage, however, the man is really there, but, he may be considered as a pure element, in Bell's formalistic scheme, if he is thought of as merely a figure of a certain size—a mass capable of movement. On the stage, man is an element considered as representational when we think of that moving mass as Macbeth or Willy Loman.[7] We shall accept as representational all patterns from our life experience, such as the pattern of striving to the peak of one's effort then relaxing, whether this is presented representationally by a striving man or abstractly by sounds increasing in volume and subsiding.

There is, however, one important aspect left out of our scheme of possibilities. Besides pure elements and elements seen as representational, we also have the representation seen as symbolic. Thus in many Renaissance pictures of the Annunciation certain lines, colors, and shapes represent a white lily, which in turn suggests purity. This presents us with the possibility of making relational patterns of meanings: purity, womanhood, conception, etc. The same period that engendered these paintings also brought forth the morality plays, which are structured by relational patterns of symbolic meaning. These symbolic elements and their relationships, however, are not what the formalist usually has in mind when he talks about pure form, so we shall pass over them here, to take them up in our later discussion of poetic structure and thematic analysis, where they play a much more important role.

Now, keeping in mind the four combinations of elements and

relationships and the distinctions between pure elements and elements seen as representational, let us see what these combinations would mean in terms of the drama.

Our first combination, pure elements in representational relational patterns, might result in a drama consisting of colored forms, lights, and meaningless sounds arranged in a pattern of intensity building to a climax—a pattern, that is, which could be taken as representational of several effort patterns and possibly most basically of the sex act.

The second combination, elements seen as representational in representational relational patterns, might be illustrated by John Gielgud and supporting cast representing Macbeth with his friends and foes in the pattern of a treacherous act and its consequences. This is, of course, the typical dramatic situation and the farthest from pure form.

To demonstrate the third possibility, pure elements in pure relational patterns, one might imagine colored forms, lights and meaningless sounds in patterns built entirely on the basis of achieving pleasing sensuous relationships between the elements —relationships generally based on unity and variety. This would be the purest pure form.

The final combination, elements seen as representational in pure relational patterns, is problematic but the effect might be approximated by thinking of actors in a series of vaudeville sketches where the sketches themselves may have a representational structure but the arrangement of sketches in the whole program might be made entirely in terms of unity, contrast, and variety. The form of Happenings, which usually employ representational elements, sometimes falls into this category, but these more often exhibit an *unusual* representational relationship of elements (taken from the structure of rallies, streetcorner incidents, etc.) than a *pure* relationship of elements.[8]

Examples one and three, involving the use of pure elements, come the closest to what Bell might take to be pure form in the theatre. Where nonrepresentational elements are employed, the formalists generally brush over the distinction between representational and nonrepresentational relational schemes, and, indeed, the distinction is a problematic one. Indeed the distinction was ignored by the workers at the Bauhaus, who—accepting the stage as an architectural space and consequently within the bounds of its architecturally centered program—stripped the theatre bare and gave us some intensely interesting experiments and theories on pure theatrical form. They presented entertainments such as the *Mechanized Eccentric* by L. Moholy-Nagy which consisted of progressions of sounds, lights, and shapes whirring, plunging, spinning, hissing, and all elaborately scored as a formal experiment—"a concentration of stage action in its purest form."[9] In his manifesto, "Theatre, Circus, Variety," Moholy-Nagy proclaimed, "We envision TOTAL STAGE ACTION as a great dynamic-rhythmic process, which can compress the greatest clashing masses or accumulations of media—as qualitative and quantitative tensions—into elemental form."[10]

It is interesting to note, however, that just as Bell would welcome back the representational elements if they could be divorced from that which they represent, so the experimenters at the Bauhaus wrestled with the problems of reintegrating man as pure form into the space of the stage, where instead of his usual "splotchy make-up and tattered costuming," formally designed masks and costumes would place him within the visual whole.[11]

The Bauhaus experimenters, especially Oskar Schlemmer, however, asked themselves "how long . . . can any rotating, vibrating, whirring contrivance, together with an infinite variety of forms, colors, and lights, sustain the interest of the spectator?" How long, in other words, can the stage do without man and his meanings —man who is the "creator, of possibly the most important element of theatre: SOUND, WORD, LANGUAGE."[12] The relatively short period of time before the Bauhaus was closed in 1932 and the very basic nature of their investigations prevented these

men from going far into the meaning-centered verbal theatre, yet
a possible direction was pointed by Moholy-Nagy in terms which
recall our fourth formal category (representational elements in
pure relational patterns).

> The creative arts have discovered pure media for their
> constructions: the primary relationships of color, mass,
> material, etc. But how can we integrate a sequence of human
> movements and thoughts on an equal footing with the con-
> trolled, "absolute" elements of sound, light (color), form,
> and motion? In this regard only summary suggestions can
> be made to the creator of the new theater. For example, the
> REPETITION of a thought by many actors, with identical
> words and with identical or varying intonation and cadence,
> could be employed as a means of creating synthetic (i.e.,
> unifying) creative theater. (This would be the CHORUS—but
> not the attendant and passive chorus of antiquity!) Or mir-
> rors and optical equipment could be used to project the
> gigantically enlarged faces and gestures of the actors, while
> their voices could be amplified to correspond with the visual
> MAGNIFICATION. Similar effects can be obtained from the
> SIMULTANEOUS, SYNOPTICAL, and SYNACOUSTICAL repro-
> duction of thought (with motion pictures, phonographs,
> loud-speakers), or from the reproduction of thoughts sug-
> gested by a construction of variously MESHING GEARS.[13]

Searching in their very systematic way for a basic *Gestaltung*,
the artists and students of the Bauhaus have supplied us with both
experiments in pure theatrical form and intimations that these
experiments must ultimately yield to the impure theatre of man,
language, and meaning. Their decision interestingly enough coincides with the usual results of those who, probably following the
same formalist impulses, investigated pure literature. W. K. Wimsatt's conclusion to his investigation of the possibilities of pure
poetry is typical:

> The music of spoken words in itself is meager, so meager
> in comparison to the music of song or instrument as to be

hardly worth discussion. . . . The art of words is an intellectual art, and the emotions of poetry are simultaneous with conceptions and largely induced through the medium of conceptions. In literary art only the wedding of the alogical [our "pure form"] with the logical gives the former an aesthetic value. The words of a rhyme, with their curious harmony of sound and distinction of sense, are an amalgam of the sensory form; they are the icon in which the idea is caught.[14]

The Bauhaus concept of a pure theatre of moving lights, bobbing shapes, and meaningless clangs must be questioned on another count, however, for it is clearly arguable (and in keeping with the position developed in the earlier chapters of this book) that the Bauhaus has missed the point; that these experiments may be pure but they are not drama. (No distinction between "drama" and "theatre" as representing literature versus spectacle is intended here.) That is, assuming the point of experiments in pure form to be the formal manipulation of the basic elements of an art, these experiments have failed to work with the basic elements of *drama* which, in the Aristotelian tradition pursued here, have been understood to be human actions. They have instead broken the dramatic elements down to the elements of other arts. Thus when colors, shapes, lights, etc. are arranged you get a kind of pure kinetic sculpture[15] and when sounds are arranged you get music, but even in combination these forms do not add up to drama. In the sense used here, *pure* (absolutely nonrepresentational) *dramatic* form would be a contradiction in terms.

This point, while ultimately inescapable, does not warrant overstrict application. The experiments and theories on pure theatre, no matter how we must finally classify them, were necessary extensions of an aesthetic trend into the complex realm of drama where any clear analytic light must be welcomed. If we now see Bell's theories of pure form as principally applicable, if at all, to his own field of the plastic arts, still their tentative extensions into drama have been valuable in stressing the visual and aural aspects of the dramatic image.

When we turn to the conventional drama, the complex of causes for these complex art works makes it difficult to say exactly what effect the possibilities for formal manipulation of the elements have upon a playwright's dramatic structure. A playwright might make an effort to choose "colorful" locales which would permit the designer one or more interesting sets, and some playwrights twist their plots to provide the costumer with the chance to dress the leading lady in a series of "stunning" gowns. Even so, sets and costumes contrived in this way are at least as important for their meaning (as an *evening* gown, as *expensive, risqué,* etc.) as for their pure form.

The pastoral setting was important for the Elizabethan author—especially in *The Winter's Tale,* where it contrasts markedly with a repressed court setting—and it is difficult to believe that Tourneur was not conscious of the effects of dark and light when he plotted the evil of debauched nights in court in his *Revenger's Tragedy.* Of course, in those times the poet was the "scene designer," and the contrasts of colors and fabrics, lines and shapes with which the present-day designer works, were caught up by Shakespeare and his contemporaries as contrasts in imagery, which are less likely to be looked at as pure form than the raw visual materials are. These images, nonetheless, give us visual and tactile experiences, if only in the imagination, and the pure sounds of the actors' words are usually composed with care; if sound without meaning seems paltry of effect, it is by no means negligible, especially on the lips of a good actor.

The case becomes clearer, however, when we consider not just the verse organization of words, or the design of a single set or costume, but the aural and visual effect of drama as actions. This brings us to the artistic raw materials of moving speaking actors in a given delimited stage space. Surely playwrights have been sensitive in their composition to the formal possibilities afforded here. This is particularly evident in the Elizabethan drama, where the arrangement of scenes allows for an artful variety in the number of people present on the stage, the amount of movement, the intensity of sounds—both of voices and of the supporting sound effects.[16]

Consider, for example, the variety in the scenes building up to and succeeding the murder of Duncan in *Macbeth*. Scene v of Act I opens on Lady Macbeth alone with the letter. The Messenger's surprising tidings are given in two brief speeches; very shortly Macbeth himself enters and the swift pace of Lady Macbeth's plot rushes the couple to the end. Scene vi, by contrast, opens with the sound of hautboys and a procession fills the stage. The speech sounds in this scene are slower, more lyric, as Duncan and Banquo comment on the birds and the air which "recommends itself / Unto our gentle senses." (I.vi. 2–3) Scene vii again begins with a flourish and a procession, this time of servants with dishes. The servants quickly pass, leaving a single brooding figure, Macbeth. Lady Macbeth enters, building the tension in her relentless driving of her husband's ambition. After their exit we get an aural contrast in the gentle tones of another two-person scene between Banquo and his son in the first ten lines of Act II, Scene i. There are four people on stage for the brief exchange between Macbeth and Banquo, then we have another soliloquy by Macbeth. Scene ii, when the murder is committed, alternates between brief monologues and passages shared by the two principals. The speech sounds come in jerky rhythms, a kind of intoxicated outpouring:

> *Lady Macbeth:* Did you not speak?
> *Macbeth:* When?
> *Lady Macbeth:* Now.
> *Macbeth:* As I descended?
> *Lady Macbeth:* Aye.
> *Macbeth:* Hark!

(II.ii.17–19)

Knocking punctuates the end of the scene, to be picked up in the next scene as an accompaniment to the prose rhythm of the famous "Porter's Speech." After the Porter opens the gate, the stage gradually fills with people.

This same variation of the raw materials can be illustrated in many other plays of Shakespeare and his contemporaries, but it is certainly not limited to them. From the Greek chorus, with its elaborate composition of verse, music, and dance, on down through the ages the formal possibilities of drama have been variously explored.

In the very different plays of the realistic period formal variety was still a factor, and the better authors carefully avoided the monotony of scenes between the same number of people broken at regular intervals by similar entrances.[17] Ibsen, who, as a director, had been involved with the visual form of many productions, accommodated this formal consideration into the structure of his own works. Consider, for example, his last play, *When We Dead Awaken*. This opens with a long (fifteen pages) dialogue which, despite whatever movement the director can inject into the scene, is essentially just a conversation between two seated people, visually very static. At the end of this conversation, Ibsen introduces a third person who talks with the couple, but before the entrance of this person the playwright calls for the following "business," not necessary for the forwarding of the plot: "Visitors to the baths, most of them ladies, begin to pass, singly and in groups, through the park from the right and out to the left. Waiters bring refreshments from the hotel, and go off behind the pavilion."[18] The effects achieved here are primarily of form; the same variety is achieved when a group scene follows an intimate dialogue no matter who the people are, and Ibsen could have broken up his static scene with *any* group of extras.

All of these examples have been offered as illustrations of abstract formal schemes, taking the sounds, lines, colors, movements, etc. as pure or meaningless elements. When I suggested that most sensitive dramatists like to vary the number of people on stage and the sound of the dialogue from scene to scene, I was considering the actor not as representing a Scotch lord with dangerous kingly ambitions, but as a mass; any object with similar visual properties could be substituted for Macbeth; meaningless sounds could be substituted for Shakespeare's poetry, as long as these sounds reproduced the tempo, rhythm, loudness, and timbre of a regular reading of the lines. It should be added that the examples used illustrate only a very small number of the possibilities for formal organization of the primary raw materials of the drama.

To what extent can such analysis be justified? To what extent do these abstract considerations really affect drama and why? A glance back at the illustration from *Macbeth* will indicate the usual place of formal considerations in dramatic construction. It is not likely that Shakespeare conceived a pattern of scenes such that a dialogue would be followed by a procession, followed by a monologue, followed by varied dialogue, etc., then thumbed through Holinshed until he found the Macbeth story to fill this scheme. The developing events of Macbeth's involvement in evil are the basic determinants of the nature of the scenes in which this story is played out, but within this outline, which gives a certain amount of freedom, considerations of variety of sound and visual materials play a part and have their own effect upon the composition. The effect of the formal organization of dramatic raw materials on dramatic structure is analogous to that which makes a poet alter a word or two to accommodate the metric requirements or to complete a rhyme. Where these formal considerations override sense we get "Old Mother Hubbard" verses like:

> She went to the hatters to get him a hat.
> When she came back, he was feeding the cat.

A work of art is an image complete in itself (the formalists' argument) offering its own finished experience. At the same time, this image bears analogies to other aspects of our experience (the referentialists' argument) through which it gains in interest and power. The work of art captures and presents only certain aspects of experiences at any one time, as in a picture one normally presents the shapes and colors of people but not their movement, sound, or smell. Although the most obvious aspect of experience which can be captured is probably physical appearance, this does not exhaust experience; we also have experience of meanings and their relations and we have the experience of formal relations, such as the symmetrical relation between our two hands, the repetition of trees in the forest, etc. These formal relations of our experience may be presented by using the pure elements of a medium as matter for their form and without representing the physical appearance of things in the real world. This is the basis for music and nonrepresentational painting.

Since the work of art *presents* experiences for us, these experiences can be elaborated in ways other than that of perfecting the details of appearance, as one might perfect the likeness in a portrait to fit the sitter. Thus the materials brought to the work of art—both raw materials and ideas—may, to some varying extent, be taken "abstractly" (separate from whatever representational function they may have) to be arranged pleasingly, as we might make a pleasing pattern of colored blocks. This is the purest side of art, contrasting with the mere likeness of the common portrait, and here, if anywhere, nonrepresentational elements are being manipulated in nonrepresentational patterns of relations, because this arrangement of colored blocks may be made entirely in terms of unity and variety. Although these relationships are certainly observable in life, it is much more convincing to assume that they are not *imitated* from life but spring spontaneously to mind as ways of arranging artistic materials to satisfy us through some inner psychological need for balance, unity, and variety of stimulae.[19] However, mere pleasant arrangements of pure elements are usually recognized as of very little artistic value and classed as interior decoration, *Tafelmusik*, etc. The distinction is admittedly a difficult one to draw theoretically, but it is one that most sensitive people make automatically when comparing, say, the work of Mondrian or Franz Kline to the exercises of design school students.

In sum, there is in the successful work of art (as there is not in the two types of work which fall off either end of the spectrum of art: the work of interior decoration and the mere likeness) a tension between the perfected image complete in itself and the (often multiple) analogies it bears to our common world of experience, especially since *any* aspect or aspects of experience may be selected and combined in the art image. For present purposes we need hold only that this analysis is true of drama. Without arguing the case, however, I suggest that it is true for the other arts as well, although differences between the aspects of experience typically presented make considerable differences in the nature of the images and the degree of obvious representation they appear to have.

It would take a discussion of the nature of relations well beyond the scope of this work to mark any fast distinction between representational and nonrepresentational relational schemes. For our purposes, however, this is not necessary, because the tenor of our analysis has been to show that both pure and representational form have their place. In this connection, it would be well to note that pure form represents the other side of the coin mentioned in the chapter on actions, where it was held that the artist makes each action the epitome of time through keen awareness of purpose and given circumstances. We now see that he will also perfect the relational patterns.

The foregoing description of the formation of the art image does not explain everything about art, but it should explain the examples from *Macbeth* and *When We Dead Awaken* which preceded it; it should explain the fugal fun Shakespeare created by doubling Plautus's twins in *Comedy of Errors*; and it should explain, in our final example below, how Eugene O'Neill shaped materials from his own life into patterns representing his assumptions about human actions in time—while at the same time making interesting arrangements of the physical elements of production.

In *Long Day's Journey into Night* the tragic descent of O'Neill's mother (Mary Tyrone in the play) into doped confusion is physicalized in a setting which gets progressively dimmer, going from the bright morning sun, to midday, late afternoon and fog, to midnight in James Tyrone's sparsely lit house: a progression which is *physically present* in the intensity of the stage lights. There is an effective progression in the speech rhythms, too, as the characters go from short speeches and quick changes of subject to long reminiscences while drugs and drink suspend time. It seems natural that this long day must have happened just that way in O'Neill's experience, yet we know from the information in the Gelbs' biography that it did not.[20] The image of a day was perfected and form had its say.

The perfect form for the artist to copy probably never occurs in life, nor does it pop full-blown from the intuition as Croce would argue. Joyce Cary, criticizing Croce's position, emphasizes that "the essential thing about the work of art is that it is work," and speaks of the writer's need to fix his vision in words, images, rhyme, etc. "All these details . . . had to enforce the impression, the feeling that he wanted to convey."[21] Cary, just as O'Neill, just as Shakespeare, *perfects* the image, and pure elements and pure relations are part of the whole.

Discussions of pure form spread over a wide and amorphous area. I have attempted to include in my analysis all logically consistent meanings of these terms which bear on dramatic structure. There are, however, two aspects of structure which, though not within the realm of pure form as we have defined it, are commonly associated with it. Because both of these have an undeniable influence upon the making of a dramatic production we must examine them briefly.

The first of these is championed by those theorists who want to say that the kind of form Bell was talking about is actually "significant form," and that these significant forms signify—or "speak a language of,"—emotions. When these ideas occur among dramatists—most often today as an inheritance from Gordon Craig and Adolphe Appia—we find them expressing the sadness of a sad play in horizontal lines, dark costumes, long slow moves by the actors, etc. As a prominent theatre text informs us: "All the types of visual and auditory stimuli can be patterned to reinforce a particular emotional tone."[22]

Experience bears out the contention that these patterned stimulae, although not representational in the literal sense, do stir emotions, and this has been a consideration in the shaping of the dramatic image ever since the Greeks equated various verse meters with various emotions. However, forms which express emotions are not pure. (Bell's forms, remember, yielded *only* the "aesthetic emotion.") These expressive forms are representative of *something*, even if only of a pattern of emotions. (We must assume here that there is a sense in which, say, the rhythm of bodily movements in a state of sadness might be considered a pattern of emotion.) While the expressive quality of abstract patterns of stimulae present many problems, I would argue that these are, in effect, cases of one more aspect of our temporal experience compounded into the elaborated image which is the work of art, not cases where rules indigenous to art alone have dictated the structure.

The second kind of form which is sometimes taken to spring pure from the roots of art itself is conventional form: patterns such as the sonnet or the sonata. It is hard to find any such overall formula in widespread use in drama that closely regulates the structure of the work. As Aristotle contended, tragic form is clearly imitative of an action, and the playwright—from Sophocles, to Shakespeare, to Arthur Miller—more likely draws his tragic pattern from assumptions about life than from the rules of art. This is by no means to deny that artistic traditions play a large part in the playwright's vision and interpretation of life. The conventions of five-act structure, for instance, undoubtedly affected certain Elizabethan plays, at least loosely, and the same period exhibits numerous conventional rhetorical forms in the drama.[23] Nevertheless, the *idea* of tragedy is not the same as the *rules* of a sonnet, even with traditional plot devices added on.

Melodrama represents a slightly different area of conventional form because a pattern clearly exists which may be filled with materials the way movie studios grind out "westerns." However, a realistic view, in keeping both with Bell's ideas and our own, would have to say that the melodrama is more formula than form. While we are moved by the *pattern* of the melodrama we are usually moved carelessly, indifferently, and largely by associations *outside* the artwork—appeals to patriotic or moralistic convictions, etc. Probably, also, the memory of the pattern as experienced in good *original* works aids the effect of its copy in lesser plays. For Bell, pure form has an intense interest *in itself*. Thus the abstract patterns of melodrama, filled with clichés which are usually attached to the emotions through well established literal meanings and associations, are the opposite of the very *concrete* pure form.[24]

What really is at issue in the area of conventional forms is not necessarily a pure form but merely an inherited form. Those who, like Henri Focillon, have traced the history of various forms have usually found them to be representational in origin (at least in the wide sense used here) and kept alive by appeal to some universal of human experience.[25] Even so, when great artists use conventional forms, as they often do, they intuitively pick a form with particular relevance to their own ideas and they rarely leave their borrowed forms unaltered.

The elements of experience may be related to one another in many different ways: Today is the same as yesterday in some significant ways; it is different from yesterday in others. Today is warmer than yesterday, later than yesterday. Today's headache is the result of yesterday's party. The list could be expanded at great length. In just this same way any major work of art presents a rich complex of materials and ideas, and it is possible to see these elements in many different relationships. We shall want to ask if any particular relationships seem to be typical of a given genre; if, in other words, the mode of structural thought differs from narrative to poetry to drama. In the next chapter we shall pursue this inquiry.

Chapter VII

THE STRUCTURES OF NARRATIVE AND POETRY

In one sense the structure of drama is quite obvious to any intelligent person who has seen a few plays. This person could go home and write his own play, and, although the product might be trite, the structure would probably be adequate. Indeed, Sardou is said to have gained his knowledge of dramatic structure by reading the first act of a Scribe play, then completing the other acts by himself. What this means is that given a model, one can copy it, as Sardou did, or describe it, as most playwriting texts do. In other words, the dramatic structure is obvious to us because we know it already. Almost intuitively we look out upon the world and relate certain of the experiences we perceive in terms of dramatic structure. However, it is not *necessary* to relate experience in this manner; there are many other ways of seeing experience.

An analogous situation exists in our experience of space, where until recent times, it was assumed that man naturally saw space through the framework of Euclidean geometry. In fact, Kant took the Euclidean postulates as *a priori* truth—as the *method* of our perception. Mathematicians have since proved that our experience of space may be organized in different ways. They have demonstrated that, while it is difficult to break the Euclidean habit, we may train ourselves to see space in other structures.[1] Just so, we must break the habit of perceiving drama in the well-made play form in order to fully appreciate, not only other structures, but the true nature of the well-made play itself as an organizer of experience. We must distinguish what is peculiar about the organization of experience made in drama by contrasting it with similar ways of ordering *the same kinds* of materials as narrative or poetry. The following analyses of specific non-dramatic works are offered only for what they may contribute to the better understanding of drama, hence they do not purport to be complete descriptions of the art of narrative or poetry.

Story, the product of narrative art, is often taken to be the structural basis, not only of drama, but of moving pictures, novels, and some kinds of poetry. Aristotle was quite positive that story was the soul of drama, that it provided the necessary and complete structural foundation for a play. Actually Aristotle used the word *mythos* (*Poetics* 6. 1450a 37–38) which meant a little more than "story."[2] In any case, the perfectly common-sense observation made by Aristotle is followed in a perfectly common-sense manner by almost all. The most natural way to describe a play is to tell its story, and, if one does not reflect critically on the definition, this same story would seem to be all that anyone could mean by "structure," because the idea leaps into one's head: the story is the framework.

There is, of course, some truth to this thought, but it is basically misleading. While a drama may be "based on" a story—as the Greek dramas were based on myths and as Shakespeare based many parts of his plays on Holinshed and Plutarch—the story does not serve as the structure of the drama. It is obvious, for example, that the Oedipus myth of a child cast out, patricide, and incest does not form the structure of the play *Oedipus*, where action takes place after all these things have happened. Even among the Elizabethan playwrights, who followed the chronicles closely, the story has an artistic existence of its own as a narrative of events, even though the events may be worked into the drama in the same order as they were given in the story.

It is true that a story often contains dialogue and that characters in plays often tell stories, but this does not alter the basic fact that in the story the events are described, while in the drama perhaps those very same events are acted out. In this discussion "story" is understood to mean simply, "a narrative of events." Under other circumstances it might be useful to make some further distinctions often included in the popular understanding of "story," especially the idea that a story relates events which did not actually happen or which happened differently, and the idea, which follows from this, that a story is contrived artfully (as opposed to an "account"). We shall leave these somewhat problematic distinctions for other hands.[3]

An example of "artless" story may be found in a short account of the last days of Bataan and Corregidor told by an army nurse.[4] It will not be necessary to reproduce any large section of the story to give the reader the general effect:

> Conditions at Hospital Number 1 were not too good during the last few weeks we spent there. Patients were flooding in. We increased from 400 to 1,500 cases in two weeks' time. Most were bad shrapnel wounds, but nine out of ten patients had malaria or dysentery besides. One night we admitted 400 patients, most in worse condition than usual.

They'd been left at first-aid stations near the front because of the shortage of gasoline.

We were out of quinine. There were hundreds of gas gangrene cases, and our supply of vaccine had gone months before. There was no more sulfapyridine or sulfanilimide. There weren't nearly enough cots so triple-decker beds were built from bamboo, with a ladder at one end so we could climb up to take care of the patients, who were without blankets or mattresses.[5]

In spite of the Red Cross roof markings on the hospital several bombs were dropped on or near the hospital buildings on April 4th:

We remained frightened until two hours later when someone heard the Jap radio in Manila announce that the bombings had been an accident and wouldn't happen again. So after that, we wouldn't even leave the hospital for a short drive. We felt safe there and nowhere else.

. . . .

The morning of April 7 we were all on duty when a wave of bombers came over. The first bomb hit by the Filipino mess hall and knocked us down before we even knew planes were overhead. An ammunition truck was passing the hospital entrance. It got a direct hit. The boys on guard at the gate were shell-shocked, smothered in the dirt thrown up by the explosion.[6]

The rest of the account may be summarized thus: After the bombing on April 7th most patients were evacuated to another hospital, and the following night the narrator herself was taken off to Corregidor. She briefly described waiting for the boat to Corregidor and the blowing up of the Navy ammunition dump. On arrival in Corregidor there is again a brief description of the base hospital and a breakdown of the cases. She gives a description of the constant bombing and shelling the island fortress underwent, briefly touching on the gruesome results when a group was caught outside the gate one night. "The surgery was over-

flowing until 5:30 in the morning. There were many amputa-
tions."[7] After an unspecified number of weeks our narrator was
ordered to Australia. The transportation to Mindanao and from
Mindanao to Australia is briefly described.

Considering this brief account in the light of the analyses of
structure in the preceding chapters, what conclusions may be
drawn? In the first place, one can see that the story is structured
mostly by choice of materials: little more has been done than to
aim the camera and snap. In such a simple account of more or less
familiar events, a profound analysis of the assumptions underlying the nurse's structuring of reality would seem out of place. This
is especially true because she is of the same age and nation as the
rest of us and bases her story on an ordinary "common sense" view
of things. Yet, of course, assumptions *are* at work; this is not
"raw experience," just because it seems familiar and artless.
Probably assumptions play a greater part in such a story, where
they are taken for granted, than in major art works, which dredge
up and illuminate our basic assumptions, the way Pirandello so
disturbingly chipped at our comfortable assumptions about the
difference between illusion and reality.

Given a set of assumptions it is possible to point briefly to the
interests which have guided the narrator in choosing from the
many impressions she received in those hectic months. She has,
naturally enough, the interests of her vocation, and in this very
short story the data mentioned, out of all that she took in, consist
mostly of: (1) the date and time of day—as she might write them
on a patient's chart; (2) an account of the hospital building—its
location, number and kind of beds; (3) a report on base morale
—always superb; (4) the number of patients and a rough break-
down of types of cases; (5) brief descriptions of the clothing and
food the nurses received; (6) accounts of the most important
bombings. These are the principal materials of the story and they
are handled in her typical fashion: time of bombing, severity of

bombing, damage to hospital, damage to patients; morale remained superb.

The story, then, relates in the order in which they happened, certain events chosen from among others through the interests indicated above. The first event is the first bombing of the hospital. Because the bombings recur, there is repetition. Because the nurse has selected special days: first bombing, worst bombing, last day there, days on a new base (Corregidor), the repeated incidents have some variety. There is progression because the war at that time went from bad to worse. The story closes with the short account of the nurse's trip to Australia. This is an abrupt and inconclusive end; only our knowledge of history fills in the complete story of Bataan and Corregidor.

The structure is "later than," or "this . . . and this . . . and this." No story, though, can avoid a kind of non-sequential relation of "this compared to that"—this bombing compared to that bombing, for example. A few general observations or summary reports on the status of the medical department are added. The story opens with a general account and when the nurse goes to Corregidor the same type of account is repeated. A kind of patterning of the emotional material of the nurse's experience is observable in the tight-lipped factual reporting she adheres to despite the pathos of the actual situation.[8] Of course much is left out. Most obviously wanting is tactical information on the course of the battles which might give us a feeling of purpose and outcome. While this would make a more interesting story, it would not raise it to the level usually considered "art."

Speaking from the point of view of the larger structures—and ignoring such important considerations as the need for a more precise and evocative use of language—what appears to be lacking from the nurse's story that would give it some claim to art is an overall pattern that adds up to an image of our experience. In short, there is no Basic Pattern of Events. Certainly there are events and they may be seen in some kind of pattern. But the events in this account, interesting or illuminating as they may be, are finally meaningless without our independent knowledge of the heartbreaking campaign they fit into. The nurse has related her own actual experience. It is individual and, as it were, accidental. The ending, in which the nurse flies to safety in Australia, cannot be construed as a typical pattern for nurses; it cannot be construed as atypical. It stresses neither a fatal pessimism of death as the soldier's inexorable end, nor the whim of chance that some are saved. In short, the pattern is meaningless.

History has certainly supplied many artists with patterns for their stories—Shakespeare's "history plays" are an obvious example—but, in a sense, all stories are based on history. Certainly someone could make a story of the battles of Bataan and Corregidor which would exhibit a meaningful pattern of events. It would differ from the usual history because we do not ordinarily consider tactical information as making an "artistic" story—we demand, rather, a pattern of events in some human life. The "artistic" story, however, could certainly be based upon actual happenings.

Standing at what might be considered the opposite pole from the factual account, the folk tale exhibits a pattern of events the meaning of which is strikingly clear. Aesop even sums up the meaning and passes it on in a moralizing phrase, such as "Pride shall have a fall."

If the nurse's story is basically an account of events chosen by interest and ordered by the ordering of the experience in reality, *The Three Bears* is a story in which a simple fanciful tale of a young blond tresspasser is manipulated for the demands of pattern. The main charm of *The Three Bears* lies in the repetitions in three's by which the story progresses: Goldilocks tries the Big Bear's porridge and finds it too hot; she tries the Mother Bear's porridge and finds it too cold; she tries the Baby Bear's porridge and finds it just right. The events of the story are arbitrarily motivated—getting the bears out of the house and the choice of some objects rather than others for Goldilocks to try and the bears to find disrupted. Franz Boas has described the use of such repetitions in primitive narrative:

> Rhythmic repetition of contents and form is found commonly in primitive narrative. For example, the tales of the Chinook Indians are often so constructed that five brothers, one after another, have the same adventure. The four elder ones perish while the youngest one emerges safe and successful. The tale is repeated verbatim for all the brothers, and its length, which to our ears and to our taste is intolerable, probably gives pleasure by the repeated form. Conditions are quite similar in European fairy tales relating to the fates of three brothers, two of whom perish or fail in their tasks, while the youngest one succeeds. Similar repetitions are found in the German tale of Redridinghood, in the widely spread European story of the rooster who goes to bury his mate, or in the story of the three bears.[9]

The Three Bears and the stories of similar pattern mentioned by Boas have what the nurse's story lacks—a very strong, if arbitrary, pattern to the events. But can *The Three Bears* be given what is denied to an account of supreme human bravery and suffering, an account of events which in themselves are both real and meaningful to an adult American? Our analysis would force us to say, "yes." *The Three Bears* exhibits a meaningful pattern, while the nurse's account does not. The pattern of events found in the story of Goldilocks' consumer sampling does not reflect any pattern of what we today consider profound or important events. Indeed, this type of structure has disappeared from most contemporary adult narrative and drama. Yet we must be careful not to confuse the profundity or importance of the real life event with the profundity or importance of the art work which takes it for subject.

Apart from the overall pattern of events, much of the charm of the three bears type of story lies in the repetition or near repetition of a *verbal formula*. This not only has its meaning as an

117

image of the repetitions of life, but it has an immediate sensuous appeal, which Boas assures us the primitive audience did not miss, of repeated sounds and formulas.[10] Repetitions are, of course, common elements in narrative, drama, poetry, and especially music, as we shall see in the next chapter.

The foregoing simple examples of narrative probably show off their structure more clearly than more sophisticated works and so serve well as brief illustrations to contrast with dramatic structure. In the vast area between the transparent narration of facts represented by the nurse's account and the fanciful folk stories heavily hung with pointed moral meanings and the immediate appeal of formal patterns, as in *The Three Bears*, lies the bulk of our important narrative art. Before summarizing the similarities and differences let us examine the structure of poetry so that the three major literary genres may be discussed at once.

Drama has been termed an image of man's interactions in time. Perhaps, then, consideration of a poem which also concerns itself with the effect of time on man will best clarify the different structures of the two genres. Shakespeare was extremely sensitive to the passage of time and objectified his feelings, especially in plays like *Pericles* and *The Winter's Tale*. But he also expressed his experience of time in non-dramatic forms, which is the subject of many of the sonnets. The nature of this expression appears in the following example:

> When I do count the clock that tells the time,
> And see the brave day sunk in hideous night;
> When I behold the violet past prime,
> And sable curls all silver'd o'er with white,
> When lofty trees I see barren of leaves,
> Which erst from heat did canopy the herd,
> And summer's green all girded up in sheaves,
> Borne on the bier with white and bristly beard,
> Then of thy beauty do I question make,
> That thou among the wastes of time must go,
> Since sweets and beauties do themselves forsake

> And die as fast as they see others grow;
> And nothing 'gainst Time's scythe can make defence
> Save breed, to brave him when he takes thee hence.
>
> (Sonnet XII)

Without exhausting the subtleties of the verse, we may observe the more obvious structural features. The first part of this poem (lines 1–8) supplies the occasion for the statement made in the last part. ("When I do count . . . Then . . . do I question make.") More important from our point of view than the grammatical form of the statement, however, is the manner in which experience has been given a structure, or how the elements have been *related* to make the sonnet.

Shakespeare, in the first eight lines, provides five comparisons which grow in impressiveness and sense of universality from the pretty violet, to tall trees, to the necessary crops. In these comparisons the relation is of a present faded state with a recollected prime. In lines nine through twelve the images of decay in nature are a warning that "thy beauty" must decay. The concluding couplet states the argument (13) and presents a way out (14) in the form of "nothing . . . Save. . ." Although this is a rough summary, the structure here is one of a comparison and a conclusion of the form: a faded violet is to a violet in its prime as you in the future are to you now, but the round of death and decay is palliated for the individual by the presence of children, whose youth defies Time's removal of the parent.

It is important to notice that although we progress through the poem (a short progression compared to the course of 3924 lines through *Hamlet*), the terms of the comparison are conceived of as all present to the mind at once. There is no action here except the thinking process of the "speaker"—the imaginary first person of the poem. The *structure* of the poem does not provide an image of our experience of time even though there are verbal images within the poem of the effects of the passage of time. The structure is an image of a process of thought which brings signs of physical decay and death into juxtaposition with the "brave" thought which opposes them. There is, to be sure, a movement of thought in the form: "when . . . then . . . and," but this is a logical movement, and the experiences mentioned in the poem (as opposed to the experience of logical sequence in the statement of the poem) could have been gathered in any order.

Put in another way, while it is obvious that it takes time to read a poem, the essential experience gained from this temporal labor is not one of passing time, but of a juxtaposition of static images. A photograph of the great slabs at Stonehenge may give a very strong feeling of the passage of time, but the experience of seeing the picture is a static, not a temporal one. Poems, unlike pictures, usually do not present a single image, because there is generally at least an implied comparison, and, unlike pictures, they are not static, because there is a movement of thought. Even in the short poem examined here the effect is heightened by the fact that the last line comes as a mild surprise after the gloom of the preceding thirteen.

Clearly these remarks apply primarily to short lyric poems. Narrative poems offer more movement. What I am trying to establish is a typical kind of poetic structure, or relationship of the elements, as opposed to typically narrative or dramatic structures.

If Sonnet XII is compared to the nurse's story, however, the nature of the orderings of experience becomes clearer. The incidents related in the narrative were ordered by the sequence in which they happened to the nurse, which is the normal structure for simple narrative.[11] No one really cares, though, in what order the speaker of the poem may in real life have counted the clock, seen the day, beheld the violet, curls, trees, etc. The images move from decay to bloom, because the poet gives us the examples of faded beauty before he mentions the fresh beauty of the young man in line nine. This opposes the natural order of the experience of nature, but on the other hand, it is a common logical movement of thought: decay reminds one of its opposite—prime. This poem is (as most poems are) a movement of thought relating images through their meaning.

The speaker progresses not only from sense perception to sense perception but in an ordered emotional movement from despair to hope; however, nothing in the nature of temporal experience demands this particular movement. In fact, the movement could be reconstructed in reverse, as "Children are the only defense against mortality. So keep this in mind together with the thought that, though young and fresh today, you are mortal like the violet, dark hair, and leaves of grass." This is not to imply that the order of the thoughts in the poem is a matter of indifference. Shakespeare had a specific purpose in going from the despair of withering time to the hope of progeny. But another person observing these same phenomena may construe them in a different way—following hope by despair, for example.

It is interesting to observe the turns Shakespeare played on the idea, expressed in the final line of the sonnet, of a child to succeed the father. In *Lear* despair follows hope, because the child—Cordelia—dies: the movement is tragic. In *The Winter's Tale, Cymbeline*, and *Pericles* the child is presumed dead but restored alive to the father at the end: the movement to hope is essentially comic.[12]

This analysis, although inadequate as an analysis of *poetry*, brings to light the structural features that are relevant for a comparison with the structures of drama. It should be acknowledged, however, that the formal aspects of the poem have been slighted; the metrical and rhyming schemes of the sonnet, the shifts of thought after the eighth and twelfth lines, the conventional use of the concluding couplet have all been passed over. In the particular sonnet under consideration, we have slighted in description, though I hope not in personal appreciation, such masterful strokes as the reiteration in "breed, to brave" which emboldens the final

defiant line. Certainly "rhyme and reason" invigorate one another, as Wimsatt said they should in our discussion of pure form
in the preceding chapter.

While the experience of a poem is essentially a logical movement which, although it unfolds in time, is not an experience of
time, the experience of drama *is* an experience of time. The play
is a genuine image of man's struggle in time because it presents a
temporally conditioned work. Of course, there is ordinarily more
time *suggested* in the drama than is actually *presented* there, but
it is the nature of any art work to surround its immediate presen-
tational reality with a wide area of suggestion.

How might the materials of Sonnet XII have been presented in
a drama? The poem could conceivably be carried intact into a
play and set in the mouth of an "older and wiser" character ad-
dressing a young man in the full blush of youth. This would be
an example of poetry in drama and the poem would become a
single action in a structure of interaction between the two men.
The value of the speech in the drama would depend on how well
it carried forward the improvisational structure, such as an argument in which the older man might be urging the young swain
to abandon frivolous living and get married. The creation of a
forward moving argument would then be the important structural
consideration, not juxtapositions of decay and bloom, death and
new life—the important structural considerations of the poem.
However, the true dramatizing of the materials of experience in
Sonnet XII was achieved, as suggested, with a tragic fall in *Lear*,
with the happiness surrounding the restored child in *The Winter's
Tale*. In these plays the appreciation of the child who can comfort
the parent in old age is won only through experience not through
logic.

The most important point to be made here is that the relationship set up between the images in the sonnet is not a generally
useful relationship in the structure of the drama. It is not "dramatic" because it does not matter which event happened first and

because the greatest value is gained when the events are considered simultaneously. Thus the poem does not give us the basic offering of the drama, an image of our experience in time. The relationship of bloom and decay could be used *in* a drama, but it is not the kind of relationship which gives a basic organization to drama.

The kind of relationship which typically structures the drama is that in which events are so ordered that they have significance only when one follows another in a specific order; often this is a cause and effect relationship, but it need not necessarily be. The person who is pursuing one course of action and who receives a piece of news that makes him reverse his course is an example of the effect of one event on another. Compare the situation late in *Macbeth*: The tyrant has retired within the walls of Dunsinane castle to "laugh a siege to scorn," but news of his wife's death, then hard upon it the announcement of the "moving wood," make him decide on the suicidal open battle (V.v). Clearly the decision to leave the security of the castle must come *after* Macbeth has heard of the dire blows to his security.

The discussion of narrative and poetry may finally be summed up in a few observations on the structure of these genres as they compare with drama. It is extremely important to realize that narrative structure is not something that can be found exclusively in the novel or short story, dramatic structure exclusively in the play, and poetic structure exclusively in a book of verse. Each of these genres is likely to include the others, sometimes even to take the structure of another genre as a basic shaping principle. René Wellek and Austin Warren have pointed out how confusing genre criticism can be.[13] I am only interested in showing how the *typically* dramatic, poetic, or narrative structure functions, wherever it is found.

Poetry depends basically on a structure which relates ideas and images to one another "spatially." Although poetic images may be *of* time, the poetic image is not structured temporally. The narrative structure, on the other hand, is closer to the dramatic: it is concerned with a pattern of events. The primary difference lies in the fact that the *time* of narrative is a time of telling. The structure depends upon the selection and ordering of the events in a single mind—that of the narrator. Susanne Langer's phrase, "virtual memory," is indicative of the image which narrative presents, though she does not limit the phrase to narrative.[14] It can be seen that the narrated events on Bataan and Corregidor are structured personally by the nurse's memory. There is little in the story that gives us an experience of passing a period of consecutive time on the islands: as we might have gotten had the nurse dramatized, say, the strain of the night on Bataan when 400 badly wounded men were admitted. In short, we are told about the high points—events which are certainly moving—but we do not experience time passing. Even in the folktale the fun is clearly in the narrator's grouping of events, not in an actual temporal sensing of the series of tests of the bear family's property.

Cleanth Brooks says of modern—or, Jamesian—narrative art, "The general tendency was back toward drama with the emphasis on direct presentation rather than the mediation of a special expositor."[15] This implies the use of a dramatic structure in the narrative, yet narrative as such will always depend on the teller, no matter how much more sophisticated he is than the army nurse in our example above.

Joseph Frank, modernizing Lessing's distinctions between the temporal and spatial arts, describes a spatialization in contemporary literature which is particularly well illustrated, he feels, by Djuna Barnes's novel *Nightwood*, and by some of Eliot's and Pound's poems, which have "the space-logic implicit in the modern conception of the nature of poetry."[16] Here the structures of narrative and poetry blend as they sometimes do in a motion picture— either in isolated sequences by Eisenstein, or some of the compositions of Maya Deren. Drama, as the image of man in time, never enters here.

It may clarify the distinction to consider finally an example of narrative structure and an example of poetic structure both used in a drama. Surely narrative in structure is the long speech by James Tyrone in the last act of *Long Day's Journey into Night* in which he confesses to his son how he harnessed his talent for playing Shakespeare, admired by Booth, to a trashy popular success.[17] What gives it a place in the theatre and fits it into the total dramatic structure of the play is the relation of the image we see in the last act of this long play of an old man at the end of his career, married to a woman lost to narcotics, with the earlier images in the first and second acts of this same man as quarrelsome and penny-pinching. The progression of time in this "long" day has brought a truly dramatic change.

In the same way, the internal organization of the elements of Macbeth's "Tomorrow, and tomorrow, and tomorrow" speech (V.v. 19–28) is poetic, yet that which impels it and that to which it leads (a total disregard for life in a suicidal battle) find their places in the progressive time of Macbeth's downfall—not in, say, a comparison of age and youth or foul and fair.

Chapter VIII

MUSIC AND DRAMATIC STRUCTURE

In Aristotle's day music appears to have been primarily an accompaniment to the drama, dithyramb, and other forms of poetry or dance, though Aristotle in the *Poetics* does give it a separate existence (*Poetics* 1. 1447a 13–26). Today, though many plays still utilize music in some way, music has risen to independent stature—to such autonomous strength, indeed, that the former handmaid becomes the pure model of all the other arts for such men as Appia and Pater.[1] Ever since music and drama were separated, many people have been concerned to reunite them in theory or practice. There are many theatre people who think of their art as in some way musical and musicians who see music as somehow dramatic.

This chapter will attempt to discover what basic similarities in the structures of music and drama might permit a rapprochement, and just what kinds of critical analogies and practical combinations these similarities can support. The extent to which analogies between music and drama have been carried, and the extent to which practicing artists have felt their plays were "musical" or their compositions "dramatic," requires some demonstration to point up the need for the more sober comparison of the two structures to follow.

Racine was fascinated by the musical qualities of the verse drama.[2] He attempted unsuccessfully to compose an opera with Lully, *L'Idylle de la Paix*, but later in life the musical quality of Racine's work found excellent support in Jean-Baptiste Moreau's settings for some of the chants of the biblical dramas. These were acclaimed as a true synthesis of the arts.[3]

The nineteenth century inspired numerous minglings of the arts, and Strindberg, a prey to so many influences, was certainly prey to this one. Many of the stage directions in *The Dream Play* and *Easter* indicate that he was writing with "musical" effects in mind. He composed *The Dance of Death* to the Saint-Saens music, but finding Ibsen had used it before him, he used the *Entry of the Boyars* as a theme underlying the play.[4] He saw his late plays as in some ways similar to chamber music, an influence that reached even to the titles, as *The Dance of Death* and *The Ghost Sonata*. Part of the chamber play idea involved a concept no more specifically musical than that of intimate presentation; however, Strindberg's concepts of themes and their working out, and the careful way he selected bits of music from Beethoven, Haydn, etc. to underline his dramatic composition testify to a real sense of the mixing of dramatic and musical form.

Though T. S. Eliot has cast off most nineteenth century critical ideas, including the desire to imitate one art by another, he still can see an amalgam of music and drama according to their basic orders:

127

We can never emulate music, because to arrive at the condition of music would be the annihilation of poetry, and especially of dramatic poetry. Nevertheless, I have before my eyes a kind of mirage of the perfection of verse drama, which would be a design of human action and of words, such as to present at once the two aspects of dramatic and of musical order. It seems to me that Shakespeare achieved this at least in certain scenes.[5]

In another place he is slightly more positive:

In the plays of Shakespeare a musical design can be discovered in particular scenes, and in his more perfect plays as wholes. . . . A play of Shakespeare is a very complex musical structure.[6]

A contemporary English author of more or less naturalistic plays testifies to how a musical consciousness can haunt the composer-in-words. In his directions to Mark Rydell, New York director of his *Roots,* Arnold Wesker said that "his play was fashioned very much like a musical composition, and would Mr. Rydell, in directing, bear that in mind—slow sections and fast."[7] The words of the first act, indeed, are supposed to fit to the music of the *L'Arlesienne Suite.*

Many musicians have felt their art to be in some way deeply dramatic, even when that music had no text. One of the most dramatic forms has been felt to be the sonata, particularly when handled by Beethoven.[8] Of course Beethoven gave us *Fidelio,* but even "pure" music often has a dramatic theme, like that of the hero, running through it.

We have avoided so far the obvious example of Wagner just as we have avoided the opinions of the theorists for the opinions of practicing artists, but we may suitably include here what Eric Bentley, champion of "thought" as opposed to "arty" effects in the drama, said of the work of the master of music drama:

Every good play has a rhythmic structure and a symphonic unity. Wagner's introduction of a symphonic pattern into music drama is the redramatizing of opera by genuinely musical means.[9]

Perhaps the best exhibit we can offer is the account Jean-Louis Barrault has published of Racine's *Phèdre* analysed as a symphony. Barrault draws from all levels of musical analysis: he uses the larger forms when he makes four movements out of the five acts (by combining Acts III and IV); within the movements he distinguishes sections and themes; and he compares speeches and actions to drum taps, the single dying note of a violin, etc.[10]

How much distortion of dramatic form, musical form, or both is involved in such cross references, and what realistic bases for comparison and combination of the two arts exist? To answer this question, let us compare in some detail the structural processes of music and drama, that is, the relationships which function to bind the parts into a whole composition.

Percy Goetschius, who has at least the distinction of having put his analytical formulas to the test over and over again, offers a clear and generally accepted account of musical structure, which we may borrow for our comparison. He describes the basic units of analysis:

> The basic unit of all musical formations is the single *tone*. A brief succession of two, three or more tones constitutes the *figure*. Two or three such figures form the motive or *phrase-member*. [Current usage applies "motive" to what Goetschius calls the "figure." In our discussion we shall comply with current usage.] Two or three members make a *phrase*, which is the smallest complete musical sentence (usually four measures long). Two phrases form the *period* (eight measures); and two connected periods make a *double*-period (generally sixteen measures).
>
> Beyond this, the primary forms rarely extend; a decisive, strong *cadence* brings this portion of the piece to a fairly complete stop, as a rule. This portion is known as a *Part*.[11]

Goetschius illustrates with an example, which we reproduce here, and explains:

The *figure* in this example, the index of the whole, occurring six times, consists of five notes. Two of the figures form the first *member*, to which a second member, partly independent, is added, to complete the first four-measure *phrase*, called the antecedent, because its cadence is not a complete one and therefore involves a "consequent" phrase to round out the entire period. Note the similarity in the construction of these two phrases, and, at the same time, the contrast in their *harmonic* plan, the antecedent being based largely upon the tonic, the consequent upon the dominant harmony. Note the complete, final, perfect cadence at the end of the period. This definitely concludes the first Part. Note also that this part is repeated.[12]

From Beethoven's "Sonata No. 2" redrawn from Percy Goetschius, *The Structure of Music*, p. 148. Copyright Theodore Presser Co., Philadelphia. Used by permission.

The principle of musical motion which multiplies these basic units Goetschius suggests by the word "continuity":

By continuity is meant the never-failing evidence of purpose, the conception and arrangement of each member as a recognizable progressive growth out of the members which precede it. No meaningless episodes, no halting, no capricious, silly insertion of some foreign passage, but the un-

130

broken certainty of a continuous plan or idea which runs through the whole piece like a silver bar, holding all its members inseparably together as a unified total.[13]

This kind of musical motion is impelled by a sense of "striving for goals" as the first motive strives toward the high E (e^3) or as the concluding cadence strives toward the tonic. Musical units are multiplied and held together by repetition and variation in larger and larger units. The means may be catalogued as: exact repetition, sequence, inversion, transposition, change of mode, extension-contraction, and augmentation-diminution. Variety is also obtained by modifications of the rhythm or harmony. There is a kind of punctuation, consisting of rests and/or cadences, helping to define these units.

Obviously this account leaves out a great deal that is necessary to explain music as we hear it, most notably an account of the function of rhythm and harmony, but the same principle of motion through repetition and variation can be extended to other aspects for a fuller description. Our analysis describes the Beethoven "Sonata No. 2" quoted above; it also describes the tunes we whistle, from "Old Black Joe" to "Oh, What a Beautiful Morning," and, as Leichtentritt points out, it describes such primitive music as we have records of (to the extent that this music has any form at all.)[14]

The most striking difference between the description of the structure of music offered by Goetschius and our description of dramatic structure is that Goetschius has analysed music down into much smaller units, starting with the single tone. A comparable break-down of drama would require one to start with the speech phoneme and build up the way the structural linguists have done.[15] Only one of the many complications this kind of analysis would entail is the problem of what to do with the gestures and movements of the actors. Clearly the units of analysis presented here are not strictly comparable.

On the other hand, whether one wants to look at our basic unit (the action) as the equivalent of the motive ("figure" in Goet-schius), the member, or the phrase, the structural principles of generation in the two arts can be meaningfully compared. The musical units are related in a temporal structure which plays with the two possibilities that time offers (repetition and change), and the composer explores the formal relations which may be derived from these, that is, sequence, inversion, transposition, and so forth. Dramatic structure, on the other hand, is always Heraclitean —the dramatic character, unlike the musical theme, never steps twice into the same river. Of course, no one knows whether the nature of Time is finally musical or dramatic, repeating or unique. In our arts we have two images of its possibilities.

Since repetition is so basic to musical structure, an examination of its uses in the two arts should point up the basic structural similarities and differences. Let us consider a number of dramatic phenomena that might be claimed to be analogous to musical repetition: (1) repeated phrases or words, (2) repeated scenes, (3) the reentrance of the same character, (4) reentrance of catch phrases or themes, (5) the repetitions of poetry in verse drama.

In drama there are, of course, many examples of the literal repetition of phrases or words. This is a favorite stylistic device of Tennessee Williams, well illustrated by the passage early in *A Streetcar Named Desire* where Blanche greets her sister:

> *Blanche:*   Stella, oh, Stella, Stella! Stella for Star! (She be-gins to speak with feverish vivacity as if she feared for either of them to stop and think. They catch each other in a spas-modic embrace.)
> *Blanche:*   Now, then, let me look at you. But don't you look at me, Stella, no, no, no, not till later, not till I've bathed and rested! And turn that over-light off! Turn that off! I won't be looked at in this merciless glare! (Stella laughs and com-plies) Come back here now! Oh, my baby! Stella! Stella for Star! (She embraces her again) I thought you would never come back to this horrible place! What am I saying? I didn't mean to say that. I meant to be nice about it and say—Oh,

what a convenient location and such—Ha-a-ha! Precious
lamb! You haven't said a *word* to me.[16]

This device lends a kind of poetry to the dialogue (an effect considered later) and serves as a decorative addition to the speech
pattern, giving a kind of naturalness to emotional speech. Essentially, though, Blanche's lines are filled out with what Bronislaw
Malinowski has called "phatic communion"—speech used just to
maintain contact with the other person, not as a means of trans-
mission of thought.[17] It hardly serves as a basic structural determinant in the action.

There is a much better case for an analogy to music in the
structural repetition of *scenes*. Racine's *Phèdre* offers an excellent
example, for the first two acts contain, as the major part of the
action, five confessions of love. Hippolyte confesses his forbidden
love for Aricie to his companion, Théramène; then Phèdre confesses to her companion her forbidden love for Hippolyte. In the
second act Aricie confides, again to a companion, her love for Hippolyte; then we have the two parallel scenes in which Hippolyte
confesses his love to Aricie and Phèdre confesses her love to Hippolyte. The repetition in Act I of scenes of confession of forbidden
love might be likened to the repetition in varied form of a musical
period. It could never equal the phenomenon of exact repetition in
music, yet even so, the first two acts of *Phèdre* seem to bog down
dramatically in too much repetition, because these confessions follow roughly the same pattern and take roughly the same time, giving a monotonous rhythm to the opening of the play.

The circumstances which permit Racine to repeat love confessions, first to a companion, then to the person loved, are interesting in terms of our theory of dramatic structure. The repetitions
are possible only because the persons involved are not permitted
to interact with each other before their scenes take place—though
we must note that their relations to one another are altered, between Acts I and II, by the report of Thésée's death. There are, in
a sense, five first scenes. This lack of progression is undramatic

and helps give a static quality to the beginning of *Phèdre*, a sacrifice Racine was willing to make in return for the creation of irony—essentially a poetic kind of relation.

Henri Bergson noticed the frequent use of repetitions in comedy, which, for him, meant mechanization—the complete negation of the fundamental law of life.[18] Parallel scenes are often found as a comic device, as in Goldoni's *The Servant of Two Masters*, where the servant performs a like task for each master. Again, the parallelism is only possible because the masters are not permitted to compare notes. In any drama, we are being invited to see life as patterned. In the examples of repetition just cited, the playwright assumes more than the ordinarily conceded amount of patterning in life. As mentioned, this has often a comic effect in drama.

Another possibility of analogy at the level of the scene exists where the opening scene in a drama might be repeated at the end of the play, corresponding to the restatement of the themes at the end of the sonata form. This is, to be sure, a structural device we would not expect to find in a play, because the drama usually conceives of life as changing, hence the ending will most often represent a profoundly altered situation. (Perhaps no better example could be found than *Oedipus*.) However, some recent playwrights, who view life itself as repetitious, have made use of the formal device of repeating their opening scene exactly, or almost exactly, at the end. Ionesco's *The Bald Soprano* and Beckett's *Waiting for Godot* are good examples. Though we have just compared a whole play to a form that may constitute only one movement of a musical composition, there is usually considered to be a completeness to the sonata form, or "first movement form," which permits the comparison, particularly to a one-act play like *The Bald Soprano*.

The reentrance of a character is sometimes thought of as a repetition and compared to the reentrance of a theme in music. There is no denying that this is repetition of a kind, but it is obviously not repetition of a motive. In music the true comparison would be the reentrance of the viola of a string quartet, for example, after that instrument had been silent for a time, although this would not be considered repetition in music. The reentrance of a character or simply his or her return to prominence in the scene sometimes brings with it another kind of repetition, however, treated by many as the exact duplicate of musical repetition. This takes the form of a little catch phrase which the character repeats each time he finds himself in a particular situation, as Gaev in *The Cherry Orchard* repeats his billiard phrases when he is confused.

Repetitions of images (and hence the themes they may suggest) have been traced by a number of recent critics. Cleanth Brooks, who sensibly avoids identifying image patterns with the structure of the play, has pointed out, for example, that Macbeth returns a number of times to the image of the naked babe and the image of clothing.[19] In like manner the musician may return a number of times to a certain melodic theme. However, the repetitions of images in a play are part of a poetic structure which is subordinate to the shaping force of the patterns of events. On close inspection, too, one can see that the repetitions of images in a play provide no analogy to either the precisely defined repetition in music—the exact and immediate repetition of a whole section such as the eight quoted measures from the Beethoven sonata—or its reasonable extension. The repetition of images or themes prominent in verse drama depends upon a logical structure of meaning, not on the repeated perception of some significantly extensive sensual pattern.[20]

Certainly in verse we have repetition of rhythmic patterns and sounds (where rhyme, alliteration, etc. are used), but whatever structural analogies may be found between poetry and music (a subject to which Calvin S. Brown, among others, has devoted considerable thought),[21] they do not, by the fact that dramas have often been written in verse, prove an analogy between dramatic and musical structure, because Ibsen and many others have proved that it is possible to construct a drama without verse.

Actually, exact repetition in literature is more often found in primitive than in modern works. Primitive song, which merges indistinguishably with dance, drama, and poetry, is full of exact repetitions.[22] Homer repeats certain formulas word for word; primitive rituals may repeat the same prayer before a succession of altars. These are all equivalents to classical musical form, but our image of life has become more dynamic, a progression of cause and effect. If our assumptions about life should ever so change that we come to feel that striving is futile, that our idea of cause and effect is illusion, perhaps drama would assume a form more closely allied to the repetitive form in music (we have noted hints of such a tendency in Ionesco and Beckett). Even then it is doubtful that a thoroughgoing formal equivalence in the smaller formal elements would be felt, for while it is conceivable that the general outline of a scene might be repeated, it is unlikely that whole sections would be repeated word for word, which would provide the only true equivalent to the repetition of the musical motive or phrase.

Victor Zuckerkandl offers a discussion of repetition in his theoretical treatment of music which may summarize what we have attempted to say here. He points out the large proportion of musical composition which is just repetition, then mentions a passage from Beethoven's *Pastoral Symphony*. The passage consists of:

> A brief tonal formula, comprising a mere five tones, in three variations—as if I should say: "I gave him apples, apples gave him I, I apples gave him"—repeated thirty-six times in all, followed by eight more repetitions of half the formula. . . . And hardly have we got through it before it begins again, and the whole thing is repeated tone for tone![23]

A striking comparison with the drama is then made:

What is true of repetition on a small scale is equally true of repetition on a large scale. Innumerable compositions proceed according to a basic plan in accordance with which their often quite extensive first part is first repeated note for note, only to reappear again in a slightly altered version after an interlude that is often very short. Imagine a play of which the first scene should be played twice and which after the second scene, should begin at the beginning again! But the situation is even more paradoxical. In many compositions this interlude follows the pattern of a process of gradual intensification leading to a climax; and what appears at the climax, the event for which we looked with such tension and which actually forms the culmination of the entire development, is nothing but the repetition of the story that we have already heard twice through. What would be sheer idiocy in a narrative, a drama, a poem—this beginning all over again—in music conveys the most powerful effects.[24]

Dramatic structure is bound by its meaning, by the obvious presence of a representation of man. Its structure must move always forward, the way we assume man's life moves forward in a pattern of time set on its one-directional course. The kind of time pattern we delight in in music can return upon itself. It is illustrated by the breaking and withdrawing of the waves, the circular dance, etc.[25] The kind of time which the theatre presents flows in a straight line. It is the time which brings to pass the effects of our decisions.

It must be acknowledged that at least part of the structural difference here is due to the fact that repetitions in drama are usually repetitions of *meanings* while musical repetitions involve nonrepresentational elements. Repetitions of stage position, costume colors, sounds, etc. in drama often are not noticed by most of the audience and, in any case, rarely determine the course of the drama. On the other hand, a musical passage exactly repeated can well be said to have a different *meaning* by its position in the piece—as coming at the beginning or the close.

137

Further, those who press the analogy of music and drama are often influenced by the sense of "striving" which Goetschius and others have noted in music. (See p. 131.) There does indeed seem to be a structural similarity here to the typical patterns of drama, which build to a climax where the turning point of the hero's fortunes and the peak use of nonrepresentational elements (the loudest, or, perhaps, the quietest point in the play) coincide.[26] If drama and music are shaped by different structural principles, still, within the broad outlines of the dramatic form, there is room for a musical arrangement of the materials, just as we found there was room for a narrative and a poetic arrangement of the materials.

The drama is full of sound. Besides the constant din of the words, there are footsteps, bells, snatches of song, and so forth. These sounds are part of man's life in time and therefore a part of the dramatic image of that life. They are there: raw materials to be patterned. However, the possibilities for creating structures of sound in the drama are limited by the overriding demands of dramatic structure. Music, on the other hand, because it is so pure in its materials, which means so self-limited, can develop the sound patterns of the voices or the footsteps *as sound*. Music makes patterns which delight us because in their abstract organization we hear echoes of the sounds and rhythms of life so purified that we can appreciate them as sounds, not as a woman's footfalls or the scream of a siren. In this development, which takes a raw pattern of sound and organizes it into a symphony, the sound is freed from literal connotation and developed in patterns which derive from our experience of a free rhythmic time.

Drama benefits from a kind of "feedback" from music because sounds, which are by-products of the acted script and which have received a rough kind of patterning in the design of the play—a patterning that must be fairly simple because so many elements (such as characterization, plot, and truth to appearance) must be considered—return in their infinitely more developed form from the hands of the musician who has had the opportunity to explore and develop them as pure sounds. The dramatist recognizes in this music some of the quintessential sounds of drama. To take one compelling example, he recognizes in certain modulating chordal sequences the essence of transition and he uses the device at its most obvious in the organ music that accompanies most daytime "soap operas." At a much more elevated level the dramatist's recognition of "developed sounds" in music suggests the possibility of grand opera.

One of the greatest challenges in the arts is to blend the disparate structures of music and drama over an extended composition. The challenge has been successfully met only a few times; however, the problems encountered and the terms of success can tell us a great deal about the two structures. Thus we may turn to the detailed examination of musical and dramatic structures in a piece from one of the successful operas.

The Beaumarchais-Mozart *Marriage of Figaro* suggests itself for a number of reasons. Both play and opera have enjoyed popular and critical acclaim for excellence in their respective mediums. Moreover, Mozart is considered to have been highly successful in making the opera work as both music and drama.[27] More important for our present purposes is the fact that Mozart achieves whatever dramatic success he may claim while utilizing traditional musical forms to carry the dramatic content.[28] For example, the piece to which we shall devote some close attention below, the trio No. 13, is built on the sonatina pattern, freely handled, as is the case in other, purely musical, compositions by Mozart.

It strikes one immediately, of course, that Mozart and Da Ponte have chosen to cut a good deal of material from the play. While they have retained much, considering the operatic necessities, and stayed remarkably close to Beaumarchais, a comparison of the libretto and the play text shows how many lines have fallen by the way. We see, for example, that almost the entire trial scene has been dropped from Beaumarchais' third act. Indeed, Beaumarchais' last three acts are combined in the opera into two acts which only coincide with the divisions of the play at the end. A glance at the scene we quote below will show why the cuts must be made. The opera progresses through a section of dialogue which would be spoken in less than thirty seconds in a piece which plays on record for slightly more than three minutes: roughly six times as long. At that rate, a setting for the entire play text would have lasted all night.

What sort of material strikes the librettist and composer as dispensable to the opera? As we have seen, the trial scene is cut, probably because it adds an intellectual type of confusion (the legal niceties of Figaro's agreement with Marceline) to an already complex plot. It may be said that the opera does not suffer from this exclusion. This is the kind of scene that would be likely to be cut by anyone who wanted to shorten the play and is not necessarily pruned away on purely musical grounds.

The nature of some of the other cuts is more interesting to us. These cuts we roughly divide into two hardly exclusive kinds: single line cuts and tailoring of the characters. One of Beaumarchais' more charming bits of dialogue is the line which he gives to Suzanne in Act II as she teases Cherubino about his song to the Countess: "The nice young man, with his long, hypocritical lashes. Come, bluebird, sing us a song for my lady."[29] It is hard to sustain this much figurative language in the recitative and Da Ponte reduces the epithet to "Hypocrite!"[30] In Act III of the play, Figaro introduces an amusing diversion when he tries to convince the Count that he is in possession of all the English necessary to get by in London since he knows the phrase, "Goddamn!"[31] As one would suspect, this idea about language has no relation to music and, indeed, it disappears from the libretto.

Admirers of Beaumarchais probably would find two characters decidedly changed in the transfer to opera: Figaro and the Countess. I would argue that musical reasons may account for the alterations. In the play Figaro is both witty rogue and philosopher;

in the opera he is also a witty rogue, though perhaps a little less witty since he must be denied the extent of verbal expression he is granted by Beaumarchais, but he is not a philosopher. Music, it must appear, cannot sustain much philosophy. Figaro's long summary of a servant's life and outlook is cut away, and, like Figaro's useful bit of English profanity, it may have been cut to avoid offending aristocratic ears with distasteful words or sentiments, yet, given the necessity to eliminate dialogue, these sections are likely to seem unappealing to those concerned with a musical setting.

A number of his other by-the-way remarks drop out. A very amusing little scene at the beginning of Act IV in which Figaro bandies remarks about fortune and the relativity of truth with his fiancée, Suzanne, (at a time when fortune seems to smile) does not find its way into the opera. Mozart makes some recompense in the recitative and aria (No. 26) he gives to Figaro in the last act; however, philosophically this does not go much beyond the message of *Cosi fan tutte*: women are charming vixens. This is decidedly not the republican adventurer created by Beaumarchais.

While we would probably say that Figaro's character loses something in transition, there are those, notably Joseph Kerman, who would say that Mozart chalks up a gain for the Countess.[32] The point is debatable. Mozart and Da Ponte purify and simplify the Countess. The hints of her infatuation with the page, while not eliminated, are decidedly reduced. Perhaps more than anything the nobility of Rosina's character in the opera is attributable to the pure beauty of the music the composer has written for her, particularly the aria No. 19 ("Dove sono").

We may profit most at this point by moving in close: looking at a small section of the opera and comparing it in some detail with the equivalent section in the play. A good part of the praise for Mozart's musical dramaturgy results from the way he made his ensemble pieces carry the action instead of stringing out recitatives and arias. Edward J. Dent has shown how the arias in *The*

Marriage of Figaro form just half the sung musical numbers, while in a more typical Italian opera of the period by Martin (Vincente Martin y Soler), also on a libretto by Da Ponte, the arias make up almost two-thirds of the total.[33] Joseph Kerman is enthusiastic about Mozart's dramatic use of ensemble music, particularly trios, several of which he analyses.[34] I have chosen to analyze a trio (No. 13 in the opera score), one which contains a dramatic build and which is, at the same time, based on a classical form. Here Mozart achieved something all theatre people must admire when he managed to compose songs to contribute to scenes which depend for their effect upon stage geography, i.e. who is hiding behind which door—hardly a "musical" kind of content. This "theatrical" moment in the opera seems an excellent spot to examine with an eye to the blend of musical and dramatic structure. Thus we shall look closely at the scene in Act II (of both opera and play) in which the Count bursts in upon his wife and demands to see the person hiding in the back room. First, what changes have Mozart and Da Ponte rung upon Beaumarchais?

We quote below Jacques Barzun's faithful translation of the short scene in Beaumarchais upon which the trio No. 13 is based. Suzanne enters at the back unnoticed. The Count replies to a previous line by the Countess, then, as he speaks through the dressing-room door, our scene begins:

> *Count:* Come out, Susanne, I order you to.
> *Countess:* She is almost naked, sir. How can you intrude in this way on women in their apartments? She was trying on some old things I am giving her on the occasion of her wedding. She fled when she heard you.
> *Count:* If she is afraid to show herself, she can at least speak. (He turns again to the closed door) Answer me, Suzanne: are you in the dressing room? (Suzanne, still at the back of the alcove, hides behind the bed)
> *Countess:* (Quickly, to the closed door) Suzy, I forbid you to answer. (To the Count) No one has ever carried tyranny so far![35]

In the opera this four-line section is treated as follows: (I have bracketed those lines which have no place in the play. Reference to the diagram may make these comments clearer in the absence of a score.)

1. *Count:* Suzanne, come out at once! Come out, I wish it.
2. *Countess:* Stop! Listen to me. She can not come out. She can not come out.
3. [*Count:* And who dares to forbid it, who?]
4. *Countess:* To forbid it? To forbid it? Why common decency! She's trying on a wedding dress.

***   ***   ***

5. *Count:* Suzanne, come out at once. Come out I wish it.
6. *Countess:* Stop! Listen to me. Stop. She can not come out.
7. *Count:* Well speak at least. Suzanne, if you are there.
8. *Countess:* No, no, no. I order you to be quiet, be quiet, be quiet.

***   ***   ***

Mozart and Da Ponte have added, at the places we have indicated by asterisks, two three-part sections having no real counterparts in the play script. In these sections the characters comment on their situation. The first such section follows line four.

[*Count:* Everything is quite clear. The lover is in there.]
#1 [*Countess:* Everything is quite ugly. Who knows what might happen.]
[*Suzanne:* I understand, I think. Let's see how it goes.]

The second section of the "comment" follows line eight.

[*Count:* My wife, take warning. A scandal, an uproar, avoid for pity's sake.]
#2 [*Suzanne:* Oh heavens! A disaster! A scandal, an uproar is bound to come to this.]
[*Countess:* My husband, take warning. A scandal, an uproar avoid for pity's sake.][36]

In both "comment" sections I have shown only the brief phrases. These are repeated over and over in various combinations.

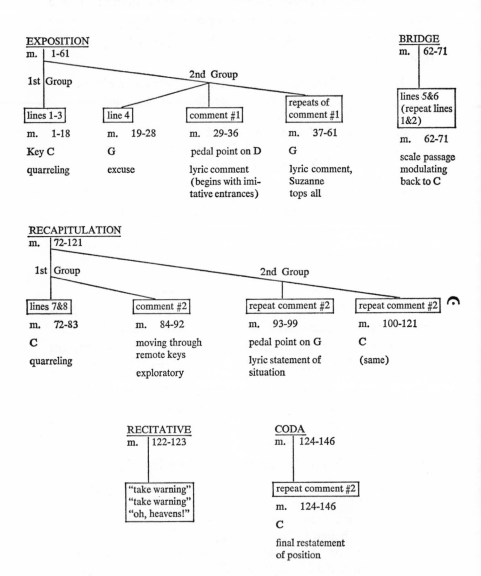

EXPOSITION
m. | 1-61

1st | Group

2nd Group

lines 1-3	line 4	comment #1	repeats of comment #1
m. 1-18	m. 19-28	m. 29-36	m. 37-61
Key C	G	pedal point on D	G
quarreling	excuse	lyric comment (begins with imitative entrances)	lyric comment, Suzanne tops all

BRIDGE
m. | 62-71

| lines 5&6 (repeat lines 1&2) |
| m.   62-71 |
scale passage
modulating
back to C

RECAPITULATION
m. | 72-121

1st | Group

2nd Group

lines 7&8	comment #2	repeat comment #2	repeat comment #2
m. 72-83	m. 84-92	m. 93-99	m. 100-121
C	moving through remote keys exploratory	pedal point on G lyric statement of situation	C (same)

RECITATIVE
m. | 122-123

| "take warning" "take warning" "oh, heavens!" |

CODA
m. | 124-146

| repeat comment #2 |
| m.   124-146 |
C

final restatement
of position

The Marriage of Figaro Trio, No. 13
See Appendix II for the score. Line numbers refer to the libretto as set
out on page 143 of this chapter.

To be clear about the progress of the drama, I now quote the rest of the scene in Beaumarchais, up to the exit of the Count and Countess. (Corresponding, in the opera, to the cue for No. 14, the Suzanne-Cherubino duet.) This material is covered by Mozart and Da Ponte in recitative.

> *Count:* (turning again) If she won't speak, dressed or undressed I shall see her.
> *Countess:* (intercepting him) Anywhere else I can't prevent you, but I trust that in my own room—
> *Count:* And I trust that in one minute I shall know who this mysterious Suzanne is. I can see it is useless to ask you for the key, but it is not hard to break down this trumpery door. Ho, there, anybody!
> *Countess:* You would bring in your people, create a public scandal—all on the strength of a vague suspicion!—We'll be the talk of the castle.
> *Count:* An excellent point, madam, I can do without help. This instant I go to my rooms and return with what I need. (He starts to go and turns back) But in order that everything shall remain as it is, will you kindly accompany me, quietly and decently—since scandal displeases you so? My simple request will surely not be denied?
> *Countess:* (upset) Sir, who would dream of crossing you?
> *Count:* Oh, I was forgetting: the door which leads to your maid's quarters. I must also shut it so that you may be fully vindicated. (He shuts the center door and takes the key)
> *Countess:* (aside) Oh what a fateful whim!
> *Count:* (returning) Now that this chamber is sealed, I beg you to accept my arm. (He raises his voice) As for the Suzanne in the dressing room, she will have the goodness to await my return. The least of the evils that may befall her then is—
> *Countess:* Really, sir, this is the most odious performance—
> (The Count leads her out and locks the door).[37]

What significant alterations may we find by comparing the quoted play and libretto?

One change, of course, is immediately apparent: a third voice (Suzanne's) has been added to the opera but was silent in the play. In addition, material which in the script comprises only four speeches that would be played in less than thirty seconds has been expanded into a musical scene which lasts 146 measures and plays in a little over three minutes. The reforming of these four lines into opera takes an interesting pattern in which the first line of the play text, the Count's "Come out!" and a quick answer by the Countess rewritten to "Stop! . . . She can not come out," from the play's "She is almost naked," are briefly stated once as the elements of the first group of a modified sonata form. The Count terminates this section and prepares us for a new kind of answer by line three of the libretto (added by Da Ponte) after which the librettist and composer turn again to the second speech of the play for the softer tones of the righteous explanation of the Countess (line four of the libretto). This is set to the first of a second group of musical themes. The softer tone leads to the first of the "comment" sections consisting of lines which have no real counterpart in the play. These comments are repeated several times; then the first demand and answer by the Count and Countess are repeated exactly as said but set to a musical bridge which leads to the appearance (as lines seven and eight of the libretto) of the second pair of lines in the play. The Count's new demand is sung on an exact musical repeat of his first theme, in its original key. The Countess' musical phrase has been varied from its first statement and is considerably more agitated, driven by a crescendo in the accompaniment which piles up chords on the repeated "tacite" ("be quiet"). Again comments by the three participants are introduced that were not in the original play, but this time the words indicate a dangerous building of tension in the progress of the scene: "a scandal," "an uproar," "a disaster," etc.

This will indicate the dramatic form of the passage both in the play and the opera. It is basically: two lines of direct action dialogue close to those in the play; a short (nine measures) section of explanation by the Countess derived from her second play speech leading to a more lyric and longer section of comment not to be found in the play, a bridge section repeating the first pair of lines; the second pair of direct action lines from the play; a concluding longer section of comment at a higher emotional temperature than the first.

What I have described, of course, is Mozart's finished form, not what he started with (which is to be found in the text we quoted from Beaumarchais). The musical form Mozart chose to carry us from the four lines of play text to the musical scene No. 13 was a modified sonata form. This consists essentially of an exposition, including the customary first and second thematic groups in the tonic and the dominant respectively, a bridge, a recapitulation of the material in the exposition, and a coda. The full sonata form has thus been modified by the exclusion of the development section. I invite reference to Siegmund Levarie's analysis of the same piece, but note that I depart from Levarie on some details.[38]

Let us see how the dramatic form fits into the musical form. Certainly the composer set the opening line brilliantly. The Count's demand is stern and brusque, utilizing two notes, the dominant and the tonic. The accompaniment, in widening chords, builds tension behind him. All corresponds to the musical demands of a first statement in sonata form. The Countess' first line, which has more desperation and uncertainty, moves conjunctly to the subdominant region and from there tries out a number of other small steps in the scale. The accompaniment in the strings is more flowing. A descending figure, also in the strings, leads to what may be taken as a second group of themes in measure nineteen (Levarie does not agree. He introduces the second theme in measure thirty-seven.)[39] Here we find the fourth line of the opera text. If this is, despite Levarie, a second thematic group of the sonata form, it would be an admirable formal correspondence with the more lyric and sustained explanation of the Countess,

"She's trying on a wedding dress," leading quite naturally and logically, through its nature as explanation rather than demand or reply, to the first of what we have chosen to call "comment" sections (measures twenty-eight through sixty-one) because this term seems to describe the dramatic situation in which all three characters pause to sing their personal comments on the situation. The dramatic mood for commenting flows out of the quieting explanation of the fourth line, and the beginning of the comment section utilizes the musical phrases to which this explanation was set. As each of the characters launches his comments, two measures apart, the interval of their first two notes widens, adding musical weight to the tensions between them.

The musical form takes advantage of the fact that direct conflict turns into introversion here to blend the "monologues" into a trio in a section in which there is little musical conflict. The highest voice line and the one with the most excitement to it is Suzanne's, most obvious in measures fifty-one through fifty-three where she has her coloratura flight up to g^2. This is directly in line with Suzanne's character in the play and the scene—she is more lively than the Count or Countess and distinctly separated from them in class.

The first comment section ends peacefully on a full chord in the dominant, as is natural for the close of the exposition in sonata form. Suddenly the Count remembers the action. He must get back to it as the composer must get back to the tonic for a recapitulation of his first theme. Both tasks are neatly accomplished in measures sixty-two through seventy-one, a modulating bridge passage in which the Count and the Countess toss out their first lines again on the way to finding new positive dramatic positions. These appear with strength at the strong musical point of restatement of first themes. One might expect that the place for a repetition of text was on a repetition in the music. This we see is not the case in the trio No. 13, for the repeated lines are set to a musical bridge, a series of chords carrying us from the dominant key back to the tonic. When the music restates its first theme, it does so with *new* lines (i.e., 7 and 8).

Actually there is a good deal of structural logic to this arrangement, and it indicates how differently the same device can function in the two arts. The musical bridge (measures 62–71) gives us a feeling of transition, of building to something. It contains a repetition of lines which, since they have already been spoken, mark time and gain impetus in the same way the chords, carrying no real melody, mark musical time. The pressures built up by the modulating chords and the tossed-off lines require a firm and fulfilling resolution. Musically the most satisfying result is the restatement of the strong first theme. Dramatically the right solution is a new attack, a carrying forward of the situation. It is significant that in spite of the advance of the dramatic situation (where the Count accepts the prohibition on *seeing* Suzanne but feels he can still trap the Countess by requiring Suzanne to speak if she is there—which he, of course, believes she is not), still the shape of the action is the same as that of lines one and two in the exposition: a line of brusque demand by the Count, a line of frantic refusal by the Countess. Dramatic dialogue rarely has this neat symmetrical form unless, as in the Greek drama, it is shaped on musical-poetical principles. A glance at the scene as quoted from Beaumarchais will confirm that though Mozart and Da Ponte have regularized the shape of the dialogue somewhat they have neither distorted it nor made it undramatic. This testifies to at least the possibility of opera as drama.

The second of our "comment" sections begins with measure eighty-four. The nine measures (84–92) comprise one of the most musically interesting places in the trio: an exploration of remote tonal regions leading into a repeat from measure ninety-three of the thematic material which carried our previous comment section, measures twenty-eight through thirty-seven. We should notice that dramatically we make the transition to comment without any quieting line of explanation such as that which the

Countess sings in measures twenty-two through twenty-eight. The transition here is made with the beginning of the comment where the Count shifts from his brusque command to Suzanne to a polite but ominous warning to his wife (accompanied, although he is unaware of it, by Suzanne's "O cielo!", etc.) The lovely modulating passage in the score is perhaps too calm for the dramatic situation it presents.

As noted above, this second comment section is at a higher point of dramatic tension than the previous one. The Count and Countess speak to one another instead of to themselves. Musically the pitch is higher and Suzanne climaxes on c^3 rather than the g^2 she hit previously. This section, comprising measures ninety-three through the fermata in measure 121, blends the three voices in a forceful development of their dramatic and musical position. They hold on a deceptive cadence in measure 121, which adds suspense to their two-measure break into recitative and a wonderful swinging impetus when the melody resumes in the twenty-three measure coda.

It is at the forceful close of the coda that music and drama run into conflict, for classical form requires, and Mozart provides, a good full close on the tonic. Naturally this stops things and it stops things on what the music makes us feel is a resolution. However, a glance back to the scene by Beaumarchais (which Da Ponte now tries to take up again in recitative) shows that no close could be considered after the fourth line in the play text, but that, indeed, this is just the beginning of a dramatic build which runs to the end of the section we have quoted. Mozart has broken into a dramatic sequence which he has been forced by musical conditions to terminate and must now pick up, at a low point in the opera, what dramatically is part of a build. Later composers recognized this problem, and Wagner would probably have solved it by going into what Mozart treats in recitative without effecting any formal musical close at all (thus not halting our sense of dramatic build). This solution, of course, was musically impossible for Mozart.[40]

He and Da Ponte might, however, have taken care to include a whole dramatic "beat" within a section requiring closure.

We must now lift our focus again to make a few more points about opera and drama before leaving our instructive example, *The Marriage of Figaro*. Soon after the trio just analysed, we come to the Act II finale. This is a very long section (939 measures) about which I should like to make a few specific comments before proceeding to a general discussion of the nature of the finale.

One of the very amusing moments of opera and play is the moment when the Count finally opens the dressing-room door to find not Cherubino but Suzanne. Both he and the Countess are startled and he turns to beg her forgiveness. Although the scene moves along fairly much as Beaumarchais wrote it, we find the forgiveness motive considerably extended—sustained on a beautiful melodic phrase. Among the lines which are dropped to make way for the musical extension is, typically, the wry remark made by the Countess, "Aren't you glad to have caught this one instead of the other? Generally speaking, you do not hate to catch this one."[41] Mozart achieves musically an effective dramatic moment not found in Beaumarchais when he brings the Count, the Countess, and Suzanne together in concord with the section, "From this moment. . . " ("Da questo momento"—measure 307 ff). This convincing musical resolution just before Figaro bursts in to stir things up again is represented in the script only by the stage direction, "The Count ardently kisses his wife's hand." (p. 143.)

The section we have just been discussing ends in measure 326 in B♭, the dominant of the key (E♭) of the finale as a whole. Here, with the entrance of Figaro, an interesting musical device which has considerable dramatic significance is utilized: the piece moves into the key of the mediant, G. Key relationships, as musicians are well aware, work to give the move into the mediant a feeling of having gone into a more brilliant area. This is, of course, appropriate for the entrance of our bustling hero, who has been absent for some time, and it corresponds exactly with the kind of things a stage director would probably do here, such as sneaking up the luminosity of the stage, or bringing in Figaro to a strong area.

Figaro enters here and the Count indicates he knows that the valet was the originator of the "mysterious" letter about the Countess. In the play the women inform Figaro that they have told the Count about this and Figaro immediately drops his deception. Dramatically this was wise, because prolonging this minor bit of trickery after the elaborate and lengthy high jinks just preceding would have bogged down the plot badly; however, Mozart keeps up Figaro's blustering denial of guilt. The composer is able to sustain Figaro's minor trick because he is able to *musically* sustain the moment.

This second act is packed with complications, and, as one may recall, Antonio, the gardener, bursts in with the news that someone had jumped out of the Countess' window. Almaviva thinks he has the culprits this time, but again he is tricked out of his victory by Figaro. His hope for defeating the valet lies now in Marceline, and, sure enough, in troop Marceline, Bartolo, Basil, and Sunstruck. The Count's forces have arrived and his star ascends. Mozart grasps this situation for a stirring ending. He has a full stage, a good balance of voices with Basil's tenor and Marceline's mezzo-soprano balancing and filling out the soprano, baritone, and bass voices that have held the scene till now. Sunstruck does not appear in the opera, and Mozart treats his seven voices, split into two opposing groups, in a rich musical texture that makes a fine dramatic climax to the act.

Beaumarchais, on the other hand, cannot stop plotting. He contrives the humiliation of Basil (he must accompany Sunstruck on his errand, musically and physically) and the act closes, not with a full stage and the build-up for the trial in the following act, but with a tête-à-tête between Suzy and the Countess in which they agree to change places in a rendezvous with the Count (the business of the final act). Beaumarchais is running over with invention, but here Mozart has contrived, through music, a better dramatic structure. He takes advantage of the build-up of people on the stage to climax an act that has been mostly duets and trios with a piece for seven voices. In the opera the weight of the last part of the finale, after the entrance of Marceline and her entourage, caps the action with what theatre people would call a most effective "curtain." This concludes one section of the action (with resounding full cadences in the voices followed by seven measures reiteration of the tonic by the orchestra), but it also forcefully presents the problem which will be our next major concern: Marceline's claims on Figaro. Beaumarchais allows the strong "curtain" to pass, concluding much more softly on a duet of plotting, as we might well expect from an author so interested in intrigue; however, the plot which Suzanne and the Countess are contriving in the play is aimed way ahead—into the last act.

For a detailed examination of the first *Figaro* finale I refer the reader to Levarie (pp. 107–123), but now I wish to turn our attention to some comments on the finale as a musical and dramatic form in general. Here the words of Da Ponte describing the difficulties of a librettist faced with this form are illuminating:

> This *finale*, which must remain intimately connected with the opera as a whole, is nevertheless a sort of little comedy or operette all by itself, and requires a new plot and an unusually high pitch of interest. The *finale*, chiefly, must glow with the genius of the conductor, the power of the voices, the grandest dramatic effects. Recitative is banned from the *finale*: everybody sings; and every form of singing must be available—the *adagio*, the *allegro*, the *andante*, the intimate, the harmonious and then—noise, noise, noise; for the *finale* almost always closes in an uproar; which, in musical jargon, is called the *chiusa*, or rather the *stretta*, I know not whether because, in it, the whole power of the drama is drawn or 'pinched' together, or because it gives generally not one pinch but a hundred to the poor brain of the poet who must supply the words. The *finale* must, through a dogma of the theatre, produce on the stage every singer of the cast, be there three hundred of them, and whether by ones, by twos, by threes or

by sixes, tens or sixties; and they must have solos, duets, terzets, sextets, thirteenets, sixtyets; and if the plot of the drama does not permit, the poet must find a way to make it permit, in the face of reason, good sense, Aristotle, and all the powers of heaven or earth; and if then the *finale* happens to go badly, so much the worse for him![42]

It would appear that we have come upon a form suited to musical structure, which needs the full resounding chords and the "noise, noise, noise" of the finale, but which is unnatural to dramatic form, according to Da Ponte. Actually a more careful look will show that a full-stage finale is just as germane to the drama as it is to opera, if we talk in terms of comedy and of the broad outlines of finale form.

There can be no doubt that there is "something about" the finale which in spite of all sober-sided naturalism endears it to the audience, because this great bringing together of the characters has been satisfying theatre-goers from Greek times through the latest musical comedy. What is the structural logic which calls for the finale? Some scholars have guessed at an origin in a concluding fertility rite in ancient comic forms. This became, by the time of the extant Old Comedy, a concluding "wedding" scene and/or feast, sometimes with dancing, of which the conclusion of *Lysistrata* is a good example.[43] Whatever the origin, the effect of the resolution of all the complicated problems which bedevil the characters seems to call for a balancing moment of full and uncomplicated celebration. Literally the atmosphere becomes lighter as the electrician sneaks up the dimmers while the cast pours on stage from the wings to sing and dance their joy. This follows a pattern of experience which, if it happens all too rarely in real life, still possesses—as pattern—the tremendous vitality of our wishing, which makes us thrill to the happy resolution of, say, *As You Like It*.

Thus we see that playwrights as successful as Aristophanes and Shakespeare freely chose to compose finales on several occasions, impelled by their dramatic instincts, not by the insistence of a composer wishing to fill out a classical form. We also recall that these authors often utilized music in their finales, which suggests that the structure of this moment of happy conclusion may well be suited to the structure of song, so binding our musical and dramatic structures as happily as the lovers are commonly bound in this last scene.

In this chapter we have found many correspondences and a few discrepancies between the structures of the drama of Figaro and the classical music by Mozart. We have looked at small details like the motive and larger ones like the piece. In spite of the structural differences we found in the theoretical analysis, it appears that a composer and librettist of talent can certainly shape a successful combination of the two arts. This might be assumed to have been proved long before this by popular acclaim, yet how many opera lovers must confess they pay scant attention to dramatic details, and even sometimes, to musical details.

One final example may illustrate the conclusion that, in spite of the fortunate fact of a number of structural similarities in the larger forms, music and drama require the greatest skill—even genius—to combine them without doing violence to either's details. Even Mozart has falsified the drama when carried away by his music, and this is partly the case with the lovely duet (No. 16) sung by the Count and Suzanne at the beginning of Act III. The very beautiful section which occurs just after the double bar (measures twenty-nine through thirty-six), particularly because it is beautiful, leaves the listener with the idea that this is a perfectly straightforward love song. As the two voices blend, one would say "a match made in heaven" rather than guess the actual dramatic fact that here we have the treacherous seducer, Almaviva, being trapped in his own trickery by a shrewd serving maid. The middle section of this ternary composition breaks into questions and answers where the Count keeps trying to reassure himself with, "We will meet?" "You will not fail me?" and Suzanne answers incorrectly only to correct and reingratiate herself with a jump to f^1 and a charming little two-measure phrase. Here Mozart captures the dramatic essence of the meeting excellently, but the framing duet sections seem much too sincere. The point is that music differs from drama, as here the music seems to be lacking a basic dramatic dimension; beautiful music seems to preclude the concept of dishonesty, perhaps even of the dramatic flaw, because how does one go about consciously composing deceitful music?

Chapter IX

ARISTOTLE

In this chapter and the two succeeding the ideas on dramatic structure set out in the earlier part of this book will be used in critical analyses of three important concepts of dramatic structure: those held by Aristotle, Robert Heilman, and the Northrop Frye-Susanne Langer school, thus refining our own concepts by comparison with a rational plot-centered concept, a concept of structure by thematic relationship, and a concept of structure by archetypal pattern.

Anyone who speaks on the form of the drama must acknowledge the immense contribution made so long ago by Aristotle. This is particularly true in my case since I have adopted ideas—the concept of the action and the importance of plot—which are

Aristotelian. The present task will be to show where I follow and where I depart from Aristotle by examining the relevant passages from the *Poetics*.[1] When Aristotle said, "Tragedy, then, is an imitation of an action" (*Poetics* 6. 1449b 24), he said a mouthful.[2] One cannot help answering, "That's it!" And yet the famous formula presents a number of difficulties if one bears down on it with the weight of modern aesthetic analysis. Let us see what that is valuable and what that is questionable can be derived from this statement, then see how it compares with the description of structure set forth in the preceding pages.

The first problem is to decide what "imitation" (*mimesis*) meant to Aristotle, because it is an important clue to the derivation of structure. The theory that art imitates nature no longer holds much weight with contemporary aestheticians.[3] Those who would preserve Aristotle's authority, therefore, would insist that Aristotle did not mean that the artist literally copied nature, making an exact likeness of the face of Socrates or, in a Socratic dialogue, reproducing each word and gesture of a philosophers' banquet. As Butcher says, Aristotle's phrase "art imitates nature" could not "possibly bear the sense that fine art is a copy or reproduction of natural objects."[4] Both Butcher and Else see imitation as referring to the *process* of art, that is, the artistic process imitates the natural process. If all Aristotle meant by his theory of imitation was that in making the art work the artist imitates (works in the same manner as) nature when nature "makes" things, then we have an interesting comment on artistic activity but little information on the art object. However, a number of the passages in the *Poetics* indicate that Aristotle, at least part of the time, had in mind a more or less literal copying of objects. A casual reader of the *Poetics*, when he reads that music imitates, will know that *mimesis* certainly is not always literal. Butcher points out that the Greeks generally felt that music was a particularly direct imitation of the emotions, and cites in support *Politics* VIII. 5. 1340a 18: "In rhythms and melodies we have the most realistic imitations of anger and mildness as well as of courage, temperance and all their opposites."[5] This is a dubious musical aesthetic, but we shall pass over it to return to drama.

Aristotle refers to the poet as imitating what *may* happen, the universal, rather than what has happened, the particular—the province of the historians (*Poetics* 9. 1451a 33–1451b 11). Of course, only an idealist could speak of *imitating* what *may* happen, but the concept had passed down from Plato and seems to have been a common theory of art at the time.[6] On the other hand, a goodly number of quotations can be marshalled to show that Aristotle, at least part of the time, used his key term, *mimesis*, in the sense of literal copying.[7] We may cite a few of these: Speaking of *mimesis* as one of the two causes of poetry Aristotle remarks: "Objects which in themselves we view with pain, we delight to contemplate when reproduced with minute fidelity" (*Poetics* 4. 1448b 10–12). "Character must be true to life" (*Poetics* 15. 1454a 24). Even the discussion of the errors that may crop up in poetry, as a description of "a horse as throwing out both his off legs at once, or . . . technical inaccuracies in medicine" (*Poetics* 25. 1460b 19–22), implies that imitation is literal even though literal imitation does not always make the best art. Though these inaccuracies may serve an artistic end and hence be justified, Aristotle adds: "If, however, the end might have been as well, or better, attained without violating the special rules of the poetic art, the error is not justified: for every kind of error should, if possible, be avoided" (*Poetics* 25. 1480b 27–30). Aristotle also spoke of imitation as implanted in us in childhood and "through imitation [the child] learns his earliest lessons" (*Poetics* 4. 1448b 5–8). Now this, of course, must mean literal imitation of speech, and action, even though distorted by the child's lack of ability.

It is pointless to push this discussion further. The idea of art as an imitation of life is certainly attractive, but it cannot stretch far enough to account for the real nature of art. What may be concluded about Aristotle is that he used this term, adopted from

Plato and common to the thought of the day, in a way that sometimes signified a quite literal copying of life and, at other times, expressed a broader idea. Most of the time, the idea of imitation seems definitely to imply something lifelike, even though liberties might be taken for artistic purposes.

The idea of imitation could be particularly important in the exploration of structure, because if the drama literally imitated the actions of men, our search for the source of structure would be over; drama would simply take the structure of the events imitated. Indeed, Aristotle himself implies this solution for one aspect of structure, "As therefore, in the other imitative arts, the imitation is one [unified] when the object imitated is one" (*Poetics* 8. 1451a 30–32). The problem is that imitation in itself does not and cannot supply the all-important clue of what to leave out. But in this we are getting ahead of ourselves, for before we can meaningfully discuss structure, we must discuss the ideas of action and plot.

The last term in the famous "Tragedy is an imitation of an action," presents fewer problems than the one preceding it. There seems to be general agreement that *praxis* meant a doing, physical or mental activity, striving.[8] There is also general agreement on the claim that doing was important in Aristotle's philosophy. Characters are happy or unhappy, brave or cowardly, as they *do* (or behave).[9] Though Butcher perhaps saw action as more inward and mental than Aristotle really meant it to be,[10] he admits that it must be shown in some outward and physical way. On the other hand, it seems doubtful that Aristotle understood actions in Stanislavsky's sense, or in the sense adapted by Francis Fergusson on the claim that he was following Aristotle.[11] However, actions, or men in action, are certainly the subject matter of drama. In fact, this helps to distingiush drama from the other arts. As Susanne Langer says, drama's basic abstraction is the act.[12] We may note, though, that the difference is probably more marked in our day than in Aristotle's, because in ancient times mankind was the universal subject of art.

For purposes of definition then, we have discovered quite a bit, but if we wish to get some clues for structure, we must move along in Aristotle to the description of the action as "serious, complete, and of a certain magnitude" (*Poetics* 6. 1448b 24–25). A discussion of structure is not concerned with the seriousness of the action, but it must be concerned with the idea of a single whole action of a certain magnitude. The implication is that when such a single complete action is found we have the basis of dramatic structure, for which the action need only be imitated:

> As therefore, in the other imitative arts, the imitation is one when the object imitated is one, so the plot, being an imitation of an action, must imitate one action and that a whole, the structural union of the parts being such that, if any one of them is displaced or removed, the whole will be disjointed and disturbed. (*Poetics* 8. 1451a 30–34)

The idea of a play as a single complete action is an appealing one, and this is one point on which the *Poetics* is clear and full. Aristotle offers the explanations of (1) appropriate size to be held in the memory (*Poetics* 7. 1451a 3–6); (2) size to encompass a change from good to bad fortune (*Poetics* 7. 1451a 9–15); (3) having beginning, middle, and end (*Poetics* 7. 1480b 27–35); (4) such that if one part is removed the whole will be disturbed (*Poetics* 8. 1451a 30–36). He also tells us several things that do not by themselves constitute unity of action: unity of the hero (*Poetics* 8. 1451a 15–16) and incidents performed by this one hero (such as Odysseus' wound on Parnassus) which have no necessary or probable connection to the rest of the incidents (*Poetics* 8. 1451a 16–30).

Looking back over these rules we can see that "having beginning, middle, and end" and "such that if one part is removed the whole must suffer," though they are now famous aphorisms of art, are least helpful. At best they describe in general terms a successful completed art work. Aristotle defines a beginning as that "which does not itself follow anything by causal necessity" (*Poetics* 7. 1450b 28–29), yet only the Unmoved Mover can get outside the causal chain. Even taking the less strict interpretation which was obviously meant here, the beginning of *Oedipus*, for example, has its importance because it *does* follow a number of things by causal necessity: an unsolved murder, a period of famine, etc. The same kind of argument could be made about the end. Yet the formula points a rule of art which would win general assent. The artist's activity of selecting and shaping his materials results—at least in the kind of works Aristotle was used to—in a form which gives a feeling of beginning, middle, and end. The difficulty with the formula is that it calls for considerable explanation.

The famous prescription for the organic art work (*Poetics* 8. 1451a 30–36) suffers from the same kind of general assent and specific confusions. Plays are notoriously alterable. They are cut and rewritten many times. Even *Hamlet* is hardly ever played complete, and who is to say what is the Ideal *Hamlet*, or *Cat on a Hot Tin Roof*,[13] from which not one word or gesture may be extracted or changed without damage to the whole? Of course, it can be said that a play altered ever so slightly is a different play, but it is a play nonetheless.

Aristotle makes a good practical point in the general dictum that a play must not be too long to be grasped in the memory and he adds that it must fit within the time alloted to dramas in the competitions. These considerations, though external (as Aristotle recognizes), are valuable aids in deciding just how much elaboration your action can stand, for there does seem to be some real, if elastic, limit to the amount of drama an audience can absorb in a morning at Athens or an evening on Broadway. (We today are perhaps easily exhausted spectators compared to the Athenians or even the early eighteenth century Englishmen.)

What seems the most instructive of Aristotle's definitions of an appropriate complete action is that: "The proper magnitude is comprised within such limits that the sequence of events, according to the law of probability or necessity, will admit of a change from bad fortune to good, or from good fortune to bad" (*Poetics* 7. 1451a 11–15). This, particularly the latter part, helps to put a structure on the events of life, thus preparing them to be made into a drama. That it admits of a change from good fortune to bad is much more informative as a description of the action which comprises *Oedipus*, than to say that it has a beginning, a middle, and an end.

The crux of the matter is that it is very difficult to say just what one single and complete action is. The idea of regarding some given segment of a man's life as comprising one complete action is dependent on making an abstraction of real events. Complete and uncluttered actions do not come ready-made from life. Furthermore, the issue is kept from going back to life experience by Aristotle's habit of using the myths as his examples of raw material for drama. He speaks, for example, of the body of stories about Odysseus. The poet's task, he indicates, is to select material that will make one complete action, and Aristotle applauds Homer for achieving this. But, as Aristotle describes the process, the poet is already operating at one remove from reality, because he is using stories, not life. The point is to get from *life* to the dramatic structure—via story or myth, if you prefer, but nonetheless consciously acknowledging the kinds of abstractions made in the process.

I suggested in the earlier chapters that the best way to give a structure to the events of a drama is through the Basic Pattern of Events. This has the latitude to carry the single purposive action through the familiar pattern of striving, success or failure, and adjustment. It can contain the pattern of change from good fortune to bad or the patterns of reversal or recognition, which are really only Basic Patterns of Events briefly suggested. The

Basic Pattern of Events can contain these and more; it can serve as explanation for the basic structure of many different kinds of drama. What is more, it suggests its own derivation. Even before art takes over we are accustomed to order the events we observe into patterns; the events of a day, a career, an adventure, a voyage, etc. Stories enforce this kind of patterning in us. But the ordering implies an active selection and grouping according to some mental concept which usually further implies an assumption that the ordering is "meaningful." A single complete entity of the magnitude of a drama without any extraneous parts is never found in raw experience simply waiting to be imitated.

We have considered the Aristotelian conceptions of imitation and action and in so doing have discussed aspects of structure in its limiting phase (the concept of the whole). But, besides a beginning and an end, we have also a middle, and we must now turn to Aristotle's suggestions on the inner structure of the play, that is, we must consider plot.

Aristotle devotes a great deal of space to plot, from Chapter 6 section 9 to Chapter 14 section 9, where he finally says, "Enough has now been said concerning the structure of the incidents, and the right kind of plot." Yet even after this he keeps returning to plot. It will not be necessary to cover in detail all the material on plot in these many chapters. Those sections in which Aristotle deals with the ideal tragic hero, the best manner of recognition, etc., are shrewd observations on a great mode of drama, but they are also essentially hints on how to write a good play (more or less the kind of thing we find today in the standard playwriting text, although these later authors aspire to well-made plays, not Greek tragedies). Aside from tips on the kinds of material that ought to be put in a perfect tragedy, however, we are interested in how Aristotle sees the abstract problem of arranging incidents. Let us, as usual, set out the evidence Aristotle gives, then see what can be made of it.

Plot is the imitation of the action:—for by plot I here mean the arrangement of the incidents. (*Poetics* 6. 1450a 3–5)

Most important of all [the parts of a tragedy] is the structure of the incidents. For Tragedy is an imitation, not of men, but of an action and of life. (*Poetics* 6. 1450a 15–17)

The Plot, then, is the first principle, and, as it were, the soul of a tragedy. (*Poetics* 6. 1450a 37–38)

For the power of Tragedy . . . is felt even apart from representation and actors. (*Poetics* 6. 1450b 19–20)

This is the impression [to thrill with horror and melt with pity] we should receive from hearing the story (*mythos*) of the Odeipus. (*Poetics* 14. 1453b 6)

The proper structure of the plot involves imitating:

an action that is complete, and whole and of a certain magnitude. . . . A whole is that which has a beginning, a middle, and an end. (*Poetics* 7. 1450b 25–28)

The incidents must have a necessary and probable connection or sequence (*Poetics* 10. 1452a 18–21). "Character must be true to life," and consistent (*Poetics* 15. 1454a 24–28). Finally, Aristotle's example of the plotting of *Iphigenia* is found in *Poetics* 17. 1455a 31–1455b 15.

We may sum up the points thus: plot is certainly the most important part of the drama for Aristotle, holding such independent authority that a mere telling of the plot of a tragedy will produce horror and fear (the tragic effects) in a listener. The plot consists of an arrangement of incidents imitating actions, not men, and the manner of this arrangement or structure depends on establishing a necessary or probable connection between incidents. Aristotle saw drama as formed around a core of "story" and this story as a series of incidents or happenings (*pragmata*) which were arranged in a probable sequence to imitate the action of life. Now perhaps this is to reduce the *Poetics* to a level which its author did not imagine, but, if we are to deal with the specifics of drama, these vague terms and phrases must be given some concrete reference.

First we must deal with the idea of structure as plot or story, what we might call the "soul of the drama" concept, and it will be well to note right away an objection to this simplification. Else sums up his observations on *mythos* as follows:

> The plot as "basic principle and as it were the soul of tragedy" is surely part of Aristotle's original stock of ideas in the *Poetics*. The plot or arrangement of the incidents is the framework, the form, of tragedy. A poem is not a living thing and cannot literally have a soul. But we have to bear in mind constantly that by 'plot' Aristotle means primarily the *shaping* of the structure of incidents, the forming process which goes on in the mind (soul) of the poet: in other words that *mythos* really signifies a working part of the art of tragedy. It is the *arché* of the poem just as the idea of house in the builder's mind is the *arché* of the house.[14] [*arché*—beginning, origin, first principle]

The concept of plotting as process, as well as imitating as process, has cogency and justification. However, if pushed to its logical extremes in the context of the *Poetics* it can only lead to what a modern would call a "process-product" confusion. Aristotle does deal with plot as story or outline of the incidents,[15] and it is plot in this sense that we shall be concerned with.

There is, undoubtedly, something extractable from a play (novel, epic, etc.) which we may call plot or story. Lamb, among others, amply demonstrates the fact. The plot or story may also be said to exist prior to the play, as the Oedipus story existed prior to the play by Sophocles, and we could even say that the specific plot of the *Oedipus Tyranus* existed before the drama of that title was completed. We must ask what is the nature of "story" in this sense and what is its relation to structure (in the sense developed in this essay—relation of the events), keeping in mind that for practical purposes "plot" in Aristotle is story.[16]

Actually the story of a play is essentially a narration of the important events of the play. In cultures such as ancient Greece, where the stories to be found in the drama had in independent and prior existence, it must have been easy to recognize the plot-story as an extractable core of a play. In this day of "originality" of plot, the concept would not be as apparent; today's audience point of view sees the plot as a kind of summary or précis made after the fact. This point (that the story, or "prose argument," is itself an artistic creation) is forcefully illustrated by W. P. Ker's reference to Coleridge:

> The prose argument of 1817 [added by Coleridge to *The Ancient Mariner*] is not the matter of the poem as Coleridge originally shaped it. It is a fresh artistic creation; it is as much form as the poem itself. And though it may be identical with the poem in the narrative argument, yet the meaning of the poem is different.[17]

The theoretical tangle arises when you try to posit story-plot as the structure (presumably the *sufficient* structure) of the play it represents. The fact is that story is itself an art work of sorts (short narrative) needing its own structure. In other words, to say that the structure of a play is a story is merely to abstract from the play another more stripped-down kind of literary work, a work that relates in unembroidered form the main incidents. But what governs the ordering and relation of events in the story? We are caught in a reductio argument. We must quickly add that Aristotle does give us a way out, but, before we explore it, we should say a little more about story.

Aristotle's view of drama saw the elements of story as extremely important—perhaps too important. Right or wrong, his theory colors the *Poetics* and leads any structural theories by the nose. The passages which best illustrate this, and which we must consider in order to clarify our ideas of structure, are in Chapters 14 and 17. For the crucial section of Chapter 14, I use Else's translation, which renders the idea of *pragmata* better than that of

Butcher: "Anyone who hears the events as they unfold will both shudder and be moved to pity at the outcome: which is what one would feel at hearing the plot of the *Oedipus*."[18] Some commentators have felt that in this passage Aristotle must have meant *mythos* to include a reading of the whole play.[19] To this Else answers:

> But there cannot really be any doubt . . . the reading of the whole play (the full text) cannot come into question here: Aristotle is still dealing with the structure of the play as such and has not gotten to the writing-out stage. . . . . The plot of the *Oedipus*, its outline or bare structure, before the play is written out, is what Aristotle has in mind.[20]

Thus plot has an extremely powerful effect. Do we suppose that this is the basic effect of a play, which is merely strengthened by character, thought, diction, melody, and spectacle? It would appear that something like this was in Aristotle's mind. The modern would insist that in the instance cited the audience is moved by a short story, in the typical way such a story may move us, but that our experience before a play is really a different kind of experience even though the same incidents may figure in both. What has been disregarded is the medium, because the plot or story exists itself as a work of art—albeit minor—in competition with, not as soul of, the play. Structure as pure relation has no ability to move an audience emotionally.

Aristotle gives us an even better look at what he considers plot to be in Chapter 17; here he actually gives a story outline for a play, as well as an outline of the *Odyssey* in much the same manner. The case is not as clear as we might wish, for when Aristotle introduces this outline he calls it *logos* (story or argument) not *mythos*, but I follow Else in regarding the difference as not important here.[21] The passage in question reads:

> As for the story, whether the poet takes it ready made or constructs it for himself, he should first sketch its general outline, and then fill in the episodes and amplify in detail.

The general plan may be illustrated by the Iphigenia. A young girl is sacrificed; she disappears mysteriously from the eyes of those who sacrificed her; she is transported to another country, where the custom is to offer up all strangers to the goddess. To this ministry she is appointed. Some time later her own brother chances to arrive. The fact that the oracle for some reason ordered him to go there, is outside the general plan of the play. The purpose, again, of his coming is outside the action proper. However, he comes, he is seized, and when on the point of being sacrificed, reveals who he is. The mode of recognition may be either that of Euripides or of Polyidus, in whose play he exclaims very naturally—'So it was not my sister only, but I too, who was doomed to be sacrificed'; and by that remark he is saved.

After this, the names being once given, it remains to fill in the episodes. We must see that they are relevant to the action. In the case of Orestes, for example, there is the madness which led to his capture, and his deliverance by means of the purificatory rite. (*Poetics* 17. 1455a 31–1455b 15)

Several things should be noted. As Else points out, Aristotle includes in the story (*logos*) material which actually takes place before the play, at least that of Euripides, opens. This confirms for Else what he has held all along, that Aristotle includes as plot all pertinent incidents of the whole story even if they take place before or outside of the stage action proper.[22] This seems to be clumsy for the playwright who is presumably trying to shape up the incidents he will actually dramatize, as an accurate idea of the form of his play can be derived only from a scenario which is limited to the actual events of the play. If we ignore for a moment the fact that Aristotle's story overlaps the bounds of the play for which it serves as outline, we may make a second comment: This story, even without proper names, sounds very much like what we think of today as plot—a brief narration of the important incidents. It is not a "tragic rhythm," nor is it a Basic Pattern of Events. In other words, this story is a specific story, not likely to recur in the same form; whereas, the Basic Pattern of Events for such a story would be something like "sacrifice-release, sacrifice-release," where the situations are colored by the shifting relations of the celebrant and the victim and the different manners of release. (Keep in mind that this Basic Pattern of Events attempts to render Aristotle's story, not the Euripidean play.)

With the plot given, Aristotle suggests our next work is to fill in the episodes, seeing that they are relevant to the action. This implies, again, a concept of playwriting which stresses logical structure, or essentially "argument." It is a process which consists of filling in the outline with incidents and characters which will, by probability or necessity, or the chain of cause and effect, lead from one part of our predetermined story to another. This is a deceptively partial view of the construction of a drama. It seems much more likely that the playwright, as any other artist, works even in the early stages with much more physical images than Aristotle's disemboweled sample of story outline would indicate. It is not my purpose to trace the creative process, but the impressions which the Gelbs list (besides the story of the famous Haitian king and his legend of the magic bullet) as stirring O'Neill (a playwright who also made great use of a plot outline) to work on *The Emperor Jones* are closer to the first materials of art: the sound of an African drum, a phrase in dialect that a negro friend often repeated.[23] In practice, a story may actually be completely changed or altered many times in order that the sequence of events may present the images the way the playwright wants them.

Aristotle offers one factor beyond story or plot as the final structural determinant. He suggests that the incidents of the plot should be arranged according to the laws of probability or necessity. This is a true structural determinant: we can shape a plot on this basis even where Homer and his kin have left no prior story for us. There are two troubles with this rule, however: it leads into certain ambiguities, and the examples Aristotle gives at several points break the laws of probability or necessity. (Is it probable or necessary that a young girl, Iphigenia, escape mysteriously from being sacrificed or that she end up wielding a knife over her brother?) Of course the Aristotelians have a ready answer for this last criticism, and we call on Butcher for the standard apology: "The rule of probability which Aristotle enjoins is not the narrow *vraisemblance* . . . . The rule of 'probability,' as also that of 'necessity,' refers rather to the internal structure of a poem; it is the inner law which secures the cohesion of the parts."[24]

Either you go outside the internal structure of the work of art to probable or necessary in life or, the other horn of the dilemma, you end up in ambiguity and circularity. What does it mean to say that the incidents, or any parts of a work of art, should have a necessary and logical connection with reference *only* to the internal structure? It can really mean little more than that the parts should be placed so that they work best, or "What works, works." Aristotle himself allows for this answer when he comments on the popular success Agathon had with several presumably improbable endings: "This [satisfying] effect is produced when the clever rogue, like Sisyphus, is outwitted, or the brave villain defeated. Such an event is probable in Agathon's sense of the word: 'it is probable,' he says, 'that many things should happen contrary to probability' " (*Poetics* 18. 1456a 21–25).

We are required to say that the incidents must be arranged so they are necessary or probable to the inner artistic structure, but then we ask how are we to judge what this necessity or probability is if we are denied outside reference. There is no logic, no necessity, to the drama itself, despite recent formalist attempts to derive syntactical systems of "formation rules" and "transformation rules" from the " 'structural' properties of any medium."[25]

Aristotle probably did not mean to leave us in this circular position. On a number of occasions he refers to life as a test for the probable and necessary, particularly in Chapter 9, where he discusses poetic and historical truth. Here he says that poetry tends to express the universal, which means "how a person of a certain type will on occasion speak or act, according to the law of probability or necessity" (*Poetics* 9. 1451b 8–10). In sections 6–9 of this chapter we get the view that what has happened (historically) is manifestly possible, and what is possible is credible. In Chapter 15 he remarks, as we have noted before, that character must be true to life.

It is undoubtedly true, as Butcher says, that Aristotle did mean the necessary and probable to refer to a higher order outside everyday particular incidents, but the ultimate reference for what is probable and necessary in the drama must, for him, be either life or pure logic. This is, at best, an ambiguous position. If your appeal is to the probable and necessary in life, you will be faced with many versions of these norms and no efficient way to arbitrate the differences. If the appeal is to a purely formal logic, you have the extremely difficult task of proving that such a thing exists.[26] If the phrase simply describes the "rightness" of the relation of parts in a successful art work, it does not say very much.

The point is that neither the Greek drama generally nor many of Aristotle's own examples really stay within strict probability and necessity. In fact, the well-made play tradition hews much closer to this structural assumption than Aristotle's examples do. The result is an ambiguity in the *Poetics*. Certainly the terms "necessity" and "probability" do mean something and in a general way cover much of Greek drama, but when closely pressed they turn vague, especially when even their own author appears to admire the "improbabilities" which Homer and Agathon make "probable" (*Poetics* 18. 1456a 21–25 & 24. 1460a 11–36).

The real trouble is that these terms cannot cover enough. The possibilities for relation of incidents available to dramatic structure cover the whole range of human life in time. As such, drama can utilize any and all the relationships derivable from the nature of time (though it is unlikely that all of them would be employed in any one era). It can utilize, besides the obvious temporal relationship of "later than," such relations as repetition, contrast, expectation-fulfilment. A structure governed by the rules of probability or necessity is not flexible enough to cover either the dramatic possibilities or the dramatic fact, even of Aristotle's day, unless these terms are so stretched as to become almost meaningless. For example, probability and necessity in their usual meanings, seem to have no more to do with the remarkable events of *King Lear* or *The Tempest* than they do with Agathon's endings or Iphigenia's dilemma, although in each instance the artistic devices may seem "right."

From the point of view of the theories of dramatic structure presented in this essay we may summarize the contribution of the *Poetics* as follows: Aristotle stated remarkably well the nature of drama, although in specific application his theories are open to ambiguity. He is particularly harmed by having to use the contemporary aesthetic of imitation, which, in spite of heroic efforts, he never successfully transcends—even though later critics have told us what Aristotle *ought* to have said. That the subject matter of drama is men in action, is irrefutable, though as a structural model the one whole and complete action is bothersomely abstract, describing the effect of a successful art work rather than a shaping process. He offers both the ideas that structure is derived from actions in life and that, as a relational structure, it is governed by probability or necessity. Both these ideas are fruitful, leading us toward a real source, as opposed to the beginning, middle, and end rule, but Aristotle has failed to carry us far enough or wide enough to really grapple with the origins of structure. Finally, his logical mind seems to have loaded the scales perhaps too much in favor of story or plot as the soul of drama. The dramatic image of man in action in time includes story, but only as an inextricable part of a whole which includes the words (with their meanings and suggestions) and even the despised spectacle: parts which cannot be listed in order of importance.

Chapter X

STRUCTURE AND THEMATIC ANALYSIS: THE SHAKESPEARE CRITICISM OF ROBERT HEILMAN

"Structure" is a word that has frequently been on the lips of those twentieth century critics associated with the "new criticism"—a group whose nucleus is usually considered to include Eliot, Pound, Richards, Ransom, Blackmur, Tate, Winters, and Brooks. Though Eliot is the only one of the group who has done a considerable amount of writing on the drama,[1] other critics, influenced by the technique so admirably applied to poems, have adapted for the analysis of drama the seminal ideas of a close attention to the language of a work and a penchant for examining the imagery and tracing what is assumed to be its "organic" relation to the work as a whole. As we suggested in the introduction, this has not always had an entirely salutary effect.

It is late to join the chorus of those who have reacted against this "new criticism" of drama—several of the most important objections to the technique are noted in this chapter—yet we are faced here with a seemingly plausible notion of structure which is definitely non-Aristotelian (Heilman, as we shall see, is contemptuous of plot) and, despite the telling attacks made upon it, still has wide appeal. Therefore the task of this chapter will not be another attack on the questionable interpretations to which thematic analysis sometimes leads, but an attempt to defend the thesis of this book—that the essential structures of drama are not spatial but temporal—against the seductively "poetic" notions of thematic structure.

There is some doubt that the kind of analysis of drama practiced by Heilman and Traversi is really the legitimate extension of the new criticism. Certainly it does not closely resemble Eliot's criticism. Also, it banks very heavily on the studies of imagery in Shakespeare done by Caroline Spurgeon and Wolfgang Clemen,[2] neither of whom could be considered in the inner circle of new critics. Nonetheless, Heilman collaborated with Cleanth Brooks on the textbook *Understanding Drama*[3] and in his own study of *King Lear* acknowledged his debt to the new criticism.[4] Probably, rather than calling the kind of analyses typified by Heilman's work a "new criticism of drama," it could be characterized more accurately as a school of thematic analysis.

The case against this school is a difficult one to state, because typical pronouncements are not so much wrong as perverse and tedious, while other statements are entirely admirable and helpful. This is the case with Cleanth Brooks' essay "The Naked Babe and the Cloak of Manliness,"[5] often cited as a milestone in the reading of Shakespeare as a pattern of imagery,[6] which, surprisingly, turns out to be a brief and guarded examination (on a text

175

by Coleridge) of the recurrence of an image in *Macbeth*. Brooks does not state that the image pattern is the structure of the play, or the meaning of the play. Robert Heilman, is not so guarded or brief. He may, therefore, supply us with a point of attack. Carrying out this attack is intended not so much to deflate Heilman as to clarify some of the theoretical points made in the discussion of structure in the preceeding chapters.

Heilman has presented his views and demonstrated his techniques in two books, *This Great Stage: Image and Structure in "King Lear"* and *Magic in the Web: Action and Language in "Othello."* A convenient brief treatment is available in his article, "More Fair than Black: Light and Dark in 'Othello.' "[7] Since the correctness or incorrectness of Heilman's interpretations are not at issue, no attempt will be made to summarize his lengthy discussion of *Lear* or *Othello*, but in the course of the two books and the article he has made a number of statements on the structure of drama, to which we may add the implications of some of his critical pronouncements. We shall, then, be employed here with an examination of Heilman's explicit and implied position on dramatic structure, particularly as it involves the materials on poetry and the drama dealt with in our seventh chapter.

Heilman sets out at the beginning of his *Othello* article the ideas on structure with which he will operate:

> The most obvious approach to the structure of drama is to equate structure with plot and then to describe plot in terms of those familiar and yet somewhat elusive elements sometimes called rising action, climax, denouement, etc. . . . But at best such descriptions of the action yield only superficial information.
>
> A likelier route into the heart of the play is to define the structure in terms of theme. . . . But all this would still be, I think, peripheral; a more central thematic approach would be to consider *Othello*, like *Romeo and Juliet* and *Anthony and Cleopatra*, a play about love. To say this would be not merely to name the subject of the play but to point out the

forces which give the play a composition of a certain kind. The central tension is between the love of Othello and the hate of Iago, the specific forms taken in this play by good and evil. The development of the drama is determined by the progress of Iago's hate, which, in endeavouring to destroy the deep and passionate but inexperienced love of Othello and Desdemona, utilizes many varieties of love itself.[8]

In *Magic in the Web* Heilman expands this idea: "If love is what *Othello* is 'about,' *Othello* is not only a play about love but a poem about love."[9] In the idea of structure just quoted, my particular objection is to the implication that *Othello*, taken as play or poem, could be accurately described as structured by turns upon the idea of love, because it has been held in the preceding chapters that a play is basically structured by patterns of events not plays upon an idea.

In the transubstantiation of *Othello* from play to poem, Heilman, after substituting a thematic structure for "descriptions of the action," calls our attention to the *language* of the plays, "to the fact that *Othello* is written in verse rather than prose."[10] This "fact" is of central importance to Heilman because he holds that "a play written in poetic form is simply not the same kind of literary work as a play written in prose."[11] To spell out Heilman's implication here (which he himself does not do): There is one kind of work, essentially crass, which is prose drama; there is another kind of work with certain superficial resemblances to drama, but which is really that higher kind of thing, a poem.

Perhaps the sense of fuzziness and ambiguity in Heilman's position results from his refusal to follow out the implications of his statements containing a strong preference for the poetic form. He tries to have his drama and his poetry too, but his desire to make the poetry rule the drama—separating it in kind from a prose drama—leads him into such typical confusions as the statement (to be quoted in context below) which makes the poetry "neither primary nor wholly secondary." Essentially Heilman tries to make

177

"the language" prove too much. Following on his statement of the importance of the fact that Othello is in verse, Heilman comments thus on the poetry:

> It is a *special language which helps determine what the play becomes*. It helps determine structure. This is not to say that poetic language is primary; but neither is it wholly secondary, an executive assistant to some antecedent principle of structure. What happens in a poetic drama is the collusion between different bearers of meaning. The poetry is an imaginative language full of secondary meanings; but the characters and actions must also be thought of as an imaginative language with more than one level of meaning—the literal and the symbolic, with ambiguities possible at both levels. There is a drama of action and a drama of words. Each is a language available to the playwright. If he uses both languages and controls them adequately, the extensions of imaginative meaning will not conflict.[12]

Heilman starts with a legitimate observation about the language of *Othello*: it is in verse. The observation is not wholly correct—because 20% of *Othello* is written in prose—but in general it is a legitimate kind of observation about language. Next, we learn that poetic language is neither primary nor secondary in determining structure, but we do not learn what place it *does* have in the ambiguous "collusion" of "bearers of meaning." Finally, Heilman tells us that characters and action must be thought of as an imaginative language, which moves entirely away from any concrete differentia in the language (like verse-prose) by which these plays can be distinguished in kind. So what the argument really says is that *Othello* is imaginative and multidimensional while some plays are literal and dull. One cannot disagree, but one is hardly struck by the perspicacity of the insight.

But Heilman's "new critical" emphasis on the *language*, which he seems secretly to hope will prove that *Othello* is "really" a poem, has led him to state, "There is a drama of action and a drama of words." This statement jars uncomfortably with Heilman's insistence that "the poetry in a poetic drama is an integral part of the work."[13] There is no flat contradiction here, but it does leave open to question how Heilman sees the poetry as at once integral and separate: another ambiguity.

The "drama of actions and the drama of words" become, in the later *Magic in the Web*, "verbal drama" and "actional drama." Heilman describes how he will use these terms: "I will therefore use the term 'verbal drama' for poetic language, or, more generally, for all the effects traceable, initially or finally, to what characters 'say' and how they say it; and the term 'actional drama' for what characters 'do.' "[14] This distinction cuts radically across the description of dramatic structure I have set forth, where I analysed drama as being built from the materials of speech and spectacle which unite in actions, and where, in effect, all drama is "actional."

Heilman recognizes that:

> "Doing" and "saying" are not always properly distinguishable; saying is often a very important way of doing. . . . Actional drama and verbal drama work in collusion; both are imaginative languages, each potentially ambiguous and polysemous; they are fused in a harmonious structure of meaning. The play about love and the poem about love, though they have different structural foci, are one; they are *Othello*.[15]

Again Heilman can be seen trying to preserve the drama, which even he cannot deny, and at the same time he attempts to make something essentially undramatic out of it. The result is ambiguity.

Despite this ambiguity in basic definitions and theories, Heilman's critical practices point the direction we must assume he favors. His analyses are essentially thematic. He reads the play finally as a poem. There will be no attempt to follow these readings through their lengthy development, because the issue here is not whether the reading is right or wrong. The point is that the method yields a kind of information which, though plausible, leads away from the central facts and strengths of the play and of the contribution which poetry (understood in the strict sense) can make to it. One would hardly suspect from Heilman's comments what a very good *play Othello* is.

A few examples may sufficiently demonstrate the method which Heilman himself describes in these terms: "In the structural interplay of dramatic and verbal elements, the utmost importance is to be attached to the astonishing repetitiveness of Shakespeare's imagery."[16] Heilman realizes that the exploration of Shakespeare's imagery is not new and he cites particularly the work of Caroline Spurgeon, but adds that she did not fully explore the structural implications of the image clusters.[17] Let us see how Heilman operates with images (keeping in mind that, when he wants them to be, characters, properties, and actions as well as words, are all part of the essentially poetic or imagistic "language" of the drama-poem):

> At the most obvious level of perception *Othello* works in terms of a startling contrast—that, of course, between the 'fair' maid, as she is so often called, and her black lover. . . . Desdemona, we know, is innocent; and the very language of the play, as we shall see, has had the effect of making Othello, at the end, doubly black.
>
> But Shakespeare does still more than give us a sharp contrast with a symbolic increment: he finds other complications in the black-white issue. To equate black and villainy is easy; but we get beneath surfaces and into the real terrors of experiences when black and white become indistinguishable. . . . The method of Iago's evil is planned confusion; the use of the 'heavenly' to produce 'blackest sins' . . . . In effect; the fair Desdemona will be made black: good becomes evil, and the world is thrown into utter disorder. . . . In this doctrine, love—love for the fair Desdemona—is a mode of order; absence of love is chaos—disorder—darkness. In the very next speech after these words of Othello ["and when I love thee not, / Chaos is come again" (III.iii.91–92)], Iago begins his campaign to restore the anarchy that preceded the creative fiat 'Let there be light'.[18]

The reading is certainly ingenious, but its effect recalls very strongly, and in a derogatory sense which was certainly not intended, Heilman's statement that the language of drama is essentially "ambiguous and polysemous." Perhaps Heilman's meanings include *too* wide a sweep of ambiguity, because when one opens the doors this wide one blurs specific meanings in a flood of uncontrolled associations. Consider how Heilman moves from the specific black-white contrast, through absence of love, to chaos, to disorder, to darkness. He intends to take in heaven and hell, foul and fair, light and dark, day and night, and chaste and pure in the same wide net. Naturally with this almost universal scope an amazing number of things can be fitted into what Heilman designates as "the pattern." These include the most casual references to a "fair maid," "tonight," "devil," etc., all patiently listed by Heilman. If a reference does not quite fit, he contrives to make it fit. "At the beginning we have not only 'sooty bosom' and 'black ram' but the *oblique* [my emphasis] introduction of darkness in the Duke's phrase 'foul proceeding.' "[19]

One more example will illustrate how Heilman extends his readings to cover the properties and actions. Commenting on the fact that several scenes in *Othello* take place at night, Heilman says:

> Lights could be assumed; necessary properties could be taken for granted. . . . [But] Lights are symbolic as much as darkness is; they may dispel, or try to dispel, or ironically emphasize a failure to dispel, the evil or ignorance or chaos symbolized by the darkness.[20]

Thus, when in the brawl in front of his house Brabantio calls "Light, I say! Light" (I.i.145), Heilman comments:

> In effect, Brabantio seeks the light of knowledge, and he finds the light; if not altogether pleased by what he finds, he nevertheless accepts it. In any case, he does not act in ignorance: in this sense he conquers the Iago night.[21]

No one can prove that Shakespeare's lines do not suggest the interpretations noted, because obviously they have been suggested to Heilman. On the other hand, Heilman's readings seem remote from the central concerns of the play itself. By taking meanings which are literally in the play (though sometimes their context seems to deny the extensions Heilman makes), then making his own ordering of them, Heilman comes up with a structure which certainly has a relation to the play, but could hardly be called *the* structure of the play. R. S. Crane has commented on this tendency toward abstraction in Heilman and his fellows. "It requires no great insight to find an inner dialectic of order and disorder or a struggle of good and evil forces in any serious plot; or a profound dialectic of appearance and reality in any plot in which the action turns on ignorance or deception and discovery."[22]

The fact that most people do not see *Othello* and *Lear* the way Heilman does does not prove him wrong, but with the kind of structural principles he has proposed, it is impossible to explain why the actions of these two plays are ordered as they are. Of course plot *could* be just a convenient frame for a poem about nature or love (turns on a theme), but the explanation that these plays are basically *plays*, and structured in the manner described in the previous chapters (as patterns of events with essential time sequences), seems to fit the given facts better. On this count too Crane's comments are enlightening:

> One would not care to embark upon a discussion of the structure of *Othello* without first taking account of Mr. Heilman's observations. I do not think, however, that he comes very close to defining any principle of structure for *Othello* that could conceivably have guided Shakespeare in constructing the poetic whole. . . . What he exhibits are rather some of the material antecedents of the tragic structure in the conceptions of love and jealousy which the writing of the play presupposed and some of the consequences of the structure in the imagery and thought by which it [the structure] is made effective in the words; and his only warrant for "equating" the combination of these aspects with the struc-

ture of the play is his prior assumption . . . that the structure of *Othello* must be of this sort.[23]

I have found fault with Professor Heilman's comments, yet a number of these are not only eminently just, but represent the opinion of most commentators (for example, the storm in *Lear* does, in a sense, represent chaos). My primary objection is not to the observations per se, but to what Heilman does with them—with the extensions he makes of them. If Heilman sees these thematic patterns as functioning in a way which has little to do with drama (or poetry either), then what *is* their function? To what extent is Heilman's analysis useful and at what point does he get off the track?

No one would want to deny that the contrasts of black and white, light and dark, foul and fair, etc. play an important part in the language of *Othello*. In fact, this is almost too obvious to merit comment. What is in question is the place of such thematic groupings in the play itself. We might reasonably say that these clusters exist ready in our minds. Mention black, one thinks of white; heaven, one thinks of hell, and so forth through any number of opposites. We may also associate ideas which revolve in the same system of meanings, like hell, fire, devil, chaos, etc. These groupings form, as Crane suggested, a kind of raw material for art. They are not very interesting in themselves, because they are rather commonplace as well as being abstract and general. On the other hand, since the mind seems bound to work in terms of such relationships, they do figure in art, but ordinarily as exemplified in specific cases: Othello is far more than black; Desdemona far more than white.

Constellations of meaning do exist, however, and poets utilize them in many different ways. An excellent brief example to which Heilman calls our attention is Iago's "An old black ram/ Is tupping your white ewe" (I.i.88–89).[24] These words reverberate with associations, most of which are unpleasant; but it seems more reasonable to assume that Iago is so intensely wrapped in the specific circumstances of the moment, that when he shouts up through the night to incite Brabantio, he uses the most loaded phrases that come to his fertile imagination.

Consider another thematic cluster that Heilman derives from the black-white contrast, the cluster of meanings around night:

> The important poetic truth is that in *Othello* night is not just an accident; it is not an idle setting which might just as well be exchanged for something else; nor is it a property of melodrama, an incitement to fear in the easily fearful. Night is not passive but active; its reality is ever pressed upon us; it means not merely physical darkness but spiritual darkness. Everything converges upon the night scenes, and in them there is a confluence of forces—of evil intent or of ignorance—opposed to the true and the fair. If Shakespeare went no further than this in infusing night with meaning, he would have created a very effective symbol. But actually he did not aim only at this and succeed only in this. Night has still other potentialities.[25]

It is indicative of the relevance of Heilman's observations to note that one could easily guess what most of these "potentialities" are without reference to either essay or play. In any case, "Night may mean pleasant sleep . . . the night of married love . . . nocturnal disorders," and so forth.[26] Typically this position ignores whatever effect the stage conditions of the time may have had on the choice of settings after dark.

I have insisted that the specific elements of any good play must be fully significant, hence I would heartily agree that "in *Othello* night is not just an accident"; however, what night primarily means is *night*. The image Shakespeare has created of a street brawl at night, announcing what is taken to be an abduction, is particularly powerful, but its meaning is packed specifically into just what it is. This is not to say that associations do not radiate from this image; it is hard to *prevent* it since our minds work in this manner. Certainly Shakespeare appears to have used these associations to reinforce his theme as do many other playwrights.

Another dimension of this associative process is found in what the characters themselves make of the images. The tormented mind of Macbeth is particularly sensitive to the images and associations of night as we see, for example, in his speech beginning, "Come seeling night, / Scarf up the tender eye of pitiful day" (III.ii.46–53). What Shakespeare is doing here, however, is not writing an essay on night but dramatizing the movements of a mind caught in time through a brilliant improvisational structure in which one thought leads to another in the manner we illustrated in Chapter Five.

It is considered heresy by Heilman and the thematic school to admit that the least reference in Shakespeare carries less than universal significance: to suggest that when a character calls for a light to see his way in a dark castle or street he is to be understood by the alert critic as doing less than calling upon the motion of the celestial spheres and all beneath. ("It is possible to ignore the symbolic extensions of times of action, properties, and apparently commonplace words. But it is not wise to do so.")[27] I suggest that it does not hamstring Shakespeare to limit the range of *pertinent* association. To see Macbeth dramatizing himself is a very exciting and wonderful thing. To turn this into an essay on nature is to impoverish and change Shakespeare by generalizing him.

The drama is greatly enriched by the poetic play of thought of its characters, in which they utilize poetic structures of meaning "intimately wed" with the structures of pure form in the way we have discussed above. At the same time, this poetic play of thought takes place in a drama and hence is essentially an image of our life in time: it is a drama, not a poem. The drama of Shakespeare, as all drama, is actional. Of course, a common way for a character to act is through words, for verbal drama *is* actional drama, or just plain drama—there is no other. That the characters in Shakespeare so pack the action with specific significance by utilizing to the full the potentialities of language, is a marvelous and exciting thing. But the image created is of man's interaction in

185

time, which means that the *characters* invent the poetry. The poet is not understood as communicating directly with the audience. If Shakespeare wanted to communicate his thoughts in this way, to write, as Heilman calls *Lear*, "an essay on nature,"[28] he would hardly have set the immense machinery of this long drama in his way.

This does not entail a naive view which overlooks the hand of the poet; it merely asks the critic to be specific about what is created. Of course the poet-playwright creates all the world and being of Macbeth, Othello, and Lear, but the image he has created is of characters in action, including verbal action. The interesting thing about the poet's creation is that the poet too creates an image, not a lecture. Cleanth Brooks himself states in an argument against the kind of separation of poetry from drama which Francis Fergusson makes, "The most fragile lyric has at least one character, that of the implied speaker himself, and it has a 'plot'— an arrangement of psychic incidents, with a development, at least of mood."[29] The real difference between poetry and drama is the spatial structure of poetic relations as opposed to the temporal nature—the necessary sequence—of drama. To avoid misunderstanding it should be added that the drama is not only generated spontaneously by the characters. There is a kind of unity to a play which the one controlling mind of the author must give. Heilman sees an imagistic unity which exists *between* characters. This can certainly be concluded to be the work of the poet without denying that the essential image is of action in time, not of poetic interrelatedness.

Heilman describes a kind of spatial form in Shakespeare's plays which he construes as "poetic" and a basic structural determinant. It certainly is possible to consider a play spatially as well as temporally, especially when the play is studied in the text.[30] The problem is that Heilman imputes great poetic and dramatic power to the spatial or thematic structure he abstracts, in spite of the fact that often the worst prose melodramas are rich sources for just such thematic treatment.[31]

If the drama is basically different from poetry it would contradict Heilman's assertion, "A play written in poetic form is simply not the same kind of literary work as a play written in prose."[32] The tragedies of Shakespeare, for all their "poetry," are structurally more like Eugene O'Neill's *Long Day's Journey into Night* than they are like the Sonnets. Heilman's imagistic or thematic analysis can be performed easily on O'Neill's prose play, yielding results indistinguishable, at least in the plane of abstraction on which Heilman typically operates, from his analyses of *Lear* or *Othello*. If one wants to play out Heilman's game of tracing light-dark imagery in language, plot, and properties, Ibsen's *Ghosts* is a particularly rich field. The effects that Heilman finds to be the glory and crown of plays "written in poetic form" seem to be equally present in realistic prose dramas.

Falstaff speaks very little poetry. A good part of *Othello* is not poetry (verse). Obviously Heilman does not mean to limit poetry to verse—else how could characters, plot, and properties be part of the poetry—but, on the other hand, he is adamant that poetry and prose are radically different, that poetry is a "special language," that it is of vital importance that "*Othello* is written in verse rather than prose."[33] In short, Heilman has put a tremendous burden upon a radical distinction between prose and poetry without clearly defining and separating the two.

However, it is basically the kind of *structure* Heilman assumes in his view of a poetic drama that is at issue here. An excellent example of the structural implications of Heilman's reading of *Othello* as a poem—"the poem about love," as he explicitly characterizes it—is to be found in the following passage:

> When Othello says he threw away a "pearl," we recall that Brabantio, in acceding to Desdemona's departure, called her "jewel"; when Desdemona says she would rather have lost her purse than the handkerchief, we recall that Iago, who has stolen the handkerchief, has spoken of stealing a purse; we spontaneously make these connections, and, even if we go no further, our reading has brought forth linkings that cannot be expunged; but we often do go further, and seek

out the formal order that is exemplified in these images that leap out of their own contexts and carry our imaginations into other parts of the play. When to these we add many other instances in which poetic language, functioning doubly or triply, takes us beyond specific moments of action into others and on into general areas of character, feeling, and thought, we find that we have an immensely complicated verbal structure with which we must come to terms—the "poem about love," as I have called it. We are trying to describe what Traversi called "a new kind of dramatic unity."[34]

Note particularly the "spatialization" implied in "we often do go further, and seek out the formal order that is exemplified in these images that leap out of their own contexts and carry our imaginations into other parts of the play." The "new kind of unity" is, of course, not dramatic at all, but, presumably, poetic. Certainly most dramas would lose much of their poignancy if our minds could not, for example, leap out of the context of the last act of *Oedipus* to compare the blinded ragged outcast with the proud king and judge of the beginning. But the whole point of the catastrophe is that the *formal order* of a drama is not reversible and that Oedipus can never again be what he was. The basic image of the play is of a man caught in time, it is not in any basic sense a "poem of guilt and innocence" whose essential structure is based upon time-free thematic connections. The connections which do give power to *Othello* or *Oedipus*, though, do not seem to be of the kind exemplified by the inconsequential "pattern" formed by Brabantio's "jewel" and Othello's "pearl," which, after all, are common figures of speech likely to recur in any case.

What can finally be said of Heilman's interpretations? Primarily it should be said that they defeat art by leaving art behind—by verging off into a realm of generality which certainly surrounds our experience of the plays but, since it surrounds all mental functioning, its special relevance to the plays is questionable. Though it may be unfair to pick on such an obviously unfortunate statement, perhaps the following remark on *King Lear* will best demonstrate the weakness in Heilman's view of drama (and poetry). "When there is repeated speculation upon nature, the play is to that extent an essay upon nature—an essay necessarily broken up into parts which are apportioned according to, and probably modified by, dramatic necessity."[35] Though Heilman probably does not really mean to identify the drama and the essay, still, why does he repeat this idea in so many places (to use Heilman's *own* criterion that repeated ideas are important to the author)? All this leaves one with the disconcerting image of Shakespeare taking Hooker's essays and apportioning the sentences as appropriate to the various characters. The approach does not call to mind what most people perceive to be the strengths of Shakespeare's plays.

Chapter XI

FORM OR FORMULA: COMIC STRUCTURE IN NORTHROP FRYE AND SUSANNE LANGER

Hollywood in its heydey had a formula for comedy which Bella and Samuel Spewack summed up as "Boy meets girl, boy loses girl, boy gets girl."[1] Similarly, there is a certain formula-derived aspect to what are commonly called the "situation comedies" on television, such as the *I Love Lucy* series or *Leave It to Beaver*. The problem in dramatic criticism is that when you discuss comedy in terms of a basic comic rhythm, archetypal pattern, or in any sweeping reduction terms, you run the danger of putting Shakespeare and Molière on a level with the writers of *I Love Lucy*, because through the wrong end of the critical telescope the *form* of *I Love Lucy* is just as good, in its general outlines, as, say, *The Imaginary Invalid*.

One suspects that Northrop Frye could easily include a few typical examples from the *I Love Lucy* series among his samples of realistic comedy. He could identify the characters by Greek names: Lucy would presumably be a female *eiron*, the neighbor Fred, a *bomolochos*. The result of the analysis would differ in no important way from the analyses of plays by Molière or Plautus and Terence. This is not to confute Frye or suggest a possibility he has not already seen. He speaks of the characters and plot structures of ancient comedy (as he says, "less a form than a formula") as persisting down to our own day when "the audiences of vaudeville, comic strips, and television programs still laugh at the jokes that were declared to be outworn at the opening of *The Frogs*."[2]

Such an intriguing overview is concomitant with a basic notion of a pure literary design based on myth, but, on a certain level of abstraction, bearing relations to mathematical structure. This is certainly the call of the wild to a philosophical critic, bringing up again both the problems of the relevance of gross structural descriptions and the possibility of pure form in drama and putting to the test some of our conclusions in Chapters II and VI. In discussing these problems one must deal with another theorist, Mrs. Susanne Langer, less sophisticated in literature but considerably more sophisticated in philosophy, who has also explored drama in terms of a highly abstract form that again suggests analogies with logical and mathematical forms.

I shall undertake to show that in their concern with gross structural patterns these theorists look through specific plays to the myths and life rhythms they want to see behind them. Such a reductive view fails to provide the kind of detailed structural information needed by a director for the practical purposes of shaping a production or a critic for the purposes of evaluation. Put very bluntly: Can we separate form from formula, Lucy from Angelique: at this level? This is not to imply that either Mrs. Langer or Mr. Frye are insensitive to value distinctions, that they do not realize—and in many places point out—specific differences between great and mediocre drama. It does seem, however, that their type of analysis must lead to a position which would logically force them to give up these value judgments by cutting off form from content.

In the investigation of comic form perhaps the best place to begin is at the end, the happy ending which all comedies are supposed to have and from which such few "problem" comedies as *Troilus and Cressida* and *The Misanthrope* need not distract us. *I Love Lucy* ends happily, so does *Twelfth Night*, yet Shakespeare's play is presumed to be in some way more profound than a television situation comedy. The obvious answer is to say that in Shakespeare we have "all that beautiful poetry." As it will develop, this must be a part of our own answer because certainly language is a major factor in the superiority of a Shakespearean play over a television program, but the critics who speak of comic rhythm are not talking about poetry; they are talking about form. While Frye does talk about the specifics of poetry from time to time, both the gist of his book and the gist of his discussion of comic form may be summed up in the title of the section which includes this discussion, "Archetypal Criticism: Theory of Myths." The happy ending is not poetry in the sense implied when people speak of "Shakespeare's poetry."[3]

What the problem comes down to finally is trying to see how useful the notions of archetypes and comic rhythms are as structural descriptions—trying to see, in other words, in what way a happy ending, often said to be the falsification of life and betrayal of art when Hollywood uses it, becomes in Shakespeare—where it is often more contrived—a profundity. With this critical problem in mind, let us develop the positions which Northrop Frye and Susanne Langer take on comic form.

Northrop Frye is intriguingly devious when he explores different methods or critical approaches to literature in his *Anatomy of Criticism*. The effect is rather descriptive than evaluative: placing literary works in one or the other of the categories he sets up, such as "high mimetic" and "low mimetic." Nevertheless, by referring to his "Conclusion" and piecing hints together, it is possible to assemble a position which states: "In this process of breaking down barriers [between different methods of criticism] I think archetypal criticism has a central role, and I have given it a prominent place."[4] Archetypal criticism is, for Frye, concerned with locating the underlying myth. "In literary criticism myth means ultimately *mythos*, a *structural organizing principle of literary form*." (emphasis added)[5] Frye sees in archetypal criticism the possibility of escape from the proliferation of "learned and astute" commentaries. "Things become more hopeful as soon as there is a feeling, however dim, that criticism has an end in the structure of literature as a total form, as well as a beginning in the text studied."[6]

This penetration to the underlying myth, which is at the same time the structural organizing principle of literary form, is the orientation behind Frye's main discussion of comedy, located significantly, in the Third Essay, "Archetypal Criticism: Theory of Myths." He prepares us for the archetypal treatment of the comic myth by statements like the following, containing implications of an abstract literary design: "We begin our study of archetypes, then, with a world of myth, an abstract or purely literary world of fictional and thematic design, unaffected by canons of plausible adaptation to familiar experience. . . . The meaning or pattern of poetry is a structure of imagery with conceptual implications. . . . In myth we see the structural principles of literature isolated; in realism we see the *same* structural principles (not similar ones) fitting into a context of plausibility."[7] A few pages later he adds more specific details on literary design:

> This affinity between the mythical and the abstractly literary illuminates many aspects of fiction, especially the more popular fiction which is realistic enough to be plausible in its inci-

dents and yet romantic enough to be a "good story," which means a clearly designed one. The introduction of an omen or portent, or the device of making a whole story the fulfill-ment of a prophecy given at the beginning, is an example. Such a device suggests, in its existential projection, a con-ception of ineluctable fate or hidden omnipotent will. Actu-ally, it is a piece of pure literary design, giving the beginning some symmetrical relationship with the end.[8]

Both Tolstoy and Sophocles, according to Frye, use omens be-cause it gives their plots a good shape. Here Northrop Frye has obviously been bitten by the same "pure form" bug which earlier bit Roger Fry, and this aspect of his argument should be referred to the criticisms of pure form we made in Chapter VI.

With this general introduction out of the way, Frye deals with "The Mythos of Spring: Comedy." "The total *mythos* of comedy, only a small part of which is ordinarily presented, has regularly what in music is called a ternary form: the hero's society rebels against the society of the *senex* and triumphs, but the hero's society is a Saturnalia, a reversal of social standards which recalls a golden age in the past before the main action of the play begins."[9] In other words: in comedy the young hero and heroine are op-posed in their love by a member or members of the older genera-tion, typically the father, but youth wins out and a new society is crystallized around them. The nature of this happy ending is characterized by Frye: "The appearance of this new society is frequently signalized by some kind of party or festive ritual, which either appears at the end of the play or is assumed to take place immediately afterward. Weddings are most common, and some-times so many of them occur, as in the quadruple wedding at the end of *As You Like It*, that they suggest also the wholesale pair-ing off that takes place in a dance, which is another common conclusion."[10]

However, in the comedy itself we have only parts two and three of the myth. The missing part one represents an ideal state before disruption by the *senex*. "Thus we have a stable and harmonious

order disrupted by folly, obsession, forgetfulness, 'pride and preju-
dice,' or events not understood by the characters themselves and
then restored. . . . This ternary action is, ritually, like a contest of summer and winter in which winter occupies the middle
action."[11]

One more remark of Frye's is illuminating in the present context. He is speaking of the comic effect of repetition as it is used
from Jonson to the radio serials and he notes E. M. Forster's
disdain for some comic character tag repetitions in Dickens. Frye
replies to Forster, "A strong contrast is marked here between the
refined writer too finicky for popular formulas, and the major one
who exploits them ruthlessly."[12] The implication appears to be
that Molière, Dickens, and all the progeny of George Abbott line
up against poor finicky Mr. Forster.

Frye's idea of the form of comedy requires a little closer look,
particularly at his idea that it has a "ternary form," because there
seems to be a fly in the mythological ointment here. To wit: *Where
is the ternary form?* Clearly the ternary form is in the myth
behind the comedy, not in the comedy itself. As Frye says, "Very
often the first phase is not given at all."[13] But if the first part of a
ternary form is not given, you have a binary form. (Actually both
"binary" and "ternary" have very special musical meanings only
very loosely applicable to comedy, but since Frye adopted the
musical analogy, I shall accept it in this discussion.)

What I wish to suggest is that Frye is looking *through* a work
of art, made transparent by his archetypal criticism, to a myth
beyond, which contains the *real* meaning and form of the work of
art. This real meaning, which with Frye is very close to the form
("The meaning of a poem [is] its structure of imagery"[14]), is then
read back into the work of art itself.

If Frye has been influenced in his literary aesthetic by formal
analyses of music, surely Mrs. Langer has responded to this temptation to a much greater extent. In fact, it is the theory of music
first stated in *Philosophy in a New Key* which Mrs. Langer specif-

ically extends to the other arts in *Feeling and Form*. Pairing Mrs. Langer's theory of comic form with Mr. Frye's should be particularly enlightening because, while Mrs. Langer specifically avoids a number of the traps that Frye willingly steps into, her basic aesthetic of comedy derives, as does Frye's, from analogies to forms outside art, like the rhythm of sentient life and certain logical forms. Both these critics cast light upon one another here because both fall into the same difficulty with comedy (and art in general) of transcending the specific work of art for a "greater reality" beyond. In the words of Richard Rudner's criticism of Mrs. Langer's aesthetic: "The art work is no longer the aesthetic object—but simply a sign for an experience which the composer 'means' by it."[15]

As for Mrs. Langer's ideas on the form of comedy, she says, "Drama . . . always exhibits such form [an image of organic form]; it does so by creating the semblance of a history and composing its elements into a rhythmic single structure."[16] Unfortunately Mrs. Langer's descriptions of the comic rhythm, developed originally from a fairly extended treatment of biological survival, differ somewhat among themselves, but the following seems to be about the clearest statement. The comic rhythm, she says, "is developed by comic action, which is the upset and recovery of the protagonist's equilibrium, his contest with the world and his triumph by wit, luck, personal power, or even humorous, or ironical, or philosophical acceptance of mischance."[17] It represents the human being winning out over Fortune by his vital energy, displayed most strikingly in reproduction.

Mrs. Langer offers us a warning, however:

> But the fact that the rhythm of comedy is the basic rhythm of life does not mean that biological existence is the "deeper meaning" of all its themes, and that to understand the play is to interpret all the characters as symbols and the story as a parable, a disguised rite of spring or fertility magic, performed four hundred and fifty times on Broadway. The stock characters are probably symbolic both in origin and in ap-

peal. There are such independently symbolic factors, or residues of them, in all the arts, but their value for art lies in the degree to which their significance can be "swallowed" by the single symbol, the art work. Not the derivation of personages and situations, but of the rhythm of "felt life" that the poet puts upon them, seems to me to be of artistic importance: the essential comic feeling, which is the sentient aspect of organic unity, growth, and self-preservation.[18]

This statement focuses the search for form where it belongs—in the play itself—rather than in some deeper meaning, even though I would object that the comic rhythm, like most such gross and abstract patterns, has a limited usefulness. A more serious and immediate objection is that Mrs. Langer's position is considerably weakened by several disturbing ambiguities. These may be summarized as ambiguities as to where the comic rhythm is, and ambiguities as to whether the comic rhythm of a play does or does not represent anything other than itself.

The whole subject of what specifically Mrs. Langer intends the form of comedy to be and how she would work out in detail a "rhythmic" analysis of a given comedy is left extremely vague in her chapters on the drama. At best there is a confusion introduced when a theory of "significant form" in music (which was itself ambiguous: does the pattern of music *equal* or *represent* the pattern of emotion?) is stretched to the more aesthetically complex representational art of drama. It is not clear, for example, whether the comic rhythm is supposed to be physically present in the pace of the performance—the varying rhythms of line delivery, movement, and sound effects—or in that which we understand through the dialogue, movements, etc., i.e., "the upset and recovery of the protagonist's equilibrium."

To view the ambiguity from another angle, does the form of what the play *described* have the "rhythm of 'felt life' " that is of artistic importance, or does the play *itself* have this form?[19] With Northrop Frye the ternary form was obviously not in the play itself but in the archetypal pattern it suggested, which does not provide much structural information to a director or critic of the specific work. On the other hand, Mrs. Langer seems both to understand a concluding comic dance as a part of the sound and movement pattern of a complete performance *and* to understand the same dance symbolically for what it suggests, which may make an entirely different pattern outside the art work. While there is no denying that both these patterns exist, it is important to specify which you conceive to be the structure of the play.

Assuming we can reasonably settle on a locus for the comic rhythm, the other horn of Mrs. Langer's dilemma appears when we note how insistent she is that drama does not imitate any of the surface aspects of life. She is most explicit on this point in her discussion of tragedy, but these remarks clearly hold for comic form as well: "Macbeth's fate is the structure of his tragedy, not an instance of how things happen in the world. . . . Tragic action has the rhythm of natural life and death, but it does not refer to or illustrate them; it abstracts their dynamic form, and imprints it on entirely different matters, . . . so the 'tragic rhythm' stands clear of any natural occasion, and becomes a perceptible form."[20] The implications of this statement are clarified in the general position Mrs. Langer enunciates again and again, "A work of art does not point us to a meaning beyond its own presence."[21]

But if it does not refer to a meaning beyond itself the comic rhythm cannot refer to the rhythm of biological survival, and the many interesting analogies Mrs. Langer draws become pointless. Further, this comic rhythm must be an "instance of how things happen in the world." While it may abstract from the naturalistic accidents adhering to instances of comic rhythm and certainly stands clear of any *one* natural occasion, still this one rhythm, this Basic Pattern of Events, must finally be the type of natural occasion to which the rhythm of a comic drama has reference in order to have the significance most critics, including Mrs. Langer, want to accord it.

These are the difficulties which befog an attempt to clarify Mrs.

Langer's remarks on the structure of comic drama. Her basic aesthetic describes a work of art in terms of a total gestalt or single Art Symbol,[22] and the biological rhythm of survival fills the perscription well. It is possible that the ambiguities found in the location and significance of the comic rhythm are in part a response to Mrs. Langer's own sense of how reductive her structural tool is.

Before passing, let us note, among a number of obvious differences, a significant agreement in the two approaches just considered. Both Langer and Frye are impressed—I am tempted to say overimpressed—by certain similarities they find between the presumably self-generating systems of mathematics and/or logic and the form of art. Frye says, "We think also of literature at first as a commentary on an external 'life' or 'reality.' But just as in mathematics we have to go from three apples to three, and from a square field to a square, so in reading a novel we have to go from literature as reflection of life to literature as autonomous language. Literature also proceeds by hypothetical possibilities, and though literature, like mathematics, is constantly useful—a word which means having a continuing relationship to the common field of experience—pure literature, like pure mathematics, contains its own meaning."[23] As Nagel warned in the review already cited, [see note 19] when language is treated "in a purely formal or syntactical manner . . . language is not *operating symbolically* at all."[24] Such a poem would be pure nonsense. The connection of art with life would be severed.

Our two critics certainly do not want to cut art loose from life, though both are at pains to point out the many ways in which art differs from life, especially in its surface aspects. Both then go back through form or structure to a "deeper level" of reality which this form is or represents: in Langer, the patterns of feeling or sentience; in Frye, myth. Yet both critics snip away at this life line with suggestions that form may be a self-generating syntactical operation.

This leaves our comic happy ending looking very much like formula. On the one hand, with Mrs. Langer, it is the final beat in the triumph of the comic rhythm of biological survival; with Frye, it is the final crystallization of a new society around the hero in myth. But in both, as we just noted, the happy ending comes close to being merely a formal device: it becomes literally formula in the mathematical sense. At this level the formula of *I Love Lucy* looks as good as *The Tempest*.

Let us step down a moment to look at the problem from another point of view. To adapt terms from Frye, we shall descend from the high aesthetic to the low aesthetic of an early twentieth century theoretician whom Mrs. Langer has referred to, Clayton Hamilton. Clayton Hamilton quite frankly balks at some of Shakespeare's endings, happy and otherwise. Fiction, for Hamilton, must be in some sense true, but the final judge of truth is our intuition. In any case, Hamilton's intuition tells him that certain of Shakespeare's endings are false. "When Shakespeare tells us, toward the end of *As You Like It*, that the wicked Oliver suddenly changed his nature and won the love of Celia, we know that he is lying. The scene is not true to the great laws of human life."[25]

The problem of the ending in comedy is probably by its very nature a difficult one, just because comedy does not have the obvious kind of "built-in" end that tragedy finds in death. In a sense Clayton Hamilton was right to suspect Shakespeare's ending. At least he was trying to make sense of the material immediately at hand and not fobbing off difficulties on a myth. Remember Shaw's difficulty with the ending of *Pygmalion*, resolved not in the theatre, but only in a lengthy essay. Yet certainly one does not want to remain in this sceptical predicament. There must be ways of going beyond Hamilton's "intuition" that still do not lead to either pure formalism or an abstract myth or "rhythm." A little thought suggests some useful analogies. One that comes quickly to the mind of a theatre person is the opening-night party. The wedding is another happy ending preserved into our mean age.

This is not to say that the happy ending represents an opening-night party instead of the mythical triumph of spring; it is merely to suggest that the happy ending is not, in itself, untrue to life. One need not look for its justification in either ancient myth or pure form. As a meaningful image of life, it is certainly within the ken at least of those who are fortunate enough to be able to attend the theatre.

But the main point is that the happy ending is a very pleasant experience. The sorting out of characters pleases us as a final kind of ordering, and the gayety of the final dance in Elizabethan and Restoration theatres charms us with the pleasures of music and choreography. As I noted in my remarks on the operatic finale (Chapter VIII), this is an image of possibly rare but certainly treasured moments which we derive from the same source Aristophanes probably did—life, not myth. We can have, indeed *must* have, both the formal appeal of the lively perfected image and the belief, which Clayton Hamilton sincerely if naively withheld, that the image reflects a meaningful pattern of our life in time.

The Two Gentlemen of Verona is a classic example of an abrupt but satisfying conclusion. The Duke of Milan rewards the just and punishes the wicked. He pardons Valentine and awards him Sylvia:

> Know, then, I here forget all former griefs,
> Cancel all grudge, repeal thee home again,
>
> . . . .
>
> Take thou thy Silvia, for thou hast deserved her.
> (V.iv.142–143, 147)

Then at Valentine's bidding the Duke extends the amnesty, concluding in an invitation to a party:

> Thou hast prevail'd: I pardon them and thee:
> Dispose of them as thou know'st their deserts.
> Come, let us go: we will include all jars
> With triumphs, mirth, and rare solemnity.
> V.iv.158–161)

The happenings of the comedies, including the happy ending, made sense to Shakespeare and his contemporaries not as a literal copy of life but as a meaningful image of one pattern of life. This was not *The* pattern, or even the probable pattern, but a meaningful image of what a life could be like that had not yet dispensed with the miraculous. Nor would Shakespeare need an archetypal form to suggest structural patterns of celebration in an age which afforded rich festivals, "disguisings," and such diversions as were presented at the houses which the Queen might visit on her "progress."[26]

Northrop Frye's remarks on comedy are illuminating, because they lead one to relate numerous seemingly disparate plays as different aspects of a common myth. Surely these relations are one of the many "meanings" of a work of art. I wish only to point out the danger, which does not seem always to be clear to the "archetypal critic," that this method can both equalize and transcend the specific works it operates on.

On the other hand, Mrs. Langer is at pains to warn us against taking comedy as "a disguised rite of spring or fertility magic." She has no intention of equalizing the great and the mediocre in some amorphous formula. However, through a confusion over just what the comic rhythm is and a refusal to let drama imitate life on any but this very abstracted formal level, she too must end with a formula, although this is clearly not her intent.

What can finally be said on the subject of form and formula, of Shakespeare vs. *I Love Lucy*? As we suspected all along, it is what goes into the formula that counts. The ingredients must be there in the work of art to be immediately enjoyed, as the rich sound of Shakespeare's verse, the satisfaction of resolutions, the gayety, color, and music of a final dance (or, on a lower level, some of the clever clowning of Lucille Ball). Any gross pattern must be fleshed out with the specific materials ordered by the improvisational structure and shaped in larger and smaller parts by the many intermediate structures; it is thus formed with the gross pattern (Basic Pattern of Events) into a meaningful image of the life of the audience.

Our pleasure in the dramas of another age depends, of course, on "universal" elements that are still alive for us, and fortunately wedding parties and dances have not disappeared. But it also depends to an extent on a recreation of the spirit of the times. This is not, certainly, a terribly difficult task for Shakespearean drama, but it is one that is not made without some effort and stretch of the imagination. Moderns without some preparations do not swallow Shakespeare any more than Clayton Hamilton did.

By the same token, modern comedies cannot successfully or truthfully be composed on Elizabethan assumptions or ideas about life. The Duke no longer straightens us all out. We even have grave doubts if the President can. Yet, fortunately, there is still some happiness present and possible and any attractive image of it is quite welcome. Our modern objection to the happy ending as formula really applies to the degradation of the happy ending as a mechanical terminus of indifferent and stereotyped material which, since it fails to entertain and move us deeply, triumphs in the end over nothing. For is it not finally the freshness, vivacity, and broad sweep of meaning which Shakespeare resolves in his admittedly abrupt happy endings which give these, through what went before, the edge over the television product?

Chapter XII

CONCLUSION

Over the course of this book a theory of dramatic structure has been described and tested against other theories. It was held that structure—that is, relationship—orders the essentially structureless materials of our daily experience so that we may understand them. Many phenomena may be seen in terms of alternate structures, as spatial phenomena may be viewed under the aspect of different geometries. The way we see experience, therefore, depends on a number of assumptions we must make about connections between events, connections which often, as in the case of cause and effect, we cannot establish with empirical proofs.

Given this constant flood of experience and the multiple possibilities for viewing it in a framework of relationships, man has taken it upon himself to create, in works of art, his own objects for experience. What distinguishes these works of art from the many other works of man is the fact that they are ends in themselves, not descriptions and predictions about the physical world (science) or tools for the accomplishment of some goal (technology). I have chosen to regard the art object as an image, both attractive in itself and significant of some aspect—although not necessarily the most obvious surface aspect—of our experience.

I have held, further, that the dramatic artist is primarily concerned with giving us images of man's interaction in time. The difference between the arts lies largely in the way the artist chooses to look at experience—in the structure he gives it. Thus dramatic structure typically organizes experience as a pattern of events. Out of all the things we do and the things done to us, certain events have been seen as connected and as somehow significant in this connectedness: for example, the boast of a proud man and a subsequent catastrophe which brought him lower than those he boasted to. But there are many patterns which time encompasses, and any of them can be utilized in the dramatic image. Though the rising and the setting of the sun may have had nothing to do with the boastful man's downfall, the pattern of time they circumscribe may condense the events for us in a temporal image with its own contributory rhythm.

One must back away from life a little to see events in a pattern. One must stop the clock and look at events historically. But our immediate experience of time is not historical; it is always "now," because the past is gone and the future is not yet. The image of man's interaction in time—of man caught in the everchanging evermoving flux, making decisions and altering them to meet ever new circumstances—this is the image drama gives us through the improvisational structure. No other art offers this image unless it becomes to that extent dramatic. The storyteller describes events in a temporal order, but his time is a time of narration, not of the happenings of events. Poetry takes time to read, and it progresses in that reading from concept to concept, but its essential image and basic structure is logical, depending upon essentially spatial confrontations of ideas in the mind. Music is truly an image of time unfolding in time, but, freed from literal connotations, music has primarily developed our experiences of repetition and variation, where drama has developed the Heracleitean image of man in an everchanging time. A few shifts in the kinds of experience viewed and the assumptions guiding these views might bring drama and music much closer together.

The pursuit of either an absolute separation of art from art or of extended analogies between them is bound to end in frustration. In terms of the drama, I have, therefore, tried to point to the basic structural principles—those relational schemes by which experience is built into a play, in which, for example, it is important that scene one precede, not follow, scene two. Dramatic production, though, offers such a wealth of material that there is room, within the framework of the dramatic structures, to organize this material in ways typical of poetry, narrative, painting, dance, music, and architecture. Indeed, these materials must be organized and related because it is typical of the artistic image, as opposed to life, that each element and relation is significant.

The study of structure can tell us much about the nature of drama, laying bare our assumptions and interests, our ways of organizing experience. In this it can be a valuable tool for the critic in discriminating and comparing different works. It can be especially helpful to the theatre worker as an aid to realizing a production whose necessarily complex whole is effectively organized to promote clear understanding and appreciation. It can be dangerous to the "interpreter." A description of the structure of a play is in no sense a substitute for the play. The Basic Pattern of Events does not abstract the "meaning" of a play. The "meaning" is only in the play itself. Structural analysis should be a working analysis: a helpful blueprint showing the way a play was constructed, not a freestanding essay showing the creative critic's ability to organize in his own ingenious ways the same material the playwright organized in his.

Appendix I

THE CATEGORIES AND *HAMLET*

Because the categories of my analysis were explained piecemeal throughout many chapters, I thought it well to offer here a brief summary of the categories as applied to the analysis of one very well known play. Since the explication of my concepts is finished, I shall suggest for each category only the most schematic of answers, leaving the reader to expand each suggestion as far as he feels impelled and the text allows. Here one must acknowledge the critical vantage point of the director, for his experience with a play from first readings through rehearsal to performance gives him the opportunity to sense a maximum number of structures at work in the medium for which they were intended. I offer, then, a sketch of the way our categories apply to *Hamlet*.[1]

Hamlet, perhaps more than most tragedies, unites different patterns of experience within its many contours, but the Basic Patterns of Events may fitttingly be seen in the action of revenge.[2] This pattern would include (1) the events in which the disturbed state of unrevenged wrong is discovered, (2) the placing of specific guilt and the decision to revenge it, (3) the tactical events involved with bringing the revenge about before one is killed oneself. This pattern can be as mechanical as the hollowest melodrama, hiding bloodless figures in dark passages, or it can, as in the case of *Hamlet*, catch the spectator with a rhythm of emotional experience which is profoundly felt. In this case, the hideousness of the suspicions—that the incest and usurpation of Claudius were based upon a foul murder—and the realization in a man of vivid imagination of the colossal, wasteful, and finally fatal task of revenge which he *must* undertake, make this bald traditional set of events a glowing image of serious commitment.

Interpreting pattern in terms of specific plot, the events through Act III, Scene i show an increasingly intolerable state of suspicion, spying, and sensed evil. This is brought to a head in Act III, Scene ii, where suspicions become certainties and both sides (Hamlet and Claudius) realize what the other knows and that they must do away with the other or be done away with (always a lurking possibility in this play). The drama is so constructed that this point constitutes an emotional and dynamic climax with Hamlet prepared to act ("Now could I drink hot blood" III.iii. 396–407).

This energy must be discharged and is discharged in the stabbing of Polonius, whom Hamlet mistook for the king. Thus a kind of resolution is made which turns from closure back to further development: a formal effect similar to that of a deceptive cadence in music. After this pathetic false ending there is a moment of stalemate: shadow boxing with the pawns Rosencrantz and Guildenstern, and the noisy but abortive uprising led by Laertes.[3] Yet neither Hamlet nor the king confront each other directly. In this deadly lull the last "innocent," Ophelia, dies off.

With Hamlet's sudden return from sea, announced by letters in IV.vii, the clock has run out. The last movement begins appropriately with a lyric discourse on mortality by both the gravediggers and Hamlet, who has now reached the state in which "the readiness [for any end] is all." Then Hamlet and Laertes lock in combat in Ophelia's grave and the infernal conflict rolls to its end with only the short break in which Hamlet tells Horatio of his sea adventure and his "readiness."

Other configurations of tragic experience are partially present or suggested in *Hamlet.* For example, there is something of the pattern of evil eclipsing the good we see in *Macbeth*, something of the fall of the noble prince set out in the *De casibus* tales. At the same time, the power and pervasiveness of the Basic Pattern of Events based on revenge can be sensed by noting some of the other possible manifestations it might take. Consider, the suspicion of illness, the positive confirmation of this illness, and the often painful—sometimes fatal—direct battle with that illness.[4] The parallel may be strengthened by noting that between the diagnosis and the kill or cure there is often a lull of false hopes and partial cures before the contagion and the organism meet in their direct and final clash.

Many types of intermediate patterns give form to the materials of this play. The very first lines between Francisco and his relief for the watch, Bernardo, depend upon the customary form of military challenge. The form of a royal entrance, suitably altered to the theatrical conditions at the Globe, and the pattern of public announcements—the seventeenth century equivalent of a press conference—determine the stage business and the lines which start the second scene. Elsewhere one finds a funeral procession, a fencing match, traditional songs, all taking their shape within the play from suitably adapted patterns in life. A particularly interesting example of a borrowed pattern is the presence in the play-within-a-play of a dramatic form of an earlier period.[5] The conventional patterns of mourning, courting, and drinking have varying effects upon the actions and words of the characters. Intermediate patterns which shape the technical aspects of the play may be seen not only in the convention of iambic pentameter, but in the rhymed couplets which close a scene and the various rhetorical patterns Shakespeare adapted to his use.

The assumptions and interests which may have guided Shakespeare in selecting and arranging his materials primarily involve assumptions about the pervasive nature of an unavenged crime and the duty and right of a private person to take upon himself the punishment of such a crime.[6] The accomplishment of an emotional resolution to the play requires the assumption that this act of revenge will in some deep way "set things right." The lively interest of contemporary audiences in the players, plus, of course, the author's own professional interest, suggested the references to the struggle between the boy actors and the mature companies. The ghost, fencing, and poisons all must have struck the Elizabethan fancy as Moon probes, and laser rays do ours.[7]

The improvisational structure which runs from the opening to the closing of the play may be conveniently sampled in one beat of the fourth act. Here in lines 16 through 39 of the third scene we find the prince brought before his uncle by Rosencrantz and Guildenstern. The king is anxious to recover the body of Polonius so that this most unfortunate murder may be kept as quiet as possible. Claudius' action for this beat may be thought of as "to end the game" (by finding the body). The circumstances controlling his way of proceeding include the fact that neither the queen nor the people would allow him to slay Hamlet openly, yet the murder of his lord chamberlain and its implications cannot be passed off lightly.

Hamlet, who realizes that his uncle dares not attack him directly in front of the court, will attempt "to pique the king." He wants to do as much damage as he can with his one weapon: his knowledge of where the old man's body is hidden. But he knows that this is a flimsy weapon against the assembled power of Denmark and the fact that the corpse will eventually be disovered anyway.

In this situation the worried and edgy king asks "where's Polonius?" Hamlet, enjoying his momentary power, answers "At supper," probably confusing the king for a moment into thinking that the old man still lives. But Hamlet plunges on to make clear that it is the worms not the old councilor who are enjoying the meal. He continues in this vein developing in an improvisatory way the initial idea of the feast not by but on Polonius until he shows "how a king may go a progress through the guts of a beggar." Now Claudius, who has mildly remonstrated twice, comes back again, probably more firmly, to demand the whereabouts of Polonius.

Hamlet, sensing the end of the king's patience, frames a more conventional answer ("In heaven.") but still reserves a final twist by saying that if the messengers cannot find Polonius in heaven the king himself would be welcome to seek him in hell. Though there is no direct evidence for this in the lines, Claudius may well start forward at this last insult, because Hamlet quickly, if still playfully, tells where the body is. The intentions are rapidly concluded as Claudius dispatches attendants for Polonius, and Hamlet, his momentary power gone, lamely quips " 'A will stay till you come."

The beat changes markedly in line 40 as the king introduces the new subject of Hamlet's necessarily speedy departure for England. This is likely to be accomplished with a change of tempo marking the king's new firmness of purpose now that he has the body and the murderer within his grasp. The departure of the attendants to look for Polonius will have altered the visual composition on the stage but it is likely that Hamlet and Claudius will also move, probably placing the king in a new strong position in relation to Hamlet.

The beat described is interesting both as it offers a compelling image of the cheeky individual facing the power structure and, more generally, as its dynamic shape of built and resolved tension is typical of most traditional playwriting, and hence illustrates the conventional assumption about the shape of human enterprise.

The considerations discussed under the problematic category of "pure form" pervade every line and every word as Shakespeare balances and varies his lines of five iambic feet against each other in relationships at least partly governed by the principles of repetition and variation. These same structural forces tie together scenes, characters, and themes as when Polonius sets Reynaldo to spy on his son, then Claudius sets Rosencrantz and Guildenstern to spy on Hamlet in scenes (II.i and II.ii) which contrast in tone, number of players, seriousness of purpose, etc.

These brief descriptions of the Basic Pattern of Events, intermediate patterns, and improvisational structure of *Hamlet* hardly exhaust the many important ways Shakespeare related his artistic materials to form this tragedy; thematic, imagistic, and character structures are among the obvious sets of relationships left undescribed. I would claim, however, that I have included the *controlling* structures which give *Hamlet* its characteristic shape as a drama, whether or not these may be the most interesting as structures or whether they relate what one might take to be the most profound ideas in Hamlet.

SCORE TRIO, NO. 13 FROM MOZART'S
THE MARRIAGE OF FIGARO

No. 13. Susanna, or via sortite!

Terzetto

Count, Countess, and Susanna

(Susanna enters through the door she used on leaving, and halts, on seeing the Count at the door of the small room.)

Allegro spiritoso

Count

Su - san - na, or via sor - ti - te!

Countess

Sor - ti - te, co - sì vo'! Fer -

Susanna

Cos' è co - de - sta li - te _ Il pag - gio do - ve an - ma - te - vi! sen - ti - te! sor - ti - re el - la non

dò? il pag-gio do-ve an - dò?

Count

può, sor - ti - re el-la non può. E chi vie-tar-lo or

o - sa? Chi? Lo vie - ta, lo vie - ta

Countess

l'o - ne - stà. Un' a - bi-to da spo - sa pro-van-do el-la si

stà, pro - van - do el-la si stà Chia - ris - si-ma è la

Count

(Susanna hides in the alcove.)

v'or - di-no ta-ce - te, ta - ce - te, ta - ce - te!

Con-

Susanna

O cie - lo! un pre-ci - pi - zio! Un

sor - te mia, giu - di - zio, con-sor - te mia, giu -

Countess

scan - da-lo, un dis - or - di - ne, quì cer - to na-sce - rà. Con-

di - zio! giu - di - zio! giu - di - zio!

Susanna

sor - te mio, giu - di - zio! con - sor - te mio, giu - di - zio! un

Con - sor - te mia, giu - di - zio! un

ciel! un pre - ci - pi - zi - o, quì cer - to na - sce - rà, o

scan - da-lo, un dis - or - di - ne, schi - viam per ca - ri - tà!

scan - da-lo, un dis - or - di - ne, schi - viam per ca - ri - tà!

ciel! un pre-ci-pi-zio, un scan-da-lo, un dis-or-di-ne, quì

Giu-di-zio!
Be care-ful!

giu-di-zio! un

Giu-di-zio!

un

cer-to na-sce-rà, quì cer-to na-sce-

scan-da-lo, un dis-or-di-ne, schi-viam per ca-ri-

scan-da-lo, un dis-or-di-ne, schi-viam per ca-ri-

scan - da-lo, un dis - or - di - ne, qui cer - to na - sce - rà,

scan - da-lo, un dis - or - di - ne, schi - viam per ca - ri - tà,

scan - da-lo, un dis - or - di - ne, schi - viam per ca - ri - tà,

qui cer - to na - sce -

per ca - ri - tà, schi - viam per ca - ri -

per ca - ri - tà, schi - viam per ca - ri -

The following is a literal translation of the libretto. No attempt has been made to reproduce some of the longer repetitions of the dialogue.

Count: Susanna, come out at once! Come out, I wish it!

Countess: Stop! Listen to me. She can not come out. She can not come out.

Susanna: [Unheard by the others] What's all that quarreling? The page, where has he gone? The page, where has he gone?

Count: And who dares to forbid it, who?

Countess: To forbid it? To forbid it? Why common decency. She's trying on a wedding dress.

Count: The matter is quite clear. The lover is in there.

Countess: The matter is quite ugly. Who knows what might happen.

Susanna: I understand some of the matter. Let's see how it goes.

Count: Susanna, come out at once. Come out I wish it.

Countess: Stop! Listen to me. Stop. She can not come out.

Count: Well speak at least. Susanna, if you are there.

Countess: No, no, no. I order you to be quiet, be quiet, be quiet!

Count: My wife, take warning. A scandal, an uproar, avoid for pity's sake.

Susanna: Oh heavens! A disaster! A scandal, an uproar will certainly occur.

Countess: My husband, take warning. A scandal, an uproar avoid for pity's sake.

NOTES

Relevant materials on dramatic structure may appear in a wide variety of sometimes unlikely, sometimes obvious sources. To allow the more curious reader to check my arguments or to pursue a given matter further, a fairly full set of references has therefore been supplied. If, as is hoped, specialists from the different disciplines which drama touches upon may each find something of interest in this book, then certain references which appear obvious to one specialist may be enlightening to another.

In the frequent references made to it, the *Journal of Aesthetics and Art Criticism* is abbreviated as *JAAC*.

INTRODUCTION

1. A number of investigations in the field of linguistics and drama have been undertaken by Czech writers. See the bibliography given in *A Prague School Reader on Esthetics, Literary Structure, and Style,* selected and trans. Paul L. Garvin (Washington, D.C.: Washington Linguistics Club, 1955).

2. René Wellek, "Concepts of Form and Structure in Twentieth Century Criticism," in *Concepts of Criticism* (New Haven: Yale University Press, 1963), p. 54.

3. Gerald F. Else, *Aristotle's Poetics: The Argument* (Cambridge: Harvard University Press, 1957).

4. Northrop Frye's principal comments on drama may be found in *Anatomy of Criticism* (Princeton: Princeton University Press, 1957) and *A Natural Perspective* (New York: Columbia University Press, 1965). Another man with wide interests is Kenneth Burke, whose comments on dramatic structure are widely scattered but may be sampled in *The Philosophy of Literary Form* (New York: Vintage, 1957).

5. Robert Edmond Jones was much impressed by the magic and ritual of drama. See *The Dramatic Imagination* (New York: Duell, Sloane & Pearce, 1941). The mystical and musical reverberations of the stage are also reflected by Jean-Louis Barrault's *Reflections on the Theatre* (London: Rockliff, 1951).

6. See especially *The Philosophy of Symbolic Forms* (3 vols.; New Haven: Yale University Press, 1953–1957).

7. (New York: Charles Scribner's Sons, 1953), Chs. XVII–XIX. See my Ch. XI for a more detailed treatment of this position.

8. (Carbondale: Southern Illinois University Press, 1961), Ch. XI.

9. *Ancient Art and Ritual* (New York: Henry Holt & Co., 1913) contains most of her material on the drama. For a critical sketch of the school see Stanley Edgar Hyman, "Myth, Ritual, and Nonsense," *The Kenyon Review,* XI (Summer 1949), 455–475.

10. See Gilbert Murray, "The Ritual Forms Preserved in Greek Tragedy," in Jane Ellen Harrison, *Themis* (Cambridge: The University Press, 1912); and Francis Macdonald Cornford, *The Origin of Attic Comedy,* ed. Theodore H. Gaster (Garden City: Anchor Books, 1961).

11. A. W. Pickard-Cambridge, *Dithyramb, Tragedy, and Comedy* (2nd ed. rev. by T. B. L. Webster; Oxford: Clarendon Press, 1962) reviews the claims of Murray, Cornford, *et al* with some skepticism.

12. His major work in this field is *The Idea of a Theatre* (Princeton: Princeton University Press, 1949).

13. Basic texts on the psychological approach through archetypes are C. G. Jung, "On the Relation of Analytical Psychology to Poetic Art," in *Contributions to Analytical Psychology* (London: Kegan Paul, 1928); and Maud Bodkin, *Archetypal Patterns in Poetry* (New York: Vintage Books, 1958).

14. Such hints may be found in Franz Boas, *Primitive Art* (Cambridge: Harvard University Press, 1927); and Melville J. & Frances S. Herskovits, *Dahomean Narrative* (Evanston: Northwestern University Press, 1958).

15. A. B. Lord, *The Singer of Tales* (Cambridge: Harvard University Press, 1960).

16. In *The Well Wrought Urn* (New York: Reynal and Hitchcock, 1947).

17. This common criticism of the school was made recently by John Holloway in *The Story of the Night* (Lincoln: University of Nebraska Press, 1961), pp. 1–20.

18. See R. S. Crane, *The Languages of Criticism and the Structure of Poetry* (Toronto: Toronto University Press, 1953).

19. (rev. ed.; New York: Holt, Rinehart and Winston, 1953), pp. 1–2, 10–43.

20. See especially Antonin Artaud, *The Theatre and Its Double* (New York: Grove Press, 1958); and *Brecht on Theatre*, ed. John Willett (New York: Hill and Wang, 1964).

21. Statements by these and other experimenters may most conveniently be found in the pages of *The Drama Review* (formerly *Tulane Drama Review*). Peter Brook has provided a commentary on some of his work in *The Empty Space* (New York: Atheneum, 1968).

22. Pirandello is not widely known as a theorist but his revolutionary plays and such few pieces as the preface to *Six Characters in Search of an Author* have perhaps had a more profound effect upon our ideas of drama than the works of any other theatre man of the century.

23. Most influential in spreading Stanislavsky's ideas in America have been *My Life in Art* (New York: Meridian Books, 1956); *An Actor Prepares* (New York: Theatre Arts Books, 1936); and *Building a Character* (New York: Theatre Arts Books, 1949).

24. Compare Stanislavsky's method with Johannes Itten, *Design and Form: The Basic Course at the Bauhaus* (New York: Reinhold, 1964), pp. 11–12.

25. For Fergusson's experience in "Method" acting classes see his *The Human Image in Dramatic Literature* (Garden City: Anchor Books, 1957), pp. 105–111.

26. Of the recent books in English not discussed in this work note should be taken particularly of: Eric Bentley, *The Life of the Drama* (New York: Atheneum, 1964); Allardyce Nicoll, *The Theatre and Dramatic Theory* (New York: Barnes and Noble, 1962); Ronald Peacock, *The Art of Drama* (New York: Macmillan, 1957); J. L. Styan, *The Elements of Drama* (Cambridge: Cambridge University Press, 1960); Alan Reynolds Thompson, *The Anatomy of Drama*, (2nd ed.; Berkeley: University of California Press, 1966).

27. An early statement of general principles is available in Allardyce Nicoll, *Film and Theatre* (New York: Thomas Y. Crowell, 1936).

28. Two notable attempts at definition are in the *Colloque sur le mot structure*, Paris, 1959, edited by Roger Bastide and published as *Sens et Usages du Terme Structure dans les Sciences Humaines et Sociales* (Gravenhage: Mouton, 1962); and in the special issue on structure of the *Revue Internationale de Philosophie*, XIX (1965) which often refers back to the "colloque."

29. R. Buckminster Fuller quotes an M.I.T. catalogue as saying "Mathematics, which most people think of as the science of number, is, in fact, *the science of structure and pattern in general.*" In Gyorgy Kepes ed., *Structure in Art and in Science* (New York: George Braziller, 1965), p. 68.

30. *Poetry and Mathematics* (Philadelphia: Lippincott, 1962).

31. "Form" has been used in many ways, at least one of which overlaps our understanding of "structure." It is to avoid these ambiguities, and particularly the idea "form" allows of the parts *and* their relationship, that we use the more restricted term "structure." See Chapter VI, pp. 92–93 for further discussion of structure in relation to form.

32. For an interesting comparison consider the structure of the "blues." A description of their poetic and harmonic patterns seems superficial until we perceive how these simple structures reflect deep patterns of experience and return a rich fund of meaning on the individual lyrics and tunes.

33. See *Aspen Magazine*, V–VI (1968) for an attempt at a play in this mode, "Structural Play #3" by Brian O'Doherty.

34. See Peter Caws, "What Is Structuralism?" *Partisan Review*, XXXV (Winter, 1968), 75–91; and the "Structuralism" issue of *Yale French Studies* XXXVI–XXXVII (1966).

35. (New York: Harcourt, Brace and Company, 1958).

36. See Michael Kirby, *Happenings* (New York: E.P. Dutton, 1965), pp. 247–248.

37. For a remarkable analysis of the use of stage space see *The Theatre of the Bauhaus*, ed. Walter Gropius (Middletown, Conn.: Wesleyan University Press, 1961), pp. 91–101.

CHAPTER I

1. See Arthur and Barbara Gelb, *O'Neill* (New York: Harper and Brothers, 1960); and Lewis Sheaffer, *O'Neill, Son and Playwright* (Boston: Little Brown, 1968). Sheaffer, who was associated with the Broadway production, has done much research on the period represented in *Long Day's Journey into Night*. This book and that of the Gelbs provide interesting opportunities for comparing actual events with their transmutations in art.

2. *Experiencing and the Creation of Meaning* (New York: The Free Press of Glencoe, 1962), p. 154.

3. For a sampling of writings that *do* explore the modes of describing experience see Charles W. Morris, "Science, Art and Technology," *The Kenyon Review*, I (1939), 409–423; and Paul Weiss, *The World of Art* (Carbondale, Illinois: Southern Illinois University Press, 1961), Ch. III and IV.

4. See Hume, *Treatise of Human Nature*, I, pt. 4.

5. Cleanth Brooks, Jr. and Robert Penn Warren, *Understanding Poetry* (New York: Henry Holt and Company, 1938), p. 171.

6. Moody E. Prior, *The Language of Tragedy* (New York: Columbia University Press, 1947), pp. 22–23.

7. The idea of shaping the work of art by choosing to include certain things (which presumably are of interest) and excluding the rest of reality—the principle of the snapshot—can be clearly seen in the analysis of an account by an army nurse of some days in the Battle of the Philippines, Chapter VII.

8. See C. M. Bowra, *The Greek Experience* (New York: The New American Library, 1957), especially pp. 125–129; and W. C. Greene, *Moira* (Cambridge: Harvard University Press, 1944).

9. In addition to the material in Greene, see William G. McCollom, *Tragedy* (New York: The Macmillan Company, 1957), pp. 56–62 and 159. G. M. Kirkwood, *A Study of Sophoclean Drama* (Ithaca: Cornell University Press, 1958), pp. 24–26, argues that Sophocles

accepts the received myth for dramatic purposes, where Aeschylus and Euripides alter meanings.

10. See A. C. Bradley, *Shakespearean Tragedy* (New York: Meridian Books, 1955), pp. 31–35 for an interpretation of Shakespeare's idea of fate.

11. See Arthur Pap, *An Introduction to the Philosophy of Science* (New York: The Free Press of Glencoe, 1962), pp. 307–340, for a modern review of Laplace and determinism.

12. Martin Esslin, *The Theatre of the Absurd* (Garden City: Doubleday and Company, 1961).

13. Eugene Ionesco, *Four Plays*, trans. Donald M. Allen (New York: Grove Press, Inc., 1958), p. 9 and p. 14.

CHAPTER II

1. Interesting examples may be found in Elisabeth Woodbridge, *The Drama: Its Law and its Technique* (Boston: Allyn & Bacon, 1898).

2. Marvin Rosenberg, "A Metaphor for Dramatic Form," *JAAC*, XVII (Dec. 1958), 174–180.

3. *The Living Shakespeare*, ed. Robert Gittings (Greenwich, Conn.: Fawcett Publications, Inc., 1961), p. 69. See also Richard G. Moulton, whose deep interest in literary structure and addiction to graphic models are both evident in *The Modern Study of Literature* (Chicago: The University of Chicago Press, 1915).

4. Henri Bergson, *Time and Free Will*, trans. F. L. Pogson (London: Swan Sonnenschein & Co., 1910), p. 224.

5. *The Review of Metaphysics*, XI (Sept. 1957), 3.

6. See Bell's *Art* (New York: Capricorn Books, 1958), expecially pp. 15–34.

7. E. E. Stoll, *Art and Artifice in Shakespeare* (Cambridge: Cambridge University Press, 1938), pp. 43–49.

8. *An Introduction to Sophocles* (Oxford: The Clarendon Press, 1936), pp. 88–89.

9. A similar list of "narrative structures" is offered by René Wellek and Austin Warren, *Theory of Literature* (New York: Harcourt, Brace and Co., 1949), p. 225.

10. William Barrett has shown that Oriental assumptions about the nature of experience result in different structures for their art. *Irrational Man* (Garden City: Doubleday Anchor Books, 1962), pp. 54–55.

11. Translated by David Grene in *Greek Tragedies*, eds. Grene and Lattimore, (Chicago: The University of Chicago Press, 1960), I, 164. The rendering of line 1193 is in question especially as regards the use of "pattern" rather than, say, "example." See the notes in Jebb's Cambridge text.

12. *The Idea of a Theatre* (Princeton: Princeton University Press, 1949), pp. 26–32.

13. Northrop Frye, *Anatomy of Criticism* (Princeton: Princeton University Press, 1957), pp. 99–100.

14. *Ibid.*, p. 105.

15. Maud Bodkin, *Archetypal Patterns in Poetry* (New York: Vintage Books, 1958), p. 1. The article by Jung referred to is included in his *Contributions to Analytical Psychology*, trans. H. G. & Cary F. Baynes (New York: Harcourt, Brace & Co., 1928), pp. 225–249.

16. Bodkin, pp. 4–5.

17. C. G. Jung and C. Kerényi, *Essays on a Science of Mythology*, trans. R. F. C. Hull (New York: Pantheon Books, 1949), p. 99.

18. *Ibid.*, p. 104.

19. *Ibid.*, p. 135.

20. *Dahomean Narrative* (Evanston: Northwestern University Press, 1958), p. 96.

21. *Ibid.*, page 103.

22. "Perceptual Analysis of A Cosmological Symbol," *JAAC*, XIX (Summer 1961), 389–399.

CHAPTER III

1. Chester Clayton Long argues a somewhat different basic structure for this play in *The Role of Nemesis in the Structure of Selected Plays by Eugene O'Neill* (The Hague: Mouton, 1968), pp. 198–215.

2. C. L. Barber, *Shakespeare's Festive Comedy* (Princeton: Princeton University Press, 1959).

3. See Ruby Cohn, "Waiting Is All," *Modern Drama*, III (September 1960), 162–167, who argues an essentially formalist view that the waiting in *Godot* is structured by repetitions and symmetry.

4. Gillo Dorfles, "The Role of Motion in Our Visual Habits and Artistic Creation," *The Nature and Art of Motion*, ed. Gyorgy Kepes (New York: George Braziller, 1965), p. 45.

5. John Gassner, *Producing the Play* (rev. ed.; New York: Holt, Rinehart and Winston, 1953), p. 35.

6. Arthur and Barbara Gelb, *O'Neill* (New York: Harper and Brothers, 1960), p. 407.

7. See W. T. Price, *The Analysis of Play Construction and Dramatic Principle* (New York: W. T. Price, 1908), pp. 282–293.

8. See Sister Miriam Joseph, *Rhetoric in Shakespeare's Time* (New York: Harcourt, Brace and World, 1962).

9. An interesting extension of this discussion, and one of the rare perceptive treatments of small structures, may be found in Harold Brooks, "Themes and Structure in *The Comedy of Errors*," in Kenneth Muir, *Shakespeare: The Comedies* (Englewood Cliffs, N.J.: Prentice Hall, 1965), pp. 11–25.

CHAPTER IV

1. *Experience and the Creation of Meaning* (New York: The Free Press of Glencoe, 1962), p. 153.

2. For an interesting discussion of the problem of finding basic units for analysis in the arts, see Z. Czerny, "Contribution à une théorie comparée du motif dans les arts," in *Stil-und Formprobleme in der Literatur* (Heidelberg: Carl Winter, 1959), pp. 38–50.

3. *Problems of Art* (New York: Charles Scribner's Sons, 1957), p. 94.

4. *Feeling and Form* (New York, Charles Scribner's Sons, 1953), p. 306.

5. For Mrs. Langer on abstraction see, most recently, "Abstraction in Art," *JAAC*, XXII (Summer 1964), 379–392. Her systematic treatment of drama appears in *Feeling and Form*, Ch. XVII–XIX.

6. This is the suggestion of Francis Fergusson, a modern Aristotelian whose analysis of the *Oedipus* provides a good example of this thinking. See *The Idea of a Theatre* (Princeton: Princeton University Press, 1949), Ch. I.

7. See the analysis of actions in Robert Lewis, *Method or Madness?* (New York: Samuel French, 1958), pp. 29–32.

8. Susanne Langer stresses this point, *Feeling and Form*, p. 306.

9. See how Alexander Dean treats the composition of stage picture and movement in *Fundamentals of Play Directing* (Rev. ed.; New York: Holt, Rinehart and Winston, 1965).

10. A trio of articles in *TDR* present views of drama as more dependent upon literary structures than I take it to be. Joseph Kerman discusses music and drama and T. E. Lawrenson describes the baroque de-

signers' extravaganzas. Respectively, George Hauger, "When Is a Play not a Play," Conor A. Farrington, "The Language of Drama," and William L. Sharp, "A Play: Scenario or Poem," *The Tulane Drama Review*, V (December 1960), 54–84. Joseph Kerman, *Opera as Drama* (New York: Vintage Books, 1959), pp. 3–22. T. E. Lawrenson, *The French Stage in the XVIIth Century* (Manchester: The Manchester University Press, 1957), p. 154.

11. See *Film Quarterly*, XVII (Summer 1964), 26–40.

12. See Leonard B. Meyer, "The End of the Renaissance," *Hudson Review*, XVI (Summer 1963), 169–186. Reprinted in Meyer's *Music, the Arts, and Ideas* (Chicago: The University of Chicago Press, 1967).

13. For some of the problems involved see George Dickie, "The Myth of the Aesthetic Attitude," *American Philosophical Quarterly*, I (January 1964), 56–65; and Virgil C. Aldrich, "Back to Aesthetic Experience," *JAAC*, XXIV (Spring 1966), 365–371.

14. Sir Russell Brain, *The Nature of Experience* (London: Oxford University Press, 1959), p. 69.

15. A prime instance occurs in *Four Quartets* (New York: Harcourt, Brace & Co., 1943), p. 3.

16. Susanne Langer's essay "The Art Symbol and the Symbol in Art," *Problems of Art* (New York: Charles Scribner's Sons, 1957), pp. 124–139, is illuminating on this point which cannot be pursued here. A summary of the position of semiotic aesthetics, with extensive references to other articles for and against the position, may be found in Charles Morris and Daniel J. Hamilton, "Aesthetics, Signs, and Icons," *Philosophy and Phenomenological Research*, XXV (March 1965), 356–364.

17. See especially the chapter "When Acting Is an Art," in Stanislavsky's *An Actor Prepares* (New York: Theatre Arts Books, 1936).

18. Stanislavsky, p. 35.

19. Stanislavsky, p. 43.

20. Stanislavsky, p. 48.

21. Stanislavsky, p. 67.

22. Compare Heidegger's description of the significance of the humble pair of shoes in the famous Van Gogh painting to the significance summed up in a simple action. Hans Jaeger, "Heidegger and the Work of Art," *Aesthetics Today*, ed. Morris Philipson (Cleveland and New York: The World Publishing Company, 1961), pp. 415–416.

23. *Feeling and Form*, p. 306.

24. *Feeling and Form*, p. 316.

25. *Feeling and Form*, p. 307.

26. *Feeling and Form*, p. 310.

27. *Feeling and Form*, p. 48.

28. Kenneth Burke, *The Philosophy of Literary Form* (New York: Vintage Books, 1957), p. 253.

29. Iredell Jenkins, "The Aesthetic Object," *The Review of Metaphysics*, XI (Sept. 1957), 10–11.

CHAPTER V

1. Ferdinand Brunetière, "The Law of the Drama," trans. Philip M. Hayden, *European Theories of the Drama*, ed. Barrett H. Clark (New York: Crown Pubilshers, 1947), p. 408.

2. Constantin Stanislavsky, *An Actor Prepares* (New York: Theatre Arts Books, 1936), pp. 26–27.

3. The sociologist would say that the playwright composes in terms of "transactions," thus placing these events within a fairly well defined area of behavioral analysis such as that offered by Eric Berne in *Games People Play* (New York: Grove Press, 1964) and *Transactional Analysis in Psychotherapy* (New York: Grove Press, 1961). To adopt such a technical term here, however, might unnecessarily limit our frame of reference.

4. Richard Schechner's discussion of the *agon* with time and the distinctions he draws between "event time" and "set time" throw a further light upon the special situation of the monologue or piece of business. See "Approaches to Theory/Criticism," *Tulane Drama Review*, X (Summer 1966), 28–29.

5. Two observations should be made here. Because we are used to looking at structure as a static pattern it is much easier to see that aspect of our short scene, i.e., the movement from hesitancy to first decision ("We will proceed no further . . ."), than it is to see a force which relates actions before the restrospective pattern becomes discernible. Second, many other relationships and hence structures, are present in our chosen passage; for example, the pattern of visual relationships of costumes and set (colors, textures, masses), the structure of the verse (including patterns of word sounds), and patterns of imagery.

6. *Essays* (New York: Macmillan, 1924), p. 191.

7. Actually communication in clichés does provide an exchange of sorts imparting certain limited but real social gains to its participants. The decision to concentrate attention on this area of human interaction has linked both social scientists and playwrights in some absorbing contemporary studies in which Berne's game analysis approaches Stanislavski's search for the "subtext" in multi level transactions.

8. Eugene O'Neill, *Long Day's Journey into Night* (New Haven: Yale University Press, 1956), p. 15.

9. Francis Fergusson, *The Idea of a Theatre* (Princeton: Princeton University Press, 1949), p. 18.

10. Beats are discussed though not defined by Harold Clurman—certainly a man of the practical theatre—in "The Principles of Interpretation," *Producing the Play*, ed. John Gassner (rev. ed.; New York: Holt, Rinehart and Winston, 1953), pp. 285–287.

11. After watching hundreds of student scenes and auditions I have become convinced that the rhythm is the most sensitive indicator of the degree to which the actor is involved in his material. See also Constantin Stanislavsky, *Building a Character*, trans. Elizabeth Reynolds Hapgood, (New York: Theatre Arts Books, 1949), p. 236. Stanislavsky's theory of "tempo-rhythm" in movement and speech runs from page 177 to 237 with a too brief summary on pages 234–237.

12. Laurence W. Cor, "Reading a Play," *JAAC*, XXI (Spring 1963), 322.

13. See Grosvenor W. Cooper and Leonard B. Meyer, *The Rhythmic Structure of Music* (Chicago: The University of Chicago Press, 1960), for a thorough theoretical coverage of rhythm.

14. See T. W. Baldwin, *Shakespeare's Five-Act Structure* (Urbana: University of Ilinois Press, 1947), but note the problems involved in tracing this back to the questionable twelfth chapter of the *Poetics* which Else comments on in pp. 360–363 and Baldwin in his Chapter XIII. G. F. Else, *Aristotle's Poetics: The Argument* (Cambridge: Harvard University Press, 1957).

15. Baldwin, p. 347.

16. See William Archer, *Play-Making* (New York: Dover Publications, 1960), pp. 85–100 for one excellent discussion of act division originally published in 1912.

17. A close analysis of the logic of the division into episodes made by the Greek tragedians would be very valuable especially if it utilized the early and odd examples not merely the "classic" specimens.

CHAPTER VI

1. (Bloomington, Indiana: Indiana University Press, 1961), p. 2.

2. Morris Weitz in W. E. Kennick, *Art and Philosophy* (New York: St. Martin's Press, 1964), p. 344.

3. Clive Bell, *Art* (New York: Capricorn Books, 1958), p. 30. For a slightly different presentation of the position see Roger Fry, "Some Questions in Esthetics," in *Transformations* (Freeport, N. Y.: Books For Libraries Press, 1968).

4. Bell, p. 10.

5. For the problems of pure versus referential music which bear closely on the issues in this chapter see the purist Eduard Hanslick, *The Beautiful in Music* reprinted in W. E. Kennick, *Art and Philosophy* (New York: St. Martin's Press, 1964); and for a sophisticated referentialist position Susanne Langer, *Philosophy in a New Key* (New York: Mentor, 1948), Ch. VIII.

6. A distinction, not necessary to our argument, is often made between the artist's materials as physical elements—blue pigment of such and such a scientifically measurable hue—and these materials as the "prehended" medium—a blue that recedes. See Virgil Aldrich, *The Philosophy of Art* (Englewood Cliffs, N. J.: Prentice-Hall, 1963), p. 40.

7. The interesting cases of performers in certain Happenings who are merely themselves, like lecturers or musicians, I would still consider representational in Bell's context because they are *ordinarily* appreciated for what they do or represent not for the physical qualities they possess. See Michael Kirby, "The New Theatre," *Tulane Drama Review*, X (Winter 1965), 23–43.

8. It is dangerously inviting to illustrate these categories by paintings, in which the first might be illustrated by a Franz Kline, the second by any good anecdotal painting, say, Raphael's *School of Athens*, the third by a Mondrian, and the fourth by a good stilllife, say, Chardin or Picasso. However, the purity of pure form is itself so problematic and the analogy of the static patterns of painting to the temporal patterns of drama so incomplete that this effort has very slight value.

9. See *The Theatre of the Bauhaus*, ed. Walter Gropius, trans. Arthur S. Wensinger (Middletown, Conn.: Wesleyan University Press, 1961), insert opposite p. 48.

10. *The Theatre of the Bauhaus*, pp. 62–64.

11. *The Theatre of the Bauhaus*, p. 67.

12. *The Theatre of the Bauhaus*, pp. 88, 91.

240

13. *The Theatre of the Bauhaus*, p. 62. Long before this work in Weimar and Dessau, Servandoni experimented with textless visual spectacles in Paris in the middle of the eighteenth century. T. E. Lawrenson, *The French Stage in the XVIIth Century* (Manchester: The Manchester University Press, 1957), p. 159. Valuable articles on the Bauhaus and its theatre are being published in *Cahiers Renaud-Barrault*. Nos. 46, 52, and 53 contain such material.

14. W. K. Wimsatt, Jr., *The Verbal Icon* (New York: The Noonday Press, 1958), p. 165. Compare Herbert Read, "Poetry depends, not only on the sound of words, but even more on their mental reverberations." *The Nature of Literature* (New York: Horizon Press, 1956), p. 45.

15. Some of the interesting possibilities here are set forth in a book in the Bauhaus tradition *The Nature and Art of Motion*, ed. Gyorgy Kepes (New York: George Braziller, 1965).

16. G. Wilson Knight makes much of the *sound* in Shakespeare in his *Principles of Shakespearian Production* (New York: The Macmillan Company, 1936), pp. 59–78.

17. See, for example, W. T. Price, *The Technique of Drama* (New York: Brentano's, 1911), p. 169.

18. Henrik Ibsen, *The Collected Works*, trans. William Archer (New York: Charles Scribner's Sons, 1923) XI, p. 376.

19. Compare Kant's idea of satisfaction through the final harmony of the object with the faculties of cognition, *Critique of Pure Judgement*, trans. J. H. Bernard (2nd. ed. rev.; London: Macmillan, 1914), pp. 41–42; and the theories of such psychologists as Rudolf Arnheim in *Art and Visual Perception* (Berkeley: University of California Press, 1954).

20. Arthur and Barbara Gelb, *O'Neill* (New York: Harper and Brothers, 1960), Ch. XX.

21. Joyce Cary in *A Modern Book of Esthetics*, ed. Melvin Rader (3rd ed.; New York: Holt, Rinehart and Winston, 1960), p. 105.

22. H. D. Albright, William P. Halstead, Lee Mitchell, *Principles of Theatre Art* (Cambridge: Houghton Mifflin Co., 1955), p. 416. Alexander Dean tells directors that: "Composition [the arrangement of the people in a stage group] is capable of expressing the feeling, quality, and mood of the subject through color, line, mass, and form. It does not tell the story." *Fundamentals of Play Directing* (Rev. ed.; Holt, Rinehart and Winston, 1965), p. 109.

23. Madeleine Doran holds that the smaller forms received more attention at this period than the big ones. *Endeavors of Art* (Madison: The University of Wisconsin Press, 1964), p. 29.

24. Several nonrepresentational painters have objected to having their work called "abstract." Their pure paintings, they say, are more concrete than the representationalist's abstractions of a house.

25. Henri Focillon, *The Life of Forms in Art* (New York: Wittenborn, Schultz, 1948).

CHAPTER VII

1. The argument and demonstration appear in Hans Reichenbach, *The Philosophy of Space and Time*, trans. Maria Reichenbach and John Freund (New York: Dover Publications, Inc., 1957), pp. 37–81. See also W. H. Werkmeister, *The Basis and Structure of Knowledge* (New York: Harper & Bros., 1948), p. 80.

2. For a detailed treatment of the *Poetics* and Aristotle's use of *mythos* see Ch. IX.

3. See René Wellek and Austin Warren, *Theory of Literature* (New York: Harcourt, Brace, 1949), p. 16. Wellek and Warren's criterion that literature (as opposed to other uses of language) is not about something real, while it is historically generally true, seems not to be a necessary condition. In an analogous situation, numerous recognizable landscapes and portraits are among our most respected paintings. We may also ask at precisely what distance from Holinshed's chronicles did an Elizabethan play become literature?

4. Reproduced in Paul M. Angle, *The Uneasy World* (Greenwich, Conn.: Fawcett Publications, 1960), pp. 76–81. From *History in the Writing*, ed. Gordon Carroll (New York: Duell, Sloane and Pearce, Inc. affiliate of Meredith Press, 1945), pp. 84–87. Used by permission.

5. Angle, p. 76.

6. Angle, p. 77.

7. Angle, p. 80.

8. I am indebted to Prof. William McCollom for this insight.

9. Franz Boas, *Primitive Art* (Cambridge: Harvard University Press, 1927), p. 311. See also John Greenway, *Literature Among the Primitives* (Hatboro, Pa.: Folklore Associates, 1964), pp. 113–118.

10. Boas, pp. 309–310.

11. An interesting historical contrast is offered by C. S. Lewis in his description of the polyphonic technique of story-telling popular in the

middle ages when stories interwove with little concern for what moderns consider "proper" narrative sequence. *Studies in Medieval and Renaissance Literature* (Cambridge: The University Press, 1966), pp. 133–135.

12. The child signifies not only hope, but *regeneration*—the key to the "comic rhythm" for Susanne Langer. *Feeling and Form* (New York: Charles Scribner's Sons, 1953), pp. 326–331.

13. Wellek and Warren, Ch. XVII.

14. Langer, p. 306.

15. William K. Wimsatt, Jr., and Cleanth Brooks, *Literary Criticism: A Short History* (New York: Alfred A. Knopf, 1959), p. 684. The whole chapter "Fiction and Drama: The Gross Structure" is very illuminating.

16. "Spatial Form in Modern Literature," in *Criticism: The Foundations of Modern Literary Judgement*, ed. Mark Schorer, Josephine Miles, Gordon McKenzie (New York: Harcourt, Brace and World, 1958), p. 383.

17. Eugene O'Neill, *Long Day's Journey into Night* (New Haven: Yale University Press, 1956), pp. 149–150.

CHAPTER VIII

1. Adolphe Appia, *Music and the Art of the Theatre* (Miami: University of Miami Press, 1963). Walter Pater, quoted in Jerome Stolnitz *Aesthetics and Philosophy of Art Criticism* (Boston: Houghton Mifflin Co., 1960), p. 142.

2. Eugène Vinaver, *Racine et la Poésie Tragique* (Paris: Librairie Nizet, 1951), pp. 105–107.

3. Pierre Moreau, *Racine L'Homme et L'Oeuvre* (Paris: Boivin et Cie, 1934), pp. 171–173.

4. *Five Plays of Strindberg*, ed. & trans. Elizabeth Sprigge (Garden City: Doubleday and Co., 1960), p. 122.

5. T. S. Eliot, *Poetry and Drama* (Cambridge: Harvard University Press, 1951), p. 43.

6. T. S. Eliot, *On Poetry and Poets* (New York: The Noonday Press, 1961), p. 30.

7. Arnold Wesker, quoted in *The New York Times*, February 12, 1961, Sec. 2, p. 1.

8. Sir Donald Francis Tovey, *The Forms of Music* (New York: Meridian Books, 1956), pp. 229–230.

9. Eric Bentley, *The Playright as Thinker* (New York: Harcourt, Brace and Co., 1946), p. 72.

10. Jean-Louis Barrault, *The Theatre of Jean-Louis Barrault*, trans. Joseph Chiari (New York: Hill and Wang, 1961), pp. 152–165.

11. Percy Goetschius, *The Structure of Music* (Philadelphia: Theodore Presser Co., 1934), p. 147.

12. Goetschius, p. 148.

13. Goetschius, p. 144.

14. Hugo Leichtentritt, *Musical Form* (Cambridge: Harvard University Press, 1951), pp. 271–272.

15. See Joshua Whatmough, *Language: A Modern Synthesis* (New York: The New American Library, 1957), Chs. VII and VIII.

16. Tennessee Williams, *A Streetcar Named Desire* (New York: The New American Library, 1951), pp. 18–19.

17. "Supplement I," in C. K. Ogden and I. A. Richards, *The Meaning of Meaning* (8th ed.; New York: Harcourt, Brace & Co., n.d.), pp. 313–315.

18. "Laughter," in *Comedy*, ed. Wylie Sypher (Garden City: Doubleday Anchor Books, 1956), pp. 81, 107–108, 119–121.

19. Cleanth Brooks, "The Naked Babe and the Cloak of Manliness," in *The Well Wrought Urn* (New York: Reynal and Hitchcock, 1947).

20. Repetitions of phrases, characters, incidents, and symbols in a musical way is examined in E. K. Brown, *Rhythm in the Novel* (Toronto: University of Toronto Press, 1950).

21. Calvin S. Brown, *Music and Literature: A Comparison of the Arts* (Athens, Georgia: The University of Georgia Press, 1948).

22. See C. M. Bowra, *Primitive Song* (Cleveland: The World Publishing Co., 1962), esp. pp. 77–85.

23. Victor Zuckerkandl, *Sound and Symbol*, trans. Willard R. Trask (New York: Pantheon Books, Inc., 1956), p. 216.

24. Zuckerkandl, p. 217.

25. Musical patterns may also be analogous to emotional patterns as C. C. Pratt implied in saying that music may sound the way emotions feel. "Structural vs. Expressive Form in Music," *Journal of Psychology*, V (1938), 154.

26. For an example of a play where the peak of stage action and the climax

of the story do not coincide, see Robert Sherwood's *The Petrified Forest.*

27. Joseph Kerman, who in turn cites Edward J. Dent, is one of the many critics who would advance this opinion, *Opera as Drama* (New York: Vintage Books, 1959), pp. 99–100.

28. See Leichtentritt, "Forms of the Mozart Opera," *Musical Form,* pp. 204–205.

29. *Phaedra and Figaro,* trans. Robert Lowell and Jacques Barzun (New York: Farrar, Straus and Cudahy, 1961), p. 129.

30. W. A. Mozart, *Le Nozze di Figaro,* (score for piano and voices) ed. Natalia Macfarren (London: Novello and Co., Ltd., n.d.), p. 81. Translated from the Italian by Jackson Barry.

31. *Phaedra and Figaro,* p. 156.

32. Kerman, p. 108.

33. Edward J. Dent, *Mozart's Operas* (London: Oxford University Press, 1947), p. 109.

34. Kerman, pp. 73–90.

35. *Phaedra and Figaro,* pp. 135–136.

36. Mozart, (Score), pp. 96–103.

37. *Phaedra and Figaro,* pp. 135–137.

38. Siegmund Levarie, *Mozart's 'Le Nozze di Figaro'* (Chicago: The University of Chicago Press, 1952), pp. 95–100.

39. Levarie, p. 95.

40. Kerman, p. 130.

41. *Phaedra and Figaro,* p. 142.

42. Lorenzo Da Ponte, *Memoirs of Lorenzo Da Ponte,* trans. Elizabeth Abbott (Philadelphia and London: J. B. Lippincott, 1929), p. 133.

43. A. W. Pickard-Cambridge, *Dithyramb Tragedy and Comedy* (Oxford: Oxford University Press, 1927), p. 310.

CHAPTER IX

1. In order to say how we differ or agree, I must indicate what I understand Aristotle to mean. I have depended on several specialists, particularly G. F. Else, the recent date of whose work has allowed him to consider most of the previous scholarship, and Butcher, whose translation and commentary have been so widely used in this field. See

Gerald F. Else, *Aristotle's Poetics: The Argument* (Cambridge: Harvard University Press, 1957); and S. H. Butcher, *Aristotle's Theory of Poetry and Fine Art* (4th ed.; New York: Dover Publications, Inc., 1951). I have reserved the privilege of not accepting such of the commentaries for which, after sympathetic consideration, I failed to find justification in the *Poetics* itself.

2. All quotations from the *Poetics*, unless otherwise noted, are from Butcher.

3. Among numerous discussions of this problem the following stand out: Richard McKeon, "Literary Criticism and the Concept of Imitation in Antiquity," in *Critics and Criticism* ed. R. S. Crane (Chicago: The University of Chicago Press, 1952); and Jerome Stolinitz, *Aesthetics and Philosophy of Art Criticism* (Boston: Houghton Mifflin Co., 1960), pp. 109–133.

4. Butcher, p. 129.

5. Butcher, pp. 128–129.

6. Butcher, p. 121.

7. Phillip Wheelwright finds ambiguities in Arsitotle's use of *mimesis* between "copyist fidelity, on the one hand, and aesthetic form, on the other." "Mimesis and Katharsis: an Archetypal Consideration," *English Institute Essays—1951*, ed. Alan S. Downer (New York: Columbia University Press, 1952), p. 9.

8. Liddell & Scott, *A Greek-English Lexicon* (New Edition).

9. Else, pp. 70–73.

10. Butcher, p. 123.

11. Francis Fergusson, "*Macbeth* as the Imitation of an Action," *English Institute Essay—1951*, p. 31. The Liddell and Scott *Greek-English Lexicon* gives no support for Fergusson's translation.

12. Susanne K. Langer, *Feeling and Form* (New York: Charles Scribner's Sons, 1953), p. 306.

13. The published version of this play contains alternate endings. Tennessee Williams, *Cat on a Hot Tin Roof* (New York: New Directions, 1955).

14. Else, pp. 262–263.

15. Else, pp. 408–409.

16. See the intriguing theory of myth by the French anthropologist Claude Lévi-Strauss in which he treats the Oedipus story as consisting of *all*

known versions of the story and handles if multidimensionally (instead of proceeding from beginning to end). Claude Lévi-Strauss, "The Structural Study of Myth," *Journal of American Folklore,* LXVIII (Oct.–Dec. 1955), 428–444.

17. W. P. Ker, *Form and Style in Poetry* (London: Macmillan & Co., 1928), p. 99.

18. Else, p. 407.

19. Else, p. 408 n. 3. Else places Butcher in the wrong camp here (as favoring "whole play") by citing a passage of Butcher that does not relate to the question at hand.

20. Else, pp. 408–409.

21. Else translates *logos* as "argument" (of the play), then discusses "story" and then talks about this outline as plot or plot structure. pp. 503–509.

22. Else, p. 409.

23. Arthur and Barbara Gelb, *O'Neill* (New York: Harper and Brothers, 1960), pp. 438–439.

24. Butcher, pp. 165–166. In the following pages of his chapter on "Poetic Truth," Butcher argues that this "probability" is of a higher order, representing things as they "ought to be."

25. Benbow Ritchie, "The Formal Structure of the Aesthetic Object," *JAAC,* III (11–12, n.d.), 13.

26. See the criticisms of a purely formal logic in W. H. Werkmeister, *The Basis and Structure of Knowledge* (New York: Harper & Bros., 1948), pp. 174–179.

CHAPTER X

1. See especially T. S. Eliot, *Selected Essays 1917–1932* (New York: Harcourt, Brace & Co., 1932) and *Poetry and Drama* (Cambridge: Harvard University Press, 1951).

2. Caroline F. E. Spurgeon, *Shakespeare's Imagery and What It Tells Us* (New York: The Macmillan Co., 1935); and W. H. Clemen, *The Development of Shakespeare's Imagery* (Cambridge: Harvard University Press, 1951).

3. (New York: Henry Holt & Co., 1945).

4. Robert Heilman, *This Great Stage* (Baton Rouge: Louisiana State University Press, 1948), p. 4. Robert F. Goheen has approached Sophocles and Aeschylus in a similar vein; see *The Imagery of Soph-*

ocles' "Antigone" (Princeton: The Princeton University Press, 1951), and "Three Studies in the *Oresteia,*" *American Journal of Philology,* LXXVI (1955), 113–137.

5. In Cleanth Brooks, *The Well Wrought Urn* (New York: Reynal & Hitchcock, 1947). Notable exception to this essay, principally on the grounds of Brooks' "incorrect" readings, has been taken by C. J. Campbell. "Shakespeare and the 'New' Critics," *Joseph Quincy Adams: Memorial Studies,* eds. McManaway, Dawson, and Willoughby (Washington: Folger Shakespeare Library, 1948).

6. Heilman's notes in *This Great Stage* and *The Magic in the Web* (Lexington: University of Kentucky Press, 1956) supply many citations, often with comment, to articles and books on the subject. R. S. Crane, *The Language of Criticism and the Structure of Poetry* (Toronto: University of Toronto Press, 1953) supplies more citations in an attack on the thematic analysts.

7. *Essays in Criticism,* I (October 1951), 315–335.

8. Heilman, "More Fair," pp. 315–316.

9. Heilman, *Magic,* p. 3.

10. Heilman, "More Fair," p. 316.

11. Heilman, *Magic,* p. 4.

12. Heilman, "More Fair," p. 317.

13. Heilman, "More Fair," p. 316.

14. Heilman, *Magic,* pp. 5–6.

15. Heilman, *Magic,* p. 6.

16. Heilman, "More Fair," p. 317.

17. Heilman, *This Great Stage,* pp. 7–8.

18. Heilman, "More Fair," pp. 318–319.

19. Heilman, "More Fair," p. 321.

20. Heilman, "More Fair," p. 330.

21. Heilman, "More Fair," p. 331.

22. R. S. Crane, *The Languages of Criticism and the Structure of Poetry,* p. 124.

23. Crane, p. 148.

24. Cited in Heilman, "More Fair," p. 318.

25. Heilman, "More Fair," p. 328.

26. Heilman, "More Fair," p. 329.

27. Heilman, "More Fair," p. 332.

28. Heilman, *This Great Stage*, p. 11.

29. William K. Wimsatt, Jr. and Cleanth Brooks, *Literary Criticism: A Short History* (New York: Alfred A. Knopf, 1959), p. 691.

30. G. Wilson Knight makes a strong plea for the "spacial" view of Shakespeare in *The Wheel of Fire* (London: Oxford University Press, 1930), pp. 3–7.

31. See the answer to such a treatment of Hitchcock by Charles Higham, "Hitchcock's World," *Film Quarterly*, XVI (Winter 1962–1963), 3–16.

32. Heilman, *Magic*, p. 4.

33. Heilman, "More Fair," pp. 316–317.

34. Heilman, *Magic*, p. 4.

35. Heilman, *This Great Stage*, p. 11.

CHAPTER XI

1. Bella and Samuel Spewack, *Boy Meets Girl*, in *Sixteen Famous American Plays*, ed. Cerf and Cartmell (New York: Garden City Publishing Co., 1941).

2. Northrop Frye, *The Anatomy of Criticism* (Princeton: Princeton University Press, 1957), p. 163.

3. Derek Traversi's attempt to say that, especially in the late plays, "plot has become simply an extension, an extra vehicle of the poetry," if it means anything more than the far from profound observation that plot and language are parts of a unified whole, finally fails to revise the common understanding of poetry as verse. Derek A. Traversi, *An Approach to Shakespeare* (Garden City: Doubleday & Co., 1956), p. 290.

4. Frye, p. 341.

5. Frye, p. 341.

6. Frye, p. 342.

7. Frye, p. 136.

8. Frye, p. 139.

9. Frye, p. 171.

10. Frye, pp. 163–164.

11. Frye, p. 171.

12. Frye, p. 169.

13. Frye, p. 171.

14. Frye, p. 158.

15. Richard Rudner, "On Semiotic Aesthetics," *JAAC*, X (Sept. 1951), 76.

16. Susanne K. Langer, *Feeling and Form* (New York: Charles Scribner's Sons, 1953), p. 326.

17. Langer, p. 351.

18. Langer, pp. 349–350.

19. This is a confusion Ernest Nagel noticed in Mrs. Langer's thinking when he reviewed *Philosophy in a New Key* in 1943. *Journal of Philosophy*, XL (June 1943), 325.

20. Langer, *Feeling*, pp. 360–361.

21. Susanne K. Langer, *Problems of Art* (New York: Charles Scribner's Sons, 1957), pp. 133–134.

22. Langer, *Problems*, pp. 132–134.

23. Frye, p. 351.

24. Nagel, p. 328.

25. Clayton Hamilton, *The Art of Fiction* (New York: Doubleday, Doran & Co., 1939), p. 13. The bulk of this material was published as *Materials and Methods of Fiction*, 1908.

26. See O. J. Campbell, *"Love's Labour's Lost" Re-studied* (Ann Arbor: University of Michigan Studies in Shakespeare, Milton and Donne, 1925).

APPENDIX

1. Space does not allow me to give a full bibliography on *Hamlet* here. However, Gordon Ross Smith, *A Classified Shakespeare Bibliography, 1936–1958* (University Park: Pennsylvania State University Press, 1963), gives a good list. In addition, two rather unusual books may help the reader: Morris Weitz, *"Hamlet" and the Philosophy of Literary Criticism* (Cleveland and New York: Meredian Books, 1966); and Raymond Mander and Joe Mitchenson, *"Hamlet" through the Ages* (London: Rockliff, 1955). The first of these subjects the criticism and interpretation of this play to a searching philosophical analysis; the second provides the reader with a sense of how *Hamlet* has been physically realized on the stage.

2. This recognizes the possible genesis of *Hamlet* in an Elizabethan revenge formula, but does not limit the significance of even Shakespeare's basic pattern to that popular genre. See E. E. Stoll, *Art and Artifice in Shakespeare* (Cambridge: Cambridge University Press, 1938), pp. 91–94; and Fredson Bowers, *Elizabethan Revenge Tragedy, 1587–1642* (Princeton: Princeton University Press, 1940).

3. If, as has been suggested, Laertes' breaking in on the king was based on the brash intrusion of Essex upon Elizabeth, we have here a particularly interesting example of the way in which a real-life incident finds its way into art.

4. It is interesting to speculate that the multiple images of disease which Miss Spurgeon detected in this play suggest that Shakespeare himself felt the same analogy of basic pattern. Caroline F. E. Spurgeon, *Shakespeare's Imagery and What It Tells Us* (Boston: Beacon Press, 1958), p. 316. (Originally published Cambridge, England, 1935.)

5. Francis Fergusson is interesting on rituals in *Hamlet* but presses their significance well beyond what I would claim. See *The Idea of a Theatre* (Princeton: Princeton University Press, 1949), pp. 120–127.

6. Eleanor Prosser has suggested that Elizabethans, as do moderns, must have taken personal revenge as a morally repugnant act *not* a sacred duty. *Hamlet and Revenge* (Stanford: Stanford University Press, 1967).

7. For a detailed study of assumptions shared by Shakespeare and his audience see E. M. W. Tillyard, *The Elizabethan World Picture* (New York: Macmillan, 1944); and Hardin Craig, *The Enchanted Glass* (New York and London: Oxford University Press, 1936).

INDEX

and interests in, 210; improvisational structure, 210–212

Happenings, 57, 58, 92, 96, 240 n.7

Harrison, Jane Ellen, anthropological theories of drama, 4

Heartbreak House (Shaw), mechanical dialogue in, 72

Heilman, Robert, criticism of *Othello* and *King Lear,* 174–189; *Understanding Drama,* 175; *Magic in the Web: Action and Language in "Othello,"* 176, 177–179 *passim; This Great Stage: Image and Structure in King Lear,* 176; views on dramatic structure, 176–177; "More Fair than Black: Light and Dark in 'Othello,' " 176, 177–181 *passim;* on *Othello* as a poem, 177–179; on language of *Othello,* 177–184; on Shakespeare's imagery, 180–181, 183–185; on poetic play of thought, 185–188; spatial form in Shakespeare, 186, 188

Henry IV–1, use of tricks in, 47–48

Herskovits, Melville J. and Frances S., criticism of Jung's theory, 37–38

Human experience. *See* Experience

Ibsen, Henrik, use of visual form, 102

Identity, assumption of, 19

I Love Lucy, 190–191, 192, 202–203

Image of man's interaction in time, drama as, 10

Image of reality, concept of art as, 58–60

Imagery, contrasts in, 100

Images: of temporal experience, 44; objects or events as, 58–59; method of composition, 61–68

Improvisational structure; nature of time, 70–71; dialogues, 71–72; dramatic interplay, 71–72; monologues, 72–76; pressure of time, 73–77; relationships in time between characters, 77–80; of Shakespeare, 80–81, 210–212; lack of sensitivity of characters, 81; beats, 82–86; act and scene division, 86–90; in *Hamlet,* 210–212

Inge, William; use of holiday as structural device, 43; use of expectation and fulfillment, 45–46

Interests: definition, 20; effect on

drama of a society, 20. *See also* Assumptions

Intermediate patterns, 40–49; significance, 41–42; differentiated from Basic Pattern of Events, 42–43; use of holidays, 43; waiting as temporal pattern, 44; expectation and fulfillment, 45–47; preparation and foreshadowing, 47; the trick, 47–48; use of a contest, 48; rhetorical devices, 48–49; in *Hamlet,* 209–210

Ionesco, Eugene: and identity, 19; use of repetition, 23; assumption of failures of communication, 81

Irony in Greek tragedy, 21–22

Jenkins, Iredell: on audience response, 27; on the aesthetic experience, 67

Jones, Robert Edmond, on magic and ritual in theatre, 230 n.5

Jung, Carl Gustav: on ritual origins of drama, 5; archetype theory, 36–38

Ker, W. P., on prose argument in *The Ancient Mariner,* 167

Kerman, Joseph, on character of Figaro, 141; on Mozart's use of ensemble music, 142

King Lear, Heilman's criticism of, 175, 176, 182, 183, 186, 189

Langer, Susanne: drama theories, 4, 190–203; on act and actions, 51, 160; on relation of the act to past and future, 63–64; "virtual memory," 124; on comic structure, 190–203; *Philosophy in a New Key,* 195–196; theory of music and art, 195–198

Laplace, mechanistic theory, 23

Leave It to Beaver, 190

Levarie, Siegmund, analysis of *Marriage of Figaro,* 147, 153

Leichtentritt, Hugo, analysis of primitive music, 131

Lévi-Strauss, Claude: and French structuralism, 14; on Oedipus story, 246 n.16

Lewis, C. S., on polyphonic technique of story telling, 242 n.11

Life as art, 57

Literary critics, views on dramatic structure, 3–4, 6

Literature, similarities to mathematics and logic, 199

Littlewood, Joan, and contemporary dramatic theory, 7–8

Logos, 169, 247 n.21. *See also* Story

Long Day's Journey into Night (O'Neill): use of intermediate patterns, 42–43; change of beat in, 83, 84, 85; division into acts, 88; representational progression in, 106; example of narrative structure in, 125; and Heilman's theories, 187

Lord, A. B., on composition of epics, 5

Lower Depths, The (Gorky), naturalistic actions in, 69

Macbeth: fate in, 22; Basic Pattern of Events, 33–34; time element and improvisational structure, 73, 74–77; aural and visual effect of elements as form, 101–102, 103; ordering of events in, 123; example of poetic organization in, 125

Malinowski, Bronislaw, theory of speech as "phatic communion," 133

Marriage of Figaro (Mozart): comparison with Beaumarchais' play, 139–156; conversion from play to opera, cuts and changes, 139–146; analysis of Trio No. 13, 139–151; score and libretto of Trio No. 13, 213–228

Martin, Anthony, experience as work of art, 57

Mechanical Eccentric (Moholy-Nagy) as pure form, 97

Melodrama as conventional form, 108

Mimesis, Aristotle's concept of, 158–160, 246 n.7

Miss Julia (Strindberg), compressed continuous action in, 89

Moholy-Nagy, L., exponent of pure theatrical form, 97, 98

Monologues, 72–76

Moreau, Jean-Baptiste, musical settings for Racine's biblical dramas, 127

Morris, Charles, model of art, 59

Mozart's *Marriage of Figaro:* comparison with Beaumarchais' play, 139–156; score, 214–228

Murray, Gilbert, on drama as ritual, 5

Music and dramatic structure, 126–156; music as accompaniment to

Greek drama, 126; music used by dramatists, 127–128; drama used by composers, 128–129; basic units of musical forms, 129–130; Goetschius' analysis of musical structure, 129–131; principle of musical motion, 130–131; comparison of basic units, 131–132; comparison of structural principles, 132; comparison of use of repetition, 132–137; comparison of use of sound, 138–139; comparison of play and opera *Marriage of Figaro,* 139–156; the finale as musical and dramatic form, 153–155

Myth: contrast with Basic Pattern of Events, 35; in archetypal criticism, 192–195. *See also Mythos*

Mythos: of Aristotle, 111, 166, 168; in literary criticism, 193–195; of comedy, 194

Nagel, Ernest, views on formal treatment of language, 199

Narrative: structure of, 28, 110–118; as organization of experience, 110–111; comparison with drama, 123–125. *See also* Story

"New criticism," 6, 174–176

Nineteenth century drama, late, as mechanistic cause and effect, 21, 23

Objets as images, 58–59

Objets trouvés as art, 57, 58

Obligatory scene, 45–46

Observed events as art, 57–58, 60–61

Oedipus the King (Sophocles): structural devices illustrating assumption of fate, 21–22; time span of, 22; Basic Pattern of Events, 31–33; meaning of actions in, 52; the beginning of, 162

Omens or portents, use in plots, 193–194

O'Neill, Eugene, composition of *Long Day's Journey into Night,* 16–17

Othello, Heilman's criticism of, 176–184, 187–188

Patterned stimuli, 107

Pericles, time span of, 22

Phèdre (Racine), repetition of scenes in, 133–134